The National Road

ALSO BY TOM ZOELLNER

The Heartless Stone
Uranium
A Safeway in Arizona
Train
Island on Fire

THE NATIONAL ROAD

Dispatches from a Changing America

Tom Zoellner

COUNTERPOINT

Berkeley, California

The National Road

Library of Congress Cataloging-in-Publication Data
Names: Zoellner, Tom, author.
Title: The national road : dispatches from a changing America / Tom Zoellner.
Description: Berkeley : Counterpoint Press, 2020.
Identifiers: LCCN 2020001055 | ISBN 9781640092907 (hardcover) | ISBN 9781640092914 (ebook)
Subjects: LCSH: Roads—United States. | United States—Economic conditions—21st century. | United States—Social conditions—21st century. | Migration, Internal—United States. | United States—Social life and customs—21st century. | Social change—United States.
Classification: LCC HE355 .Z64 2020 | DDC 973—dc23
LC record available at https://lccn.loc.gov/2020001055

Jacket design by Donna Cheng
Book design by Jordan Koluch

COUNTERPOINT
2560 Ninth Street, Suite 318
Berkeley, CA 94710
www.counterpointpress.com

Printed in the United States of America

10 9 8 7 6 5 4 3 2 1

Tell me the landscape in which you live, and I will tell you who you are.

—JOSÉ ORTEGA Y GASSET

Contents

The National Road

Your Land

A summer afternoon in Kansas: shadows in the grass, and a diagonal slash cut into the earth.

The trench in the soil had nailed me in place, as if I had just been shown the ribs of a dinosaur skeleton. Nothing here but a rut in the ground, but what a remarkable rut, because it had been carved here by hundreds of wagons traveling on the Santa Fe Trail in the mid-nineteenth century, jangling with goods headed southwest, crossing through territory of the Pawnee and Kiowa. The ground still wore a scar of their passage. I could not have been more mesmerized looking at a full-color telescope blast of the Crab Nebula, or at the dark shroud of the Virgin of Guadalupe.

An eccentric idea took root that afternoon at the side of this Kansas highway, though it would take a few more years to fully materialize. When I grew restless with a newspaper job and looked for an excuse to get away, I remembered that slash in the ground from the Santa Fe Trail.

Could I follow its path on foot? Missouri to New Mexico: nine hundred miles chasing the ghosts of wagons. A few months later, I had forty pounds of gear on my back on a dirt road on a ridge near Little Wakarusa Creek on the path of the old wagon trail.

Green stubbles of wheat poked upward from nearby fields; farther away, I could see horses grazing in a pasture, nickering to one another. And as the ridge rose farther, it came to one of those crests so common in eastern Kansas that opens a broad vista of prairie that has the illusion of limitlessness. A cloudbank shredded the afternoon sun into lace, pouring light down on all the miles flowing westward, promising something unseen over the edge—a Denver, a Santa Fe, a Pacific Ocean. Land wedded to a democratic ideal.

How was it possible, I wondered, that all of this American land—in every direction—could be fastened together into a whole? How could all those unseen cities, all those drab little towns, all those races and languages, all those hundreds of millions of flawed human beings with vastly different stories and troubles be kept hanging together in a consensus that centered around nothing more than a four-page rulebook and a set of disputed principles that we argued about before the Santa Fe Trail was there and long after it disappeared? What are the enduring features that make us Americans?

Those questions grew sharper for me as I saw more of the country, and they again take on a special urgency. "America began as a search for community," wrote Librarian of Congress Daniel Boorstin about the settlements of religious zealots, adventurers, cotton growers, wastrels, and second-chance merchants trying to stay alive on the frigid coast of New England wilderness. And yet, in that search for order came an idea of self-government based on the Enlightenment values of John Locke and Jean-Jacques Rousseau, and John Adams's observation that the real purpose of government was to bring "the greatest quantity of human happiness." To live as an American was—supposedly—to be under a system designed to maximize the rewards of simply being alive: the love of hard work, the just compensation for invention and risk, the liberty to love and marry at will, the introspection about religion, the safety from leaders who bully and steal.

One common trope when describing America is to emphasize motion. The climb out of poverty, the race to the top, the mad desire to see what's over the mountain. Migration is our franchise: New Englanders moved out to the richer farmlands of the Upper Midwest in the 1830s; their great-grandchildren lit out to California a century later; Mormons took their wagons across a thousand barren miles to escape religious persecution; African Americans left the sweltering fields of the prejudiced South for the higher wages of the gray cities of the North, like Chicago, Cleveland, and Pittsburgh; the practice of "moving for college" or "moving for a job" is so ingrained that it has become standard practice.

But today our country is slowing down and staying in place—an effect that COVID-19 only accelerated. Approximately one out of every five Americans changed their address in 1950, but that figure is now less than one in nine. Fewer people are moving today than in any year out of the last half century. A country on the move seems to be more reluctant than ever to pick up and go, even when prospects are grim—not just in small-town America but in once-powerful mid-tier cities like St. Louis, Denver, and Memphis. In 1968, the author of the small-town requiem *The Last Picture Show* wrote of the brain-drain in rural Texas. "The kids who stayed in the country tended to be dull, lazy, cautious, or all three; those with brains, zip, and daring were soon off to Dallas or Houston," wrote Larry McMurtry. This is less true today than ever before.

The American concept of geography has undergone a powerful shift. Place is less important than it has ever been to those who can free themselves from it, yet more important to those who aren't able to leave it.

The economically privileged can live where they please in the ethereal non-space of the information sphere. St. Augustine speculated that God was a circle where the center was nowhere and the circumference was everywhere; he might as well have been describing the Internet. In his seminal 2002 book, *The Rise of the Creative Class*, the sociologist Richard Florida laid out a vision of winner cities like Portland, Washington, D.C., San Francisco, Austin, and Missoula that offered charms to lure the soldiers of the laptop army who would set their own schedules and dream transformative dreams for the rest of us. "Where once people had to go to a particular place—a telephone box, a computer—to communicate, now communications come to them, in the form of a pager, a mobile telephone, or a laptop with a phone jack," wrote *The Economist* in 1997, in the midst of the detachment revolution.

But not for most people. The shift in manufacturing capacity to Asia and the rise of corporate farming has made shells out of healthy towns like Gloversville, New York; Concordia, Kansas; and Cairo, Illinois. Those without the means or desire to move out are caught in a web of diminishing opportunities. The championship cities of urban America and its information-based trades have economies growing more entangled with London, São Paulo, and Beijing than with fading cities like St. Louis, Cleveland, or Bakersfield.

The new zones of exclusion have shut out Americans from their own country, through ways that are both literal and perceived. Winner cities have become havens of inequality and nearly impossible to navigate for those drawing old-school paychecks from retail jobs or public schools. Tiny fragments of San Francisco today contain more gross national product and fluid capital than entire midwestern cities. The liberal values of these places come under increasing suspicion by those on the geographic outside of them. Our recent simplified dialectic of "coastal elites" versus "real Americans" is actually more about location than values.

Some places in America were set up from the beginning to be sacrificial zones—a repository of industrial overspill, shabby real estate, or neighborhoods redlined by racial discrimination. The New Jersey marshes on the west side of the Hudson River became a haven of unregulated dumping of garbage and chemicals that benefitted only the shining city nearby; the town of Opportunity, Montana, was built around a giant smelter belching arsenic and heavy metals from copper mined from nearby Butte; Native Americans were pushed into some of the least valuable lands in the West; virtually every city founded by railroads created class distinctions based on the cleaving line of the tracks.

What was once a regional practice is now happening on a national scale, as entire portions of the country—primarily rural and in politically conservative regions—are written off as lost. Residents of West Virginia used to complain that they were treated as an "internal colony" by the rest of the country, stripped for coal and left empty; such can now be said of broader swaths of Appalachia, the Midwest, and the Mountain West, where joblessness and life expectancy are diverging in large proportions from those of the cities where the economic winners live. Resentment builds. National cohesiveness frays. It is commonly said that America is the first country to be based on an idea rather than a shared ethnicity. Yet our nationhood is also heavily dependent on a shared place.

Here is our lowest common denominator: we all stand on the same land. If you want to know Americans, look at where they live first. Look at the land. Geography is our bounty; it has also become a curse.

American place is not what it once was—neither in shape, nor optimism. Bank mergers have destroyed local institutions that took the long view of civic development and strategic lending. Changes in agricultural technology have made the family farm an even chancier proposition than ever before, with its emphasis on mechanization and gigantic yields. Consolidation of wealth in fewer hands leaves fewer chances for rural entrepreneurship and innovation, which opens a vacancy in the national spirit. "To be rooted is perhaps the most important and least recognized need of the human soul," wrote the French theologian Simone Weil. To live as an American citizen implies a form of ownership in the future of the country, a tiny garden patch of responsibility. But in today's uprooted America, "your land" means less than it ever did—but, paradoxically, much more.

Geography is invariably personal. I grew up in a place that didn't seem particularly meaningful to me at the time: a squiggle of bland new homes pounded into virgin Sonoran Desert to the north of Tucson, a blooming Sun Belt city whose pattern of promenade avenues was founded on the right-angled idea of urban planning first brought to the continent by William Penn in the 1680s when he laid out Philadelphia. It was only when I started to travel on my own through the United States that I began to understand the contradictions of space— why certain places are esteemed and why others are sacrificed, and how these places form individual character. "Geography is destiny" goes the old historian's chestnut. We all carry maps of our country—however big or small—around in our minds, a web of association and memory, and understand ourselves through their reading. It is a physical kind of patriotism.

At the heart of the American nostalgic subconscious lies the small town. We know this place, even if we never lived there. There's the business block, the classic Main Street U.S. of A., with adjoining retail emporiums made of masonry and darkened upper-story windows shaded with blinds. Perhaps there is a drugstore selling prescriptions and cough drops; a car dealership smelling of rubber; a café serving pizza and French fries; a theater hanging on with second-run movies; a café where a group of old men, flush with memories and obscure local wit, meet for coffee every Tuesday and linger there until ten o'clock in the morning. Nearby is the spire of a First Church, often painted white with stained glass, and, farther down, a Railroad Avenue lined with derelict warehouses with bottles scattered among the side weeds, and fronting shanty houses with sloping porches. In the more moneyed precincts is a park with poplar trees and a set of playground equipment ordered from a municipal catalog, maybe a swimming pool whose cement foundation was initially poured because of a subscription drive or bond issue before the First World War. The houses of the gentry—the doctor, the attorney, the newspaper editor, the banker—aren't far away, with their over-furnished parlors, mansard roofs, and backyard grills. At night the streetlamps cast patterns of oak leaves on the pavement, and mist crowns the grass in the hours before dawn.

On the edge of town is the high school, a modernist slab with at least one wall painted in the primary colors of the school and bearing its mascot in a fighting crouch and which keeps the town regularly supplied with minor legend, intrigue, sports lore, and alarm over the peccadillos of the young. Out on the highway you'll find a purposely zoned strip of monoculture as leveling as any force in national society: a Rite Aid, a McDonald's, a Comfort Inn, a Dollar General, where the wages are bad, the taste is salt-fat-sugar, and goods are the same from East Millinocket, Maine, to Petaluma, California.

American place takes hold of us like a hand reaching up from the bedside and creates a familiarity and intimacy that recalls the wonderful Welsh word *hiraeth*—an inexpressible longing for home, even when home as a physical place is a shifting concept. My own touchstones are scattered across the country. There is a particular staircase in the U.S. House of Representatives, for example, where I used to linger when I was part of the corps of interns that passed through the Capitol each year, a green laminated press credential hanging around my neck. I liked to stare at a mural painted above the staircase, a scene in the heroic style titled *Westward the Course of Empire Takes Its Way*, depicting a movie-ready cast of mountain men, pioneer wives, and wagoners in beaver-pelt caps struggling to mount a precipice that opened to a view of a Pacific harbor. Of course, the mural leaves out the indefensible treatment of Native Americans, the corruption of the railroads, the despair of the bankrupted, and the rest of the dismal realities of what used to be called Manifest Destiny. Yet the presence of this mythology within the seat of national power seemed fascinating to me, in all of its Coplandesque idealism and selective memory.

So many more places that I once knew, and keep wanting to see again. A knob of grassy land off the winding Conzelman Road on the north side of the Golden Gate Bridge in Marin County, California, where I used to bring a bottle of cheap red wine. Old miner's shacks clinging to the hillsides in Welch, West Virginia. Iron ramps of the DuSable Bridge folded like praying hands over the pale blue Chicago River. The Hennepin Avenue Bridge to Nicollet Island from downtown Minneapolis with a view of the sign for Grain Belt beer. The weedy backyard of a friend's house in a working-class neighborhood of Cheyenne, Wyoming, just south of the Union Pacific transcontinental tracks. The roof of The Raleigh hotel on Collins Avenue in Miami Beach, where I once watched a mammoth thunderstorm roll in from the Caribbean. The eastbound approach to Denver with the neon lights of the El Rancho restaurant up on a bluff and passing underneath a series of warning signs: TRUCKERS YOU ARE NOT DOWN YET/ANOTHER 1½ MILES OF STEEP GRADE AND SHARP CURVES TO GO. The oval town green of Lebanon, New Hampshire, whose particular New England arrangement of elms and stone buildings gives it "an aura of stability and consequence," in the words of writer James Howard Kunstler, even though its fabric mills shut down decades ago. And that spot on U.S. Highway 50 outside Lakin, Kansas, where I first spied those Santa Fe Trail ruts—a permanent etching of national restlessness that I still feel stirring inside. The columnist George F. Will once wrote that there are three essential American landscapes: the Virginia piedmont, the skyline of Manhattan, and the canyons of Utah. For wall calendars and screen savers, they can't be beat. But America may be seen in its best form among less celebrated vistas—the geographies that we don't stop to notice.

This book is a collection of essays that attempts to paint a picture of "American place" in this uncertain era of political toxin and economic re-arrangement. There are observations collected from thirty years of travel-ing through the United States and topics of more recent reporting. I had hopes that the "whereness" of America might be perceived through its territorial shards and fragments: courthouses, mountains, farms, casinos, holy sites, movie sets, newsrooms, deserts, offices, amusement parks, liv-ing rooms, jails, swamps, retail stores, laboratories, police stations, bars, hotels, military bases, beaches, city halls, slums, libraries, mines, crime scenes, and the edge of Massachusetts Bay where hungry English settlers first made contact with the original inhabitants of a nation that would become, in the words of the journalist John Gunther, "the greatest, cra-ziest, most dangerous, least stable, most spectacular, least grown-up and most powerful and magnificent nation ever known," and one that defies all attempts to define it in neat terms or easy descriptions, its immensity more detailed and chasmic than a hundred encyclopedias could capture.

While walking the Santa Fe Trail, I did not so much depend on the kindness of my fellow citizens as I was overwhelmed by it. Hundreds of people offered me rides that I couldn't accept; many others let me sleep in their yards or gave me a spare bedroom for the night. One of them was Wayne Flory, a barrel-chested farmer who wore dark suits and was a life-time member of the Old German Baptist Brethren, a pacifist church that largely shunned the vanities of the world. He showed me the spring once used by nineteenth-century wagon teams, which his church now used to initiate new members. "Plenty of water for baptizing," he told me. While

Anabaptist sects can be insular, Wayne was unapologetic about looking beyond his own land. He had visited Israel and kept a light airplane out in the barn in order to see the plains from above. He supported other Christian organizations whose doctrines were different than his, and he told me his nightly prayer, which was the essence of syncretic simplicity: "God, I love you and I trust you."

Wayne had known this Kansas acreage all his life; he had been born on it in 1924—a Tolstoy living on his own Yasnaya Polyana behind a tidy square of fence. It was the kind of house and wheat field I might have whizzed past on the highway without a second glance. Yet here was one man's intimacy with the earth that most post-farm Americans could scarcely comprehend.

I walked away down the road early the next morning, heading toward Little Wakarusa Creek. And when afternoon came, bringing with it a dazzling show of clouds and sun, a rise in the road looking west made me think of all that unknown earth. All those farms and fields, all those cities, all those people existing all at the same time (intriguing, thoughtful, angry, charismatic, doubtful people I would never, ever know), and all living on a fertile portion of the North American Plate under a rough four-page agreement called the Constitution. It brought with it a sense of wonder and fear at the size of this land and questions about who we are that remain unanswered. This book is a part of that ongoing question.

Mormon Historical Sites at Night

And it came to pass in those days, in those earlier peregrinations across the width of the continent, that I would find myself standing at strange hours locked outside the gates of a spot that was linked by blood or prophecy to the early years of the Church of Jesus Christ of Latter-day Saints, known by all as Mormons.

Why I come to these places, I don't know. I'm not a Mormon. I don't think I would ever be one. The origin story of the church is just too full of leaks, their hierarchy so rigid, their testimonies in ward houses so canned, and the whole improbable enterprise too slathered in the telltale syrup of public relations. And yet, I can't stay away.

Here is the brief version of how they got started, which also happens to be a tremendously good story. In 1824, in the town of Palmyra, New York, a poor farmer's son named Joseph Smith Jr. started telling his neighbors he was led by an angel to the top of a hill eight miles south of his farm, where he dug up a book made of pure gold. Chiseled on the pages was the story of a lost tribe of Israel who had sailed to the Americas and been preached to by the resurrected Jesus Christ. Smith translated these runes by gazing at them through a magic stone from the bottom of his hat. The resulting document was the Book of Mormon, printed at the expense of a neighbor. The golden plates were then lifted up to heaven, having been viewed in the physical sense only by Smith himself. He was lynched in Illinois, but not before he had built a church whose strongest and best-known branch would go on to settle the difficulty of what is now Utah. Today, the church counts more than fifteen million adherents worldwide. Their presence is particularly strong in the Mountain Time Zone: I grew up with Mormon friends in Arizona, and in my late twenties, I lived barely a thousand yards from the church's world headquarters in Salt Lake City, with a view of the temple spires from my window.

One of the most commonplace observations made about Mormons is the particular *American* quality of the religion: the optimism, the inventiveness, the faith in the common person, the urge for perfection and progress. Even Leo Tolstoy said this after meeting one of their missionaries on a Russian train. The Mormons do not consider humanity to be inherently sinful. Hell has no real place in their faith. Heaven will be open to just about everybody, and it is a folk saying among Mormons that if you were allowed a momentary glimpse of the lowest layer of heaven, the place where all the average criminals and atheists go, you would immediately shoot yourself in the head to get there.

Joseph Smith's theology was a quilt work of the various ideas he picked up in the course of his brief life—threads of the Bible, the Constitution, Native American myths, and the Masonic temple rituals are all sewn inside—but his deepest and most surprising principle was one of eternal progression. Every person's soul is on a journey from a vaporous state called the "preexistence" into this world of flesh and onward into an indescribable future as a godlike being. Men and women together have the power to draw souls out of the preexistence through having sex, which brings them inexpressible blessings in the hereafter, the physical pleasure of the act being only a foretaste: a shadow of the great unity to come.

That this marvelously good story—which turned into a religious empire—sprang from American ground makes it all the more intriguing. Here was a system whose foundational dramas had been staged not just in the reliquaries of the Middle East but on the blameless prairies of the new country, within ready access and plainly marked on an ordinary road map of the kinds that used to be given out at gas stations. I feel in my bones that it is a deception, and that the tall tale of the golden plates is a grotesquerie at the heart of its sunny exterior of Mormonism, and yet I am drawn to its native geography again and again. And so it came to pass that after heading home from a party with some law students near the town of Sharon, Vermont, on a December night in 2008 that I came to be standing by myself outside the perimeter of the birthplace of Joseph Smith.

Again, this was mostly an impulse. The highway sign had beckoned: Joseph Smith Birthplace. Two miles and an arrow. So I bore left and went up from the White River valley on the kind of relentless 30 percent grade that characterizes that section of New England, two miles up Dairy Hill Road to a set of modern stone cairns with a large metal fence between them, blocking the road up to his birthplace. An electronic security keypad was set into one of the gateposts. Like almost every other location of note in Mormonism's long and colorful history, Joseph Smith's birthplace had been purchased and set up as a site of tourism, pilgrimage, and discreet proselytizing by the powerful Utah branch of the church—the faction that emerged strongest from the confusion after Smith was shot to death in Illinois.

I idled there a bit, with my truck's headlights trained on the dark winter scene behind the gate. Streetlights along the narrow lane inside made pools of yellow light on the asphalt and snow. The gate looked easy enough to jump. It was slightly above twenty degrees Fahrenheit outside. My shoes were thin, but the road had been plowed of snow and my wool coat was warm. Would there be some unit of church security alerted to the presence of an intruder by motion detectors? Did this place see enough overeager pilgrims or insane rip-off prophets to warrant such attention? I decided to go for it.

His birthplace had once been a farmstead owned by Solomon Mack, the father of Joseph Smith's mother, Lucy, and had been typical of the lots sold to strivers up from Massachusetts looking for another chance. Vermont was a wild place, its greenness was not easy or soft. The earth was full of granite rocks that dented the plows, and the slopes were hard to terrace. Joseph's family was living near poverty. Lucy was a believer in omens and folk magic; his father, Joseph Sr. was restless and emotional. Joseph Jr. was born two days before Christmas 1805.

On the long walk up the slope under the church lamps, my thoughts were teeming not only with Mormonism or the fact of my trespassing, but with a strange phrase: the Lacanian Real.

I had picked up the phrase from a piece of reading I had been struggling over in graduate school that past autumn. It was by Jacques Lacan, a French psychotherapist, who made references to an abstraction he called "The Real" in a way that bordered on the mystic. Reading Lacan was rough sledding, but he talked about The Real as a chartless black hole in the heart of all being that repelled all signifiers and made a joke of language. Any definitions of the color "red," for example, led only to a string of more words, adjectives like "maroon" and "crimson," none of which have any wholeness or absolute "redness" in themselves but are only, helplessly, pointing to yet more signifiers. All of language, then, is a set of stairs winding in a circle. The world itself was but a shell around the monstrous foreign thing that had no consciousness and could only be seen by its shadow casting itself across all language. The Real had only negative shape and could never be given a rightful name, but it permeated everything and announced itself only because it left traces of itself.

As it happened, I was in the midst of a slow-burning religious crisis and had given up churchgoing after reading a book that convincingly picked apart the archeological evidence for certain key happenings in the Hebrew Bible, otherwise known as the Old Testament. By the standards of science or journalism, the collapse of the walls of Jericho, the exodus in the Sinai, and the reign of King David had likely never happened. And the next logical question, after the debasement of biblical historical truth, is what made any of it true—especially the bold theological claims of a loving God and a consciousness beyond the material world.

The Lacanian Real. That weird phrase kept echoing as I walked. A sign told me I was half a mile from the birthplace of Joseph Smith. I crested the hill and walked along a flat path toward a stronger glow on the horizon that I assumed was the visitors center just out of sight. The forest grew thicker and blacker on both sides; I was surrounded by masses of pine and birch. The walk was making me warm and I took my gloved hands out of my pockets. About fifteen paces from the top of the hill, I heard the singing: a multitude of voices grouped together, vaguely female.

One truth of the Vermont woods in the winter is that choirs do not generally sing there after midnight, and if they are, something is terribly wrong. I felt a stab of the flight instinct in my chest but made myself stand completely still. After a bit, the tune became clear: "Hark, the Herald Angels Sing."

The eeriness passed and I began to think coherently again. This was, after all, a religious site in the Christmas season (Mormons are enthusiastic celebrators, even though they believe Jesus was really born in April), and I must have been on the verge of stumbling into an outdoor meeting or a service that had gone abysmally late. If they saw me, I would have to explain myself. A trespassing midnight pilgrim, aimed toward the empty crèche of a religion that I believed to be a counterfeit. But I didn't feel like running. And so, foolishly, I kept walking toward the singing.

Why was I even here, risking arrest? There was nothing to see here. Joseph Smith himself was long gone. Everyone who had known him was long gone. There was nothing there, only a marker. This farmstead hadn't even been very important to him, his parents having given up on it three years after his birth and moving on to Tunbridge. He never visited it again. The place was significant, and signified, only because of an accident: the infant laid upon this ground would go on to charm a few thousand seekers who would then suffer some lucky accidents themselves after he was gone, preserving his system from the well of nothingness. The fence and the gate and whatever this weird singing turned out to be were here only because of that infant's eventual capabilities for telling a story of the ancient ones come back to life. Without that fence and those words, this birth scene would have been at one with the rest of the forest, which might as well have stretched in a long black annihilating wave up to Canada.

I grew closer and closer to the voices and it eventually came to me—with a mixture of relief and disappointment—that these were not live human voices. They were recorded and amplified. The church had set up outdoor speakers around the visitors center to broadcast the work of the Mormon Tabernacle Choir and, for some reason, did not shut off the sound system after midnight. It must have been on an endless loop. No human beings were there.

The choir music really should not have been a surprise: a nice touch to boost the Christmas atmosphere for visitors. Despite their thin-lipped Yankee ancestry, today's Mormons are not known for their emphasis on heavy theological discourse when it comes to greeting visitors. Sentiment always comes first. The song drained away and another carol, equally as sugared as the last, came onto the speakers, and I tried to skirt the lights around the reconstructed stone cottage on my way toward the monument that marked the site of the prophet's birth.

I walked around an arbor lit up with white bulbs, up a short hill, and there it was: the largest polished granite shaft in the world when it was dedicated at this site in 1905, on the one hundredth anniversary of Joseph Smith's birth. There was no moon, and I could clearly see the monument only through its outlines in the security light from the visitors center: a rectangular phallus with dark and dull sparkles embedded within the granite.

I found later, in the published proceedings of the dedication of this marker, that the base had been shaped from four dozen barrels of Portland cement and the shaft itself had been quarried from a boulder that weighed sixty tons. It stood 38½ feet tall, a foot for every year that Joseph Smith had lived. Hauling it up that slope had been a challenge, requiring a reinforced railroad bridge, an extra-large wagon, and a block and tackle. An engineer from Salt Lake City with some connections in the church hierarchy had been sent here, to the relative obscurity of New England, to comb through old land records and reacquire the tenant stead. A few local newspapers worried that their town would soon become a "Mormon mecca," but the church dignitaries who came out for the 1905 dedication in a special railroad car were at their conciliatory best to their Yankee hosts during lengthy orations.

This was from Charles W. Penrose, the editor of the church newspaper *The Deseret News*: "All men in their spiritual natures are the offspring of God. The Prophet Joseph Smith taught that. He answered the question that has come down through the ages. 'What am I? Whence am I? Whither am I going?'"

I drew closer to the base and read part of the inscription. *He devoted his life to the establishment of this Church and sealed his testimony with his blood.* Above me, the barren monument was a cylinder in the black winter sky. Nobody else was around, not for miles. I was alone with the nonexistent choir, which sang only to me.

This wasn't the first time I had stolen into a Mormon historical site after dark. The initial one had been, in a sense, the most generative one of all: the hill in the Finger Lakes region where the golden book was supposed to have been buried by the exterminated tribe of Israel. This was south of the town of Palmyra, which is itself barely ten miles from the New York State Thruway. All too tempting. I was barely twenty-three and was driving west with my college girlfriend, who had been teaching school in Connecticut. It was about eleven o'clock at night and she was reluctant, though tolerant of my urge.

We stopped at the giant parking lot at the base of what Joseph Smith had called "Hill Cumorah." The church staged a pageant on the slopes each summer, a masque that depicted scenes from the Book of Mormon. Church members dressed as pre-Columbian Native Americans, danced on the terraces, and staged mock battles.

There was, of course, the omnipresent visitors center. The western slope of the mountain in front of us was bathed in artificial light. It looked like a night ski run—too visible to climb without being seen. We were trespassing, after all. But to our left was an asphalt service road that appeared to go in the general direction of up. Better yet, it was dark.

I somehow persuaded Kris to walk with me up that road. She had read a lot of books but knew little of the Mormon story, except what I had told her. She was a practical girl from the Omaha suburbs. Her Lutheran church was of a stern and vinegary synod, which wouldn't serve communion to nonmembers. When we talked about other religions, even other expressions of Christianity, our private joke was that she believed them to be all "wrong and bad"—a formulation more decisive than anything St. Paul said about food sacrificed to idols. She found herself slightly creeped out when we visited the huge cathedral to Christian Science in Boston, and she was now having a similar reaction to this road to a glacial drumlin. Golden bibles and visions were not for her.

"I'm going back to the car," she told me abruptly, after we had traveled less than a quarter mile.

"We're not even close to the top," I said.

"You go. I'm going back to the car." She had that tone of voice in which there was no negotiation.

Without her, I stared up the tunnel of trees. There was no telling how much farther it was to the marker that indicated the spot where Joseph Smith said (that qualifier "said" is always the dissolving border at the edge of rational candlelight) he dug and unearthed the holy scripture of the Americas. Up top, there was a statue of the angel Moroni who had come to Joseph's bedside—the standard disclaimer: "He *said* an angel came"—in the farmhouse one night and related to him the secret place in the earth where he should dig for the golden plates. Mormon paintings have reproduced this scene in the farmhouse bedroom with as much care and downy light as a pre-Raphaelite oil of the Madonna's visitation.

The people of that day had already gulped the wine of revival. Western New York was full of newcomers from the Puritan cradles of New England, people coaxed away from their homes for a taste of easy frontier money, lacking steady congregations and the surety of the truth they had once known, thirsty for some sense of purpose amid the new forests. Dislocation breeds searching. Traveling preachers amazed their audiences with tongue-speaking and altar calls, and the Smith family had taken young Joseph to the shows. The emotionalism of these revivals, as well as the frequency of the preaching tours, gave Western New York the nickname "the burned-over district," the grasses having been suffocated brown by the tents. The people had the Pentecostal fire rip through them so often that authentic spiritual feelings had been cauterized. The town churches, though more respectable, all competed for the same kingdom keys and beat each other with the club of Scripture.

The first thing Joseph claimed to have asked the angel at his bedside was therefore perfectly understandable. Which one of the various denominations should he join? The angel replied none of them, for "they were all wrong" and their ministers corrupt.

Along with those revivals had come a strong dose of wizardry. The American frontier was permeated with what D. Michael Quinn has called "the magic world view." The average citizen believed, in addition to the Christian creed, that the earth was alive with spirits, demons, and the astral; it was not uncommon to see a divining rod hanging near the iron stove, or a Tetragammon carved into the barn beam. Folk magic was widely practiced and visions were not a ticket to unrespectability. The man who mortgaged his farm to print Joseph's first edition, generally admired among his neighbors, reported having a lengthy conversation with Jesus while the two walked down a country road. He had also seen the Savior in the shape of a deer.

Buried treasure, not religion, had been Joseph's first passion. When helping his father dig a well, he was given an obsidian rock that had turned up at a depth of twenty-four feet, and he thereafter referred to it as his "seer stone." Looking deep into the opacity of this stone gave him the power, he said, to see within the earth. Burial mounds from the Hopewell culture, vanished sixteen centuries ago, dotted the canal settlements, and a farmer who spaded into one would occasionally find a few copper tools and even some silver among the mummies. Joseph enraptured himself with these local tales, as well as entirely specious stories of buried Spanish chests from pirates, and he hired himself to local farmers as a professional money-digger, using his stone as a looking glass. This earned him the nickname "Peepstone Joe" and a court hearing in which he was accused of being a "disorderly person and an imposter" by Peter Bridgman, someone whose money he had taken in the name of finding a gold mine worked by the Spaniards. On September 22, 1827, seven years after the bedside appearance of the angels, Joseph, at the age of twenty-one, ascended Hill Cumorah and dug up the chronicles of America's lost people.

The resulting Book of Mormon, translated by Joseph Smith to a listener through a curtain, is not the most elegant piece of scripture brought into the world. The language and exhortations reach for that of the Pentateuch, yet they are drained of all the authority and the mystery. Battles and kings and smiting and wickedness march past in a cloud of grim Elizabethan dust. The throat-clearing passage "And it came to pass" occurs no less than 999 times. Mark Twain said that if these words had been excised, Smith's bible would have been no more than a pamphlet. Its turgid passages nevertheless contained answers to the arguments then engulfing Western New York—infants should not be baptized and baptism is by total immersion only, government should be by a republic, man is not a fallen being, the Masons are a debauched group. I have found it almost unreadable myself, but there are reasons why the book seems rough to modern eyes. "If his book is monotonous today," biographer Fawn Brodie has written, "it is because the frontier fires are long since dead and the burning questions that the book answered are ashes." Christians of a more traditional cast immediately attacked Joseph's book, of course, with its audacious claims of an American biblical extravaganza, ready to be debunked with even basic archeology, and how smug they must have been with the roots of their own faith system safely buried under eighteen hundred years of Middle Eastern dust.

The most frequently quoted verse of the Book of Mormon occurs near the end, Moroni 10:4. Some disgruntled Mormon missionaries have called it the only useful passage in the whole porridge. "And when ye shall receive these things, I would exhort you that ye would ask God, the Eternal Father, in the name of Christ, if these things are not true; and if ye shall ask with a sincere heart, and with real intent, having faith in Christ, he will manifest the truth of it unto you, by the power of the Holy Ghost."

Ask if these things are not true. This is serious business for the potential convert. *Knowing* that this turgid, improbable book is true is the mainspring of the Mormon faith. All of the fuzzy and sticky-sweet elements for which the church is parodied hinge on this leap away from the empirical. The subjectivity of "knowing" is the defense posture that all missionaries are instructed to adopt if challenged or cornered by historical facts they cannot answer. "Tom, I *know* this church is true," one of them said to me while we sat in the sanctuary of the small ward chapel in the small town of Mexican Hat, Utah. The most rigid logic in the world can never contradict a belief like this.

There is a trace of coercion in Moroni, too, an insinuation that those who reject the story have been asking with a treacherous heart and without real intent, turns into a closed question on an endless loop. You simply keep asking until you decide that your heart has changed. Ask enough times, and the castle of logic could eventually fall. The tessellation breaks, the winding staircase collapses. And you enter into a layer above the rational; a step closer toward immensity; a road at night.

I didn't make it to the top of Hill Cumorah. After rounding a bend at the northern hump of the hill, the trees grew in closer, the light from the visitors center faded completely, and I must have absorbed some of Kris's discomfort, because the thought of making the switchbacking ascent became less and less attractive. I envisioned her sitting in the car, steaming at this weird fancy of mine, and I decided it would be best to rejoin her. A security guard might happen by the car seeking an explanation, and it would be better if I were the one to make it, even though I had none that would sound convincing.

I made many other nocturnal visits to Mormon sites. One in particular along a roadside in Iowa, a place named Mt. Pisgah, was one of the more ominous vistas I have yet seen in America.

The moon was summer-fat that night and gave the countryside the quality of a gray rainbow, with varying shades of obscurity turning otherwise functional things—fences, barns, meadows, swales—into chiaroscuro shapes that retained the lines of their daylight selves but without the substance. Mt. Pisgah was where a wagon train led by some of the first refugees from Illinois had set up a camp and a public vegetable garden for the immigrants who were to come after them. They named it after the peak in the Bible where Moses had been allowed to see the Promised Land, but Mt. Pisgah was rank with disease and starvation, and babies were born in frigid squalor. More than three hundred—the exact number is unknown—died and were buried in a common grave.

I got out of my Toyota Camry and walked around the grassy lots a bit, wondering if the places on which I was walking had been the sites of mud cabins in which people had starved to death. They had been obedient to the visions of their prophet and his story of the golden bible from the ground, or at least the peer pressure of their friends and family members. Nearly all of them at Mt. Pisgah would have known Joseph and heard him speak in those sermons that lasted several hours and were supposed to have been spellbinding.

For whatever else he had been, Joseph was a marvelous talker, gifted with the kind of radiant charisma and energy that seems to glow forth from under the skin. Those who met him, convert and enemy alike, often commented on an odd physical detail: his eyelashes were long. When he spoke, the inconsistencies of what he was saying seemed to fade into irrelevance. Ordinary life experience drained out of the listener, leaving the memorable, the higher, and the holy. His words had transfixed and seduced them; his people had adored him. Said one of the skeptical printer's devils who helped set the type on the first edition of the Book of Mormon, back in Palmyra: "He was known among the young men I associated with as a romancer of the first water. I never knew so ignorant a man as Joe was to have such a fertile imagination. He could never tell a common occurrence in his daily life without embellishing the story with imagination." Such was the imagination of the divine that had sent his listeners out onto the freezing nothing of Iowa, toward a saline lake in the death of the desert, after the storyteller himself had been murdered.

That shocking act of violence happened in the county seat town of Carthage, Illinois, where Joseph and his brother had been taken on the orders of the governor in June 1844. The Mormons had set up a giant riverside city called Nauvoo. This was a nonsense word, but Joseph told people that it meant "beautiful" in Hebrew. More than eleven thousand of his converts had gathered there, in a virtual theocracy under the rule of the prophet, presenting a challenge to the political balance of the young prairie state as well as an irritant to neighboring towns that resented their prosperity, their secret polygamy, and their refusal to acknowledge a democratic form of government. One of Joseph's counselors, outraged when the prophet tried to seduce his wife, printed an exposé sheet and Joseph responded by ordering the printing press smashed and thrown into the Mississippi River. This is what got him taken to jail and in a position to be lynched by the militias of two neighboring towns, who had smeared their faces with war paint for the occasion and forced themselves into his cell.

I arrived in Carthage shortly after three o'clock in the morning and found no signs for the jail. The town apparently did not officially acknowledge the site where its citizens ganged up and murdered a religious figure. Though there were tourist signs directing the way to the "historic courthouse square," the jail was unmarked except by the Utah church, which had long ago purchased the site of its prophet's martyrdom and erected a visitors center.

I came here as a spur on a trip from Montana to New England at a time of year when a bubble of summer low pressure had been pushing north from the Gulf of Mexico, turning the middle Mississippi Valley into a patchwork of rain that night, and the thunderheads glided and shifted like sandbars when the rain stopped. When lightning ripped, it was like a flashbulb that brought the whole countryside into gray brightness for a moment, as though it were a sick and jaundiced form of daylight. I remembered what I had learned about lightning while living in the Midwest twenty years before: that it does not come down from the clouds so much as it *shoots upward from the earth*, the rip of electricity acting as the force that rights the imbalance of ions between the ground and the clouds. What seems like the downward thrust of the lightning is an optical illusion. The human eye never seems to resolve, in that instant, that the yellow fire is actually coming up from the ground. This inversion insults our sense of the proper, and so we unconsciously fill in the aspect of heavenly descent.

I saw the bottom of the cloud-blanket tinted maroon from the radio towers on the Illinois flatlands as I drove southward, my elbow out the open window and the odor of angry metal washing through everything and the fireflies making lime streaks in the weeds. It was one of the most beautiful storms I had seen in years.

The streets of Carthage were empty in the intermittent rain. I went in circles for a time, looking for the jail and not finding a sign. The courthouse square was completely deserted. The statue on the lawn was not of Joseph Smith but of blind Lady Justice, her scales held up. The windows of the First State Bank of Western Illinois, a Rexall pharmacy, and a coin-op laundry gave her blank stares in return. A tabby with nervous paws crossed the street.

I eventually found what I had come for. On the giant lawn in front of the two-story stone structure was an iron historic marker put up by the state. It looked like a large spatula. IN THE OLD CARTHAGE JAIL, WHICH STANDS ONE BLOCK SOUTH OF HERE, JOSEPH AND HYRUM SMITH, PROPHET AND PATRIARCH OF THE MORMON CHURCH, WERE KILLED BY A MOB ON JUNE 27, 1844. TWO YEARS LATER, THE MORMONS WERE DRIVEN FROM ILLINOIS, WHERE THEY HAD SETTLED IN 1839, TO THE GREAT SALT LAKE.

I parked my truck on a side street and contemplated the iron fence. It looked as though I might wedge an insole between the bars and shimmy up over the pointed finials, but I decided to circumnavigate the property before making a commitment. And it was lucky that I did, because at the back of the visitors center and just northwest of the jail itself, I found an open gate. I could walk right in.

This was probably still illegal, and the whole block was visible to any cruising police officer, but, given the open gate, any encounter with the cops would likely amount to nothing I couldn't talk myself out of with an apology and a friendly demeanor. I was only an "aficionado of Western history" on a cross-country drive, which was wholly truthful, even if incomplete.

The rain had slacked, but the wind was in the treetops as I walked in the security lights around the south side of the jail and to the spot where Joseph Smith had fallen from the second-story window, already wounded from two gunshots in his back. His brother Hyrum had been killed seconds before by a shot to the face. At least one eyewitness account had Joseph flashing a Masonic hand signal to the mob below—the sign of extreme distress—and calling out "Is there no help for this widow's son?" before receiving an answer with a fusillade of bullets. He dropped to the flagstones below and lay still. The militia had dragged his slackened body to the side of a wooden well, sat him up upright, and finished him off as a firing squad. Yet there was nothing there to mark the spot except a reconstructed well top that drew no water.

About twenty yards away was a half ring of benches made of stone, facing a hefty tablet bearing some of the quotes of the prophet. *That by him and through him and of him the worlds are and were created and the inhabitants thereof are begotten sons and daughters unto God.* I sat there until I heard the wind begin to pick up again and thunder growing closer, then slept for a few hours in the front seat of my truck that early morning, parked as discreetly as I could manage in the parking lot of a nearby Methodist church, the rain hammering hard on the truck's metal roof.

In the morning, I did something I usually avoid: I went to the visitors center and signed on for a tour, dreading the faux-cheery conversation I would have to summon. But I wanted to see the inside of that jail. I wanted to see the passageway down which the mob advanced and contemplate the view from that window. I was the only tourist to show up at opening time, 10:00 a.m., and the staff was good enough to assign me a fellow for a quick walk-through.

One feature of the Utah church is the famous missionary program, in which all able-bodied young men are drafted (that is to say, strongly encouraged by their families and bishops, which is just as good as conscription) to spend two years wearing an FBI-quality black suit and a name tag, swearing off bodily vices and knocking on doors in all fifty states and almost every foreign nation that does not explicitly bar them. Recruits without the sales gene are sometimes called to be docents at the historic sites, where they help out the retired married couples who have volunteered in their late middle age to be sent out by the church once again for various tasks. This is the Mormon equivalent of RV culture. I drew one from the graying group, a retired speech therapist from Idaho. He went blissfully light on the spiel after I told him, quite truthfully, that I respected his church but was not interested in joining.

The gentlemanly Elder—whom I had begun to like by this point—took me up the stairs, in the footsteps of the mob, and showed me the room where Hyrum had been shot between the eyes and where Joseph had emptied a six-shooter at his attackers before his last stand at the east-facing window.

Do visitors have a spiritual experience up here? I wanted to know, and the Elder answered that in his experience the cell itself has no meaning except for what those who already believe have been inclined to bring into the room. Any feeling derived from the inanimate, in other words, is dependent on preexisting feeling. And in the case of the Elder, it most definitely existed.

"I do feel the spirit of the Lord here," he told me, as we both stood before the window. "I'm a person who cries easily and this room used to be hard for me. But it is getting better."

There is a final American site sacred to the Mormon imagination—one of the most hallowed in the whole cosmological system—and it can be found in an empty patch of grass in a suburb of Kansas City, Missouri. I arrived here off the interstate half an hour before midnight on Easter Sunday and found it without much trouble. Here at the northwest corner of River and Walnut Streets was the plot of ground where Jesus Christ is supposed to return in glory at the very end of the world.

I parked on the street next to what is called the Temple Lot and walked up a slight incline to the field. The night was misty and alit with the displaced maroon shine of Kansas City. A train whistle sounded and radio spires winked on the horizon. It was almost midnight.

I took off my shoes and went across the cold soggy grass to look at a wood-sided yellow church building at the north end. This was the headquarters of the Church of Christ (Temple Lot), one of the dozens of small breakaway Mormon groups who acknowledges Joseph Smith and his golden plates as being of God. What distinguishes this schism from the others is that they have the amazing good luck of holding the deed for this patch of ground on which I was now standing barefoot, the one that Joseph Smith had proclaimed would be the center of the future temple of Zion and the beginning spot for the apocalypse. Smith and seven others had come here in 1831 to dedicate the spot—which was then covered with a light forest—and to bury four "witness markers" with surveying notations carved on them. For good measure, Smith declared the spot to be the site of the original Garden of Eden, where man and God had shared full togetherness for the last time. A bishop secured the land for $300, but work on the temple never got far. The Mormons did not get along with their neighbors and were harassed out of the state eight years later on the orders of the governor, who had threatened to exterminate them. "Sell all the land in Jackson County, and all other lands in the state whatsoever," commanded Smith, apparently backing away from the revelation that Christ would return to this Missouri lot, and reckoning that even the Garden of Eden had a resale value.

After his death, though, his followers took the original proclamation seriously. The deed was re-purchased in 1867 by a small Mormon faction headed by a man named Granville Hedrick, and the descendants of this group have held fast onto it ever since, resisting legal challenges and merger offers. No temple has ever been erected on the lot, though the surrounding blocks are an extravaganza of Mormon architecture. The various branches of Mormonism represented here in Independence are like the Christian sects who have fought each other for centuries over the guardianship of Jesus's empty tomb in Jerusalem.

Look at what the emptiness has sculpted: A faction called the Community of Christ, founded by the son of Joseph Smith, recently erected a spectacular nautilus cathedral to the east. The Utah church maintains (what else?) a visitors center to the southeast with tall columns and large glass windows. Sweet music pours from its outdoor speakers at all hours. Parked on the street the night I visited was a sentinel of a less well-known church: a Ford Econoline van with Missouri plates, covered in painted Bible verses and apocalyptic messages. *Repent for the Kingdom of God is here. Before the fire of God. Turn away from your imperfections for in Zion God will unveil his fiery presence.* And under that, a P.O. box number where the curious could write for more information. Around the spare tire mounted on the back was etched a final exhortation: *Question Authority.*

All of these outposts surround the Temple Lot like brigades squared around a vacant parade ground. The spot of the missing temple is the emptiness around which they revolve, the open ground that gives them all a shape and a purpose: a form of the Lacanian Real.

The next morning, a Monday, I went to visit the small museum on the ground floor of the Church of Christ (Temple Lot) church, which looks like an overgrown suburban tract home paneled with wood. The original had been burned down in 1990 by a former member who felt like the apocalypse was drawing near and that his co-religionists were doing nothing to prepare for it. Jordan Smith, twenty-five, had already demonstrated strange behavior by wearing a sword on his belt, saying the Soviet Union was about to stage an invasion of the country with chemical weapons in accordance with biblical prophecy, and claiming that God had ordered him to "cleanse the church site." One night, he decorated his face with colored paint and set fire to the building, allowing himself to be taken to jail only after performing a war dance on the front steps. On the way in, I noticed a sign on the side of the reconstructed building. CHURCH OF CHRIST SPRINKLER CONNECTION.

I spoke with a pinch-faced Elder with a wooden cane named William Sheldon, who told me there were no current plans to build a temple and, furthermore, his church would not cooperate with the other branches of Mormonism in order to do so. "I really think that they think the Lord is going to sweep us aside and they will step in. But they are all here because of this spot." The temple would exist only in the future, in the country of maybe.

I took another walk out onto the lot, this time in daylight. Obscured in the grass in the temple site, and invisible to anyone who isn't specifically looking for them, are four slabs of pink granite, located on top of the spots where the Joseph Smith party had buried their "witness markers" in 1831. They each bear a plain directional legend. Said one: NE CORNER OF TEMPLE. These stones are the footprint of the sunken cathedral under Missouri—that magnificent coming edifice that Mormons believe will trigger the descent of Christ from the heavens and the bringing in of the millennium. Then the temple will be wreathed in clouds.

For now it is only an outline staked at four points, a tent in wait. Yet there is no disappointment to the Mormon vision in the barrenness of the lot. The *yet-to-come* is a marvelous thing, a pliable thing, and a sustaining promise that covers up the sense of disappointing Missouri ordinariness.

The leaders have not hesitated in the past to wreath fields and valleys with a glory and a significance that cannot be perceived except with the eyes of willing faith. Brigham Young, who led the largest remnant of Joseph's believers into the West, believed the earth itself was a living being. He said that it respired like a living human and that it was the breath of the earth—not the mindless tug of the moon—was what made the tides go in and out. "There is life in all matter, throughout the vast extent of all the eternities," he said in 1854. "It is in the rock, the sand, the dust, in water, air, the gases, and in short, in every description and organization of matter."

I am not one to call him wrong. The atoms may very well be alive. I am equipped to see only a tiny part of the world, and the rest is concealed by night. Brigham Young was the second prophet, after all, of the religion of signs and wonders; founded on golden plates that nobody saw; that made Israelites out of the American Indians, a fabulous sepulcher of treasure out of a New York hill, gods out of ordinary believers and a Via Dolorosa in a dowdy county seat in downstate Illinois. A few impulsive words from Joseph Smith could turn a hill near his home into an ancient battlefield, a few housing tracts in Missouri into an Eden and then a Zion.

Tokens of eternity: I think I understand this. The writer Belden C. Lane has said this is one of the only ways we can conceive of a larger reality too gargantuan to be expressed in any direct language. "Metaphor, the irreducible substance of story, makes such frequent use of concrete, earthly images to define the ephemeral and obscure." Perhaps this is why the ancient Israelites refused to write the name of God and deliberately dropped vowels out of it: a sign of the unknowingness.

At some point during my wanderings around the country, my spiritual distresses eased. Knowing the full truth was never going to be in the cards; the "blessed assurance" spoken of in the old evangelical hymn would never arrive on this earth. Accepting that had been a long struggle. But I do believe this: there is a burning light at the core of the universe, a source of everything to which we are inexorably connected, and we can approach that light through symbol and metaphor—a refracting lens to view even an edge of an unspeakable brightness. I am now an ordinary congregant in the Episcopal Church; the forms and style of the old liturgy of the 1662 Book of Common Prayer and the Bible happen to be the most comfortable and intuitive set of lenses for me to put on my face and try to gaze at the light, though I recognize everyone has their own way of looking at it. And though I still cannot fathom joining the Mormon Church, I must hail its particular genius for baptizing the earth—America, in particular—with a sense of wonderment and holiness that is too easily forgotten: a half-remembered fantasy that wriggles just out of our field of vision and beckons us forward. It made the earth alive with the extra-rational, even the magical, and thereby tapped a deep human thirst for the sublime. The British essayist Joseph Addison wrote,

> Our imagination loves to be filled with an object, or to grasp at anything that is too big for its capacity. The mind of man naturally hates everything that looks like a restraint upon it, and is apt to fancy itself under a sort of confinement, when the sight is pent up in a narrow compass and shortened on every side by the neighborhood of walls and mountains. Wide and undetermined prospects are as pleasing to the fancy as the speculations of eternity or infinitude are to the understanding.

What often makes something beautiful is its *bigness*—its audacity of scope. Yet nothing physical can be big enough to completely satisfy. Long vistas of nature and the giant canvases that depict them are inspiring not just for what they are but for the magnitude of their further promises. Power lies in the unseen. Such is the mainspring of what has been called the shortest horror story ever written:

> The last man in the world sat in a room
> There was a knock at the door

Horror and beauty are close cousins because they both point to the void. The quality of a work of art, whether to frighten or to enchant, often hinges on the skill with which the artist has implied an unspeakable immensity behind the canvas without actually naming or depicting it. Hints and traces are usually enough. The imagination does the rest. Joseph Smith understood that need in his fellows and, with the magnificent paint of his words, summoned lightning from the clouds. He is best contemplated at night.

Drive

Into the car and away—away to the next valley over the ridge, away to the next town, the next exit, the unknown lump of color around the turn in the road just out of sight, leading and receding. Into the car, into the country. Here is where I feel most at ease and have since the age of majority: propped upright and relaxed at the wheel, the country spinning along outside the windows.

There is little I love more than the spell of motorized land journey, a languorous day, a vague forward-looking destination in mind and a full tank of gas. If there is an opportunity to fly, I will not take it unless the schedule makes it mandatory. I have crossed and re-crossed the breadth of the United States alone, more or less coast to coast, at least thirty times in the course of twenty years, and I've made hundreds of lesser partial crossings across all forty-eight contiguous lower states in the bargain, feeling some unspecified hunger to lay down a coat of invisible paint.

All that country means all that *driving*. Horizon plus time: an exultant combination.

My personal endurance record is twenty-eight unbroken hours. This drive connected Phoenix, Arizona, to Appleton, Wisconsin, eighteen hundred red-eyed miles without a stop for anything but fuel and coffee. I can remember little else but the glare of the sun in Iowa and the curve near the end of the odyssey where tires screeched and the white lines grew fuzzy before I recovered and pushed on through. The largest city in the U.S. where I have not been is Fayetteville, North Carolina; the only state capitol steps I have not climbed are in Tallahassee and Juneau. I can tell you that the most beautiful capitol campus belongs to Kentucky; the most impressive to Texas. The worst to Arizona, followed closely by Oklahoma. The totems of statist power function as emotional slalom flags, meant to be touched quickly as part of the drive-by—a brief tactile experience in lieu of possession.

My annual copies of the Rand McNally Road Atlas (accept no substitute, even in a digital age) have been coffee-stained and torn, phone numbers scribbled near the legends, their covers usually off their staples within a month, the page edges worn by repeated jammings into the side pocket of the door, and the repeated hasty withdrawals as I prop one across my knees at sixty miles per hour, trying to decide, with the option fast expiring, whether to take a particular exit or side road before the chance is gone. This last item is a dangerous habit that I keep resolving to break, but slowing down and pulling over for a good hard look at the map is almost physically painful, an option reserved only for major structural deliberations of the day's course, not a minor choice of way that will cost me at most two hours and could lead through an interesting canyon, or a town I'd wanted to see, or just a road I'd never traversed before.

Such choices enhance the map, strip away its semiotic essence and make it a deeper document—something I can visualize, if only partially, as the very thing that it represents instead of black lines and red dots. I am a terrible frustration for the people who have been unfortunate enough to be along for the ride. I think interstate highways are a historic crime against the country, albeit one with grudging benefits, something on the level of life insurance or five-dollar movie popcorn or the Mexican-American War of 1847. You loathe what they stand for, but occasionally appreciate them.

Other contradictions lurk within this roaring appetite. Automobiles mean *freedom*: this was one of the organizing principles of the automotive revolution so close to the preexisting national mythology and soon a cornerstone of the American Dream, that quest to punch into new territory, ahead of the rest, and conquer it in the name of home ownership, big breathing lawns, and open spaces where the children can run free. Yet the car has created some truly terrible civic decisions in the last seventy years: checkerboarding suburbs, the withering of mass transit, those big breathing spaces that look so attractive but divide people from one another and wreck the conventionally humane ideas of community, and a dependence on great gluts of oil from pusillanimous, moth-eaten dictatorships.

I have no moral high ground; I cannot preach to anyone, because I love to drive. I love it even as I jam the mosquito-nosed proboscis of the gas pump into the welcoming slot and feel the flow of the hot and heavy liquid rushing into the tank, and know that there is a shade of guilt here, that this zesty vegetative remnant of the prehistoric world is going to be converted to thick black gunk as I skate around on my vague and sometimes pointless meanderings, helping to cloud the atmosphere with carbon and sap away a resource that is all too limited. It feels vain and somewhat prolicidal. But I cannot help myself. I love it too much. Without that option to wander, I feel as though I may not be me.

I took my first major extended trip near the start of my freshman year in college. I was taking some classes at the University of Kansas and had been given the use of a former Hertz rental car sold off on the private market; it was a red Ford with plaid upholstery and an air conditioner that spat out humidity and a whiff of metal. There was only a radio, but I set a boom box on the passenger seat and made my own stereo. I was a bit on my own that summer, but I had a car that would (*let the high praises of God be in their mouth, and a two-edged sword in their hand*) take me anywhere, and near noon on the day before the Fourth of July with no classes and the weekend stretching out like a scroll in front of me, I went down to the parking lot behind the J. R. Pearson residence hall, climbed into the Ford, and started heading east, without a clear plan in mind.

I got off the turnpike in Kansas City, wound through middling neighborhood arterials for a bit, and eventually found myself on Interstate 70 (yes, I cheated) in Missouri heading still farther east. There was a rise in the road near the town of Lee's Summit, where the sky arced large and was almost cathedral-like; the distance to the horizon seemed to be nearly twenty miles, and it was as if the whole country to the east were ready to unfold and show itself to me. I had never really been east of Kansas at that time, and the older half of the continent felt wonderful and exotic. I still recall that sense of incipient *possibility* as one of the more exhilarating moments of my late adolescence. And I still take note of that particular lift on I-70, which I have traveled dozens of times since that first trip.

At that moment, I decided not to turn around and go back to Lawrence but to just keep going, damned where I was going to sleep, formulating a vague plot to see a high school friend from Arizona who had moved to Columbus, Ohio. I thought I would see him quickly then turn around and be back in time for microeconomics on Tuesday morning. On I went through Boonville and Columbia, Crystal City and Truxton, and finally to the edge of St. Louis, where at nightfall I tuned into an FM radio station playing classical music to accompany the fireworks over the Mississippi; the *1812 Overture* with cannon fire played as the Arch came into view. Off the Poplar Street exit, I parked illegally and ran down to the water, touched the river that I was seeing for the first time, wandered through the crowds in the park, knocked on the gray-plated wall of the Arch, listened as the wife of then vice president George H. W. Bush made a brief speech to the crowd, yelling "Happy Birthday, America!" at the end.

But this was not nearly enough. I kept going, over the Eads Bridge, into Illinois, where fatigue and the reality principle started to overtake me and I abandoned my plans to see my buddy in Columbus on the spot. The industrial gloaming of the Illinois side of the river was a dark lure—I have always been drawn to wrecked landscapes—and I took a highway exit that listed weirdly dystopian place names like Cahokia and National City. The scent of cracked petroleum and green undergrowth curdled outside the windows, and I zigzagged through roads that led past refineries, sinister-looking taverns, and white clapboard cottages. There was one vista I will never forget: a wide and empty field stretching away under a reddish night sky with a line of tall poplar trees far in the distance and a set of radio antennas winking red. To another observer, this landscape was a mealy and uninteresting section of downstate Illinois; to me, then, it looked utterly fascinating and ominous, like the way a roll of hay in a Provençal field or a set of café chairs might have arrested the imagination of a not-very-good impressionist painter. I cannot explain the power of this heart-pulling image, even today. And I kept moving, scarcely wanting to stop or even slow. (I have since relocated this field just south of the town of Roxana, and I'm sorry to report it does not look nearly as foreboding in daytime to me now as it did in a hazy, hell-going summer night to an eighteen-year-old.)

Where was I going now? A study of the atlas under the dome light yielded an answer: I settled on a highway tracing the northern route up the Mississippi, passing by the wheeling possibility offered by the sign that read Chicago: 254 Miles (it felt at the time a place as far away as Damascus). The two-lane highway had been deemed the Great River Road by some government entity or another and was marked periodically by signs with the image of an old-timey riverboat wheel. I followed this road past bluffs and houses with docks and through sleeping little towns, the long plate of the river water winking in and out of sight, as the night deepened and drew closer to morning. In the town of Kinderhook, I stopped to buy a Pepsi from a lonely vending machine underneath a lonely sodium lamp and drank it as I continued driving, thinking of the girlfriend I had broken up with to attend the summer session at Kansas, picturing her asleep in her narrow pullout bed back in Arizona, mouth open against the pillow, hair smelling of that morning's White Rain shampoo, an intoxicant to me then. How many miles away? Yet the world was huge and I wanted more of it.

I saw the light grow over a field of wheat-heads and reentered Missouri at the town of Hannibal, the boyhood town of Samuel Clemens, who learned here to set type and began the career that would make him Mark Twain. It was the morning of the Fourth of July, and the theme motels were jammed full of tourists who had come for some kind of fence paint-off or raft race or some other damn thing. Paying for a motel seemed a huge extravagance (although gas did not!), and I felt like I could drive well into the next day and possibly into the next night. Stopping to piss in a vacant lot that overlooked the river, I thanked my good fortune, but decided to quit the journey's forward motion then and there, and hoped that I could make it back to Kansas without falling asleep. This I did, though barely. And for years afterward, I always took note of July 3 and tried to get away if I could for some directionless nighttime driving in commemoration of this oddball trip that is still a formative experience, a founding event whose anniversary I have tried to preserve.

I don't think it is an accident that the posture of driving is one of concentration. You are sitting in a state of daydreamy relaxation, but driving is not meant to be mindless. Rather, it is something like a bench for a craftsman who enjoys his work. True road traveling requires the ability to see the land passing and, to some extent, to feel it. Without that, there would be no point. Four driving days to cross the country; a lifetime to know even a fraction of its everyday majesty. In a 1992 essay for *Harper's*, entitled "An Urge for Going: Why I Don't Live Where I Used to Live," Richard Ford wrote this: "I take it as a point of civic pride that I know where the streets go in most major American cities, where the freeways meet in Downey. Where there is at least one good Indonesian restaurant in Providence, how to get a tire changed fast in the short-term lot at the airport in Great Falls." This is the kind of universal citizenship that I long for, even if it is true that the leveling force of the Internet has made obsolete the hard-won knowledge of road journeys—made it so any moron can call up in ten seconds a photo of a Maine beach that you tried so hard to see, or detailed knowledge of a Memphis barbecue place that you happened on by accident. I am left with the hubristic pleasure of refusing to consult GPS in cities where I last visited ten years ago, stubbornly feeling my way around unaided.

The longest single American journey I ever completed went through twenty-nine major cities, totaling eleven thousand miles in a conversion van, tracing a grand arc around the country: starting in Tucson, through the Mohave to Las Vegas, then to L.A. and up the West Coast to Seattle, across to Montana and down to Salt Lake City, over the Rockies and through the Midwest (taking note again of that wonderful rise near Lee's Summit, Missouri) to Chicago, New York, North Carolina, Georgia, Mississippi, Texas, then back to Tucson again. And in those two months of constant travel, sleeping on roadsides and in Walmart parking lots, in all of that time, I realized that there wasn't a single piece of road longer than ten miles that I hadn't *already driven on* at some point. This was truly a sign of advancing age.

I have become more vulnerable to the seduction of a motel as I have gotten older, but the standard operating procedure in my feckless twenties was to make every attempt at saving forty dollars by sleeping in the car or on the ground near the car. This is most easily done in the mountainous West, where federal land is abundant and a tent can be pitched in the woods or in the desert with little fuss or fanfare. The first time I tried this was after midnight outside the town of Moab, Utah, where I pulled over, exhausted, on my way back to Arizona from Kansas after that first magical summer. The desert yawned in every direction, but I somehow felt like sleeping close to town. There was a lot across the highway from a giant patch of bare ground, with what looked like a white tarp across it. I rolled out a sleeping bag and tossed fitfully until morning, dirt in my hair. A few years later, I learned that I had spent the night across the road from the contaminated site of an abandoned uranium mill, where the core material for atomic bombs had been processed.

Yet in cities and in the East, the land is private, the lights are invasive, and the cops are prowling. The sleeping-in-the-car routine takes some practice, and I got very good at it. Total up all the nights I've slept in the reclined driver's seat of the car, shoes off, keys in the ignition, fleece pillowed up on the headrest, and it would likely add up to six aggregate months. There is a system. Churches are by far the best option in a suburb: they have empty parking lots, often in the rear, out of sight of the street, and nobody ever pays attention to a lone car there after midnight; it is assumed that someone must have left it there after choir practice or baking class. Park in a way so that the car is not skulked off in the shadows, but slightly in the glow of the security lights so as not to arouse suspicion. I have rarely been bothered in the parking lots of the Lord.

This is, unfortunately, not a dwelling option on Saturday nights (early arriving parishioners on Sunday wouldn't like the sight of a derelict in their lot), and so the next best option is a school or behind a shopping center. A residential street, out of the lights, in a solidly middle-class neighborhood also works well. For one night, you can pick your ideal neighborhood, rent free. But you must be careful. Socioeconomic redlining, unfortunately, plays a deciding role. Your position is vulnerable (what could be more elemental to our prehistoric sense of predation like the feeling of being attacked while sleeping?), and whether it is fair or not to associate poverty with crime is a debate that shouldn't be held with oneself as an exhibit under glass. The neighborhood cannot be too rich either, as the cops are more responsive in these areas and some of the more paranoid among the wealthy have their own security guards who are paid to look for unwanted folks like me outside their downy estates. And so I look, above all, for dullness when it is time to turn off the headlights.

Cops have awakened me only a few times. Two of them tapped on my window at dawn outside the gates of the famous Black Hills Passion Play in Spearfish, South Dakota, where the life of Jesus is recalled for tourists. They were polite, but still ran my license number through dispatch to check for outstanding warrants. Another officer was less genteel in a town whose name I don't recall outside the Pine Barrens of central New Jersey. He pounded on my window with the butt of a flashlight, hard, jarring me out of a deep sleep, and I woke up with shouts and thrashing. The lady who lived in the house I had parked outside of had called the police, and I was told I really ought to get moving. Though I had broken no laws, I thought it wise to be compliant. Anyway, it was dawn. I still resent that Jersey cop, because I hated that feeling of being woken by force and surprise, and I've been far less able to relax on a residential street ever since. Rainy nights are the best: nobody is out, the feeling of security is that of being at home, in bed, and the tapping on the car roof is a lulling and comfortable sound.

After waking, the usual routine is to rub the eyes, crank up the seat, then drive to the nearest gas station, generally the only business open at six o'clock in the morning, for coffee. I am not discriminate in this area: any kind of swill will do the trick. Heavy sugar, heavy lightener. Then, drive for an hour, radio loud, to a diner for breakfast and a copy of the local newspaper. A distinct sense of pleasure emerges from reading the metro news in a strange town—the prolix city council dramas, the features, the wedding announcements of people I will never meet (I wonder if they'll make it; what will happen to them), the occasional spot of good writing, a cranky letter to the editor. I will have bought the local newspaper from the rack outside and will have used it to conceal a small washcloth and a pocket-sized bottle of Head and Shoulders. At some point, I will take this package, along with my chipped plastic water glass, into the men's room and lock the door. Then, I'll empty the glass, fill it up with tap water and dump it over my head. Wash, lather, rinse, dry. Fingers through the hairs, a sponge of the armpits, other business accounted for, and back out with my empty glass and clean hair. This costs no less than six dollars and comes with breakfast. Shaving and teeth brushing is generally done at the side of the road, with the aid of the driver's side window and a bottle of water. Then, it's back in the car for another day's journey, another pass at America.

There is a quality nearly erotic about a smooth weaving through poky lanes of interstate (caught again!) with a good song on the radio and a hand draped casually on the wheel. Local radio, like the local newspaper, is always the first choice, the concentric circles of the broadcast zones eliding into each other in a chain of spheres across the country, as omnipresent as they are invisible, fueling the dreamy concentration with a hum of pop culture consensus. While it is true that distinctive local radio has been partially drowned in a corporate bathtub of iHeartMedia, enough independents can be found by periodically sending the scanner to fetch a new voice on the left side of the dial. At 4:00 p.m. EST comes NPR's *All Things Considered*, another bland continental voice as durably unifying as The Eagles, The Commodores, or Trisha Yearwood, and I remember my time as a passenger crammed with at least forty strangers in an aerial tram outside Palm Springs when the driver, feeling whimsical, put "My Girl" on the loudspeakers, and all of us began to sing, at first hesitantly, then more boisterously. Even in the mass-production zone of cultural fulfillment centers, you can perceive Walt Whitman's sense that we are all connected in matters of wordless language, despite different races and tastes, seeing the same "vapor as it flew in fleeces tinged with violet." This land contains multitudes, but it draws its people together in extravagantly conceived accidental communities of art, sound, and road.

Here's another giant contradiction: I don't even like cars. Or better said: I am indifferent to them and uncaring of their particularities. My gang of friends in junior high school went through a car fetish phase, drawing elaborate sleek designs in the recesses of their notebooks, invariably in imitation of DeLoreans, and each other, in the way that girls of a slightly younger age are supposed, by gender essentialists, to pass through a "horse phase" and read *The Yearling* and *Misty of Chincoteague* with a certain longing. I pretended to be interested (what girl or boy does not stutter through the low-grade misery of junior high school with a surfeit of pretending), but inside I could not have cared a hamster's ass about cars. I wanted a driver's license just as bad as my friends—and the day it came was like a received parole—but the style and the aesthetics of the ride never mattered. I have not washed a car since I was eighteen years old. This habit, learned mostly from my dad and done as a self-imposed obligation anyway, stopped after the summer I passed through St. Louis at night. The outward condition of the car should not matter, so long as it takes you where you need to go and can be depended upon with minimal maintenance.

The best car in a long line that I have owned was a boxy and innocuous 1985 Toyota Camry, which marched like a robot soldier nearly a quarter of a million miles before I had to let it go. Four cylinders, stick shift, a speedy merge, and a steering alignment slightly out of whack as a souvenir from the only time I have deliberately taken a car airborne on a bumpy road (knocking my friend's head against the ceiling in the bargain). At one point, the hinged lid over the gas tank refused to stay closed, and I simply drove around like that, with it flapped open to the breeze. I didn't care what the car looked like. It was an extension of me, true, but an object whose appearance was never central to its core function. The car is like your eyes—seeing outward, not regarding itself, total outer-directedness. What matters about the car is where it can take you, what it can show you.

This exposure can be as profound or as mundane as you choose to make it. I have always tried to combine the rambling with an appreciation for the local geography, although this is a lake that has no bottom. I once was taken to an over-fried lunch by a pair of elderly sisters whom I had met in a church outside the town of Superior, Nebraska. The northbound road into town was a series of prairie swales that I halfheartedly admired on approach, typically at the speed of seventy miles per hour, loving, as always, the interplay between the fixed and the fluid. During lunch, the sisters told me they had grown up at the beginning of the twentieth century on a farm just off this road. They described the spot, which I knew. It shamed me a bit to think of how they and their parents had worked themselves to the bone on that plot, lacking electricity or running water; they had deep intimate knowledge of the land that I blithely darted past without truly understanding or seeing the kinds of activity, geological and human, that had made the grassy undulation what it was.

Painful as it is to initiate *drivus interuptus*, I make it a general policy to slam on the brakes for historic markers, those bolted, steel-plated toothpick flags of memory that lend character, depth, and meaning to a rug of grass or an impasto of mountains. The best markers tell a specific story, in around three paragraphs, about an event that happened right there on that ground: a cabin that once stood, a massacre that took place, a song that was composed. I'm thinking now of the one in Smith County, Kansas, that announces the vanished homestead where Brewster Higley penned the song "Home on the Range." He had moved to that spot to escape a shrewish wife, hence: *Where seldom is heard / A discouraging word.* For all of its other virtues, Kansas has the best historic markers in the U.S.: loaded with context, site-specific, and easy to read even in the dark with your headlights aimed at the steel plate at a non-glaring angle. The worst are in Pennsylvania, which is a shame for a state so rich in American happening. Pennsylvania's memorials are as brief as a telegram, just as archaic, often pointless, and devoid of context. And they are annoyingly abundant, forcing me to stop for baffling miscellany—I like my miscellany served with a helping of purpose.

One of the finest historic markers I ever saw was one near the town of Menominee, Wisconsin, on a foggy spring night. My college girlfriend was in the car with me, patient with this eccentricity, as I hit the brakes for yet another marker, expecting a schoolhouse site or a politician's birthplace, but instead finding not a sign, but a stone monument bearing an intellectual shock. This spot on the roadside of the Upper Midwest happened to mark the forty-fifth parallel, meaning that we were exactly midway between the north pole and the equator. There was a half-crescent illustration on the iron plate, locating us on the curvature of the earth. At that moment, I had a sudden dizzying sensation, like a camera angle abruptly wheeling backward at a thousand miles a second, of being fixed on the whirling globe in a sea of blackness. It was a moment not unlike that state of weird awareness that the French author Georges Bataille terms "disintoxication" (or perhaps what Katharine Butler Hathaway would call an "arterial sentence") when the banal facades and fictions of life disappear for a moment and we become conscious of an overwhelming reality: our own mortality, the mortality of others, or perhaps just the sense of being loose in a vast and dazzling emptiness, as the historic marker was there to helpfully point out. This invisible line belted the globe; it appears in unbroken sequence across ten U.S. states, and yet this small stone in Wisconsin and a giant highway sign in Salem, Oregon, are the only two places I have seen it commemorated.

"How was it?" my girlfriend asked, wearily bemused, when I climbed back into the Ford. "Best I've ever seen," I said. It was as oddly frightening as that night field in Illinois, but I think this comfortable sense of dread is also what helps gives the country richness, drama, and adventure. I will never forget my first sight of Crater Lake under the moonlight; my heart was thunking as I passed the last ridge on the trail I was not supposed to be on, this weird shining immensity about to come into view, as though a hole in the surface of the world were about to open and devour my frame of reality.

I like to go to a source, even if the source has just announced itself unexpectedly with a sign, a brochure, or a half-remembered name on the map—Ascension Rock, for example, near Whitehall, New York, where the Adventist prophet William Miller and his followers gathered on the night of October 22, 1844, to await what Miller predicted would be the end of the world. Spook Hill in Lake Wales, Florida, where an optical illusion in the road lends the impression that tennis balls and grapefruits are rolling uphill. Bartlesville, Oklahoma, where Frank Lloyd Wright once designed a slim skyscraper for an oil services company (now the weirdest bed-and-breakfast in the Sooner State). A calm lake in Indiana where the now-neglected author Gene Stratton-Porter kept a country house and wrote book after book. The house in Ketchum, Idaho, just barely visible from the road, where Ernest Hemingway ended his life. To see what they saw, the approximate shape of the terrain, the same line of mountains, the same approximate oxygen, perhaps shuffle the same dirt. It is meaningless and brimming with portent, all at once.

The map of personal history plays a role, too. Life feeds best on new experiences and does not benefit from endless retracing, but I sometimes cannot escape the draw. In Seattle, I had to stop again at the neon-lit and self-consciously gothic B&O coffee shop, where I downed two espressos in preparation for an awful all-night drive back to Missoula, Montana, after a final and irrevocable breakup with a woman I had been with for two years and now understood I would never marry. This was the night before my thirty-fifth birthday; a man's biblical allotment is supposed to be seventy years, and if this was true, that night was an exact chronological fulcrum, the biological equivalent of the halfway mark between pole and equator. In Cornwall, Connecticut, I revisited the grounds of a failing prep school where I taught for a summer, down the road, the geography nerd wants to add, from the house of Charles Van Doren, former Columbia professor disgraced in the quiz show scandals of the 1950s (I never bothered him). I also saw the school had destroyed the horseshoe court that I had been so proud of setting in concrete. *All flesh is as the grass.* In San Francisco, I cannot reasonably avoid driving past houses of various friends or corners where certain conversations took place. In Phoenix, I sometimes relent to a drive-by of the house in which I grew up. In Denver, I slept in the car on a lovely rainy night a few blocks from downtown St. Joseph's Hospital, where I was born in the maternity ward forty years ago. These places are imbued only with as much meaning as we choose to assign. They are emotionally prepackaged, and sometimes feel phony and cheap.

So much better are the encounters that can never be planned and the sights that bring a certain calm transcendence. There is great happiness to be found in a banal view; Edward Hopper understood this, as did Richard Ford, who has written about the pleasures of the "literal landscape" in the ambiguously zoned and utilitarian swaths of central New Jersey. Willie Nelson's wistful line about "seeing things that I may never see again" while on the road never made sense to me; I want to see certain American spots again and again, as many times as I can. There is such unexpected beauty in the visual bric-a-brac of the roadside: those great sad homes on the edges of small towns in western Maryland lit by electric candles in front of window curtains; a room you spot on the second floor of a town house with a ceiling fan and a poster of Morrissey; the way the concrete shell of a car wash is angled to the street in a crossroads at the edge of a Texas town; the rails shining in orange sunset in a railroad yard in Council Bluffs, Iowa; the empty-eyed slab of the Michigan Central Station in Detroit looming like the corpse of an assassinated monarch over the ruined prairie kingdom; a towering apartment block in Philadelphia once owned by Father Divine; the way the skyline of Pittsburgh explodes into view at the northeastern end of the Fort Pitt Tunnel; a riverboat casino in Missouri where I won five dollars on the first hand of blackjack I ever played and stopped cold right there and walked out (this may serve as a metaphor for the whole driving experience; don't linger); a middlebrow country club in Alabama where I plundered a shower in the locker room; the Dollar General store in Murfreesboro, Arkansas, where I bought boxer shorts when running low; a highway bridge near the Okefenokee Swamp in Georgia where I once stopped, got out, and felt the night close in like a perfumed blanket. Ours is a country where memory and fresh experience twist together.

Is there a self-indulgent side to all this? Isn't there something breathtakingly arrogant, and annoying, about blowing into a town, making the rapid-scan, glancing at the courthouse, zigzagging along the river, perhaps downing a Reuben-on-rye at the diner before getting the hell out after sixty minutes and feeling as though the place has been notched, "owned," placed gently like a poached duck into an invisible bag of the mind? Thinking that you've understood a damn thing at all because you spied the house in Cadiz, Ohio, where Clark Gable grew up? (No time to take the tour, thanks.) What have I gained, really, with another cruise at the posted speed limit through another town or city, in a stack of previously cruised tens of thousands of settlements, among Dutch colonials and auto part shops and plastic kiddie castles in municipal parks? I will have almost certainly initiated conversation with no one, understood no new precepts, forged no new understandings. A polite and to-the-point exchange with the diner server is usually as far as my generalized shyness will allow me to transgress on the privacy of my fellow Americans.

Part of what really motivated me in the ten years I spent as a newspaper reporter was a license to speak to strangers: a built-in excuse—if not a self-preservation imperative—to drill through the thin layer of ice that encloses us as we walk around the planet minding our own business. I could "interview" anyone as long as a plausible construct could be formulated. This took effort and caused embarrassment, at first, but I learned to be dulled against my own insecurities and just start talking. The story provided license to interact, and some of the most enjoyable conversations I remember having with total strangers involved subjects far removed from what the interview was supposed to be about. Yet stripped of this identity and on the road within my moving metal walls, I am once again encased in a comfortable and useless silence, not living in practice with my own self-image as a wandering collector of brief, affable, and somehow meaningful exchange.

But this silence does have exceptions. An interesting life tale from a man I once sat next to at a firehouse fish fry in Emmitsburg, Maryland. A woman in San Antonio, Texas, who told me how much she distrusted her parish priest. The hard and genuine handshake I got from a man who had surveyed the highest point of land in the state of Nebraska and seemed happy to have his work appreciated. But I am sad, and somewhat guilty, to report that the drive is mostly solitary.

The arrogance has an acquisitive dimension, too. In trying to see as many U.S. places as possible, I think I might be attempting a repressed version of trying to *own* those places for a moment, to capture them and make them mine, as a tourist will try to possess, frame, and mount the Grand Canyon by taking a photograph from Bright Angel Point. One might well decide to deposit Alpha Centauri in a private bank account after a few glances. Nature never agrees to confiscation, of course. Not even our bodies truly belong to us.

In literature, there is a school of both fiction and nonfiction that strives for the encyclopedic prison: a book that seeks to explain the entire world in one document, to be the universal key to a subject. Pliny the Elder traveled all over the known world in the first century, obsessively writing down nearly everything he saw and cataloging the world's then store of knowledge into a mammoth *Naturalis Historia*, which included lapidary descriptions of dolphins, olive trees, volcanoes, statues, and wars. The French Enlightenment author Denis Diderot attempted to pour the world into his *Encyclopédie*; Honoré de Balzac wrote as though he were preserving the miniaturist details of Paris for another civilization. Melville decorated *Moby Dick* with every allusion he could drag: this great American novel takes place on five continents and three oceans. Jack Kerouac made motion a life's subject; John Dos Passos made the kaleidoscope of the nation a character in the U.S.A. trilogy. Former *Chicago Daily News* foreign correspondent John Gunther tried to report the entire world of the 1940s in a series of doorstopper books: *Inside Europe*, *Inside Africa*, and *Inside South America*. James Michener's novels read like admixtures of melodrama and Homeric charts. There is something at once noble and pathetic about this Sisyphean ambit, and I understand it perfectly.

Trying to "write" the world is trying, on some level, to own the world: a bit like the original sin of wanting to have the knowledge of God. The urge to drive may be a cousin to that ancient blasphemy of wanting to be everywhere and know everything all at once, which takes on a military aspect—aggression for the sake of possession—and always ends in futility and absurdity. *When Alexander heard from Anaxarchus of the infinite number of worlds, he wept, and when his friends asked him what was the matter, he replied, "Is it not a matter for tears that, when the number of worlds is infinite, I have not conquered one?"* The driving urge may also be an extension of Eros, the life force, the hand-maximizing urge, that thirst for living as much and as fully as the boundaries of biology will allow. And so I suppose my urge to knock off courthouses, touch the sides of civic monuments, see over the next ridge, and puncture the next county line is an oblique method of trying to pack as much Americana into the manuscript of memory as possible, to know my country in a more sensual and tactile way at the expense of a more fixed and certainly, arguably, more satisfying perspective from the porch of an owned house.

And this leads to an essential question: What the hell do I think I'm trying to accomplish? Would it be better to heed the advice, expressed on a refrigerator magnet I once saw, GROW WHERE YOU ARE PLANTED? Richard Ford wanted to know the same thing about himself regarding the number of homes that he'd rented over the years. He says: "One never moves without an understanding of that staying is the norm and that what you're after is something not just elusive but desperate, and that eventually you'll fail and have to stop. But those who'll tell you what you *have to do* say so only because that's what they've done and are glad about it—or worse, are not so glad."

I know I have been, on some level, sacrificing depth for breadth, and occasionally not very good breadth. There was *always* a schedule to keep, an obligation on the other end: a job, an impatient friend, a school calendar, a deadline. Severing the rope to a "real" life and becoming a complete and rootless hobo is an act I've never been able to pull off, though I look at hitchhikers, the graybeard RV crowd, and the young van-lifers with envy. Our physical bodies all come to occupy a tiny patch of land, or get scattered to the breeze, and so why not wander far on the slackened leash while it may still be done, knowing that we'll be rounded back home at night? And so why not stack up summertime experience like harvested wheat?

An ancient Norse metaphor for life is a great hall with a window on each end. A sparrow flies through the first window and flutters on to the next window. That is life: a flight from one obscurity to the next, though a bright and fascinating chamber, full of portraits, ornaments, and filigree. But the bird cannot stay. It is hustled in and out, with barely enough time for a long look. The drive is ancient, and so is the paranoia that something important might be missed on the journey; an irrecoverable truth; a vision that could heighten the experience, delight the senses, perhaps make the whole ineluctable puzzle make sense. And thereby a horrible dilemma: Do I stay in one place? Or do I keep moving?

Which option is ultimately more futile?

I can only act in doses, and immersed in an idealized theory of self on the drive, I do not have all the time in the world to dawdle in the village and jaw with the citizens, and, at least in praxis, there is that constant febrile ever-urge to get hustling right along, into gear, through the light, around the bend, and hell-and-gone and going next to who knows where within the limits of land and road. There is never enough time to stay; something else beckons from the unseen: this is the needful fiction that fuels the drive.

Spillville

In the summer of 1893, the Czech composer Antonín Dvořák took his wife and six children to the frontier town of Spillville, Iowa, for a three-month stay. This was not a random choice.

Dvořák had been living near Gramercy Park in New York City and working as the director of the National Conservatory of Music of America. Though he had managed to compose his Symphony No. 9, *From the New World*—a grand triumph at its New York Philharmonic premiere and to this day his most popular work—the babble and chaos of the city grated on his nerves. The composer's secretary, Josef Kovařik, offered a suggestion: Why not take a vacation in Spillville, a prairie town populated almost exclusively by immigrant Czechs? It was an idyllic place where Dvořák could speak Bohemian on the dirt streets, drink pilsner, play the card game *darda* with his countrymen, and perhaps find some further inspiration for his music.

Upon his arrival in Spillville, Dvořák did all of that and more. He took early morning walks along the Turkey River and found a white oak stump on which to sit and listen to songbirds. He played the organ in the loft of St. Wenceslaus Catholic Church during morning Mass and strolled the brick sidewalks in the evening under kerosene lamps. People in town began to call him "the master." He would later describe the summer as among the happiest of his life.

He wrote in a letter home: "These people—all the poorest of the poor—came about forty years ago, mostly from the neighborhoods of Písek, Tábor, and Budějovice. And after great hardships and struggle, they are very well off here. I like to hear stories about the harshness of the early winters and the building of the railroad." The residents of nearby frontier towns expressed a grudging admiration for the industriousness of the Bohemians in Spillville but frowned on their drinking, their ineptitude with English, their Catholicism, and their clannishness. In larger cities such as Chicago, the Czechs picked up an unflattering nickname: *bohunks*, or *hunkies*, the likely antecedent of the slur *honky*.

On an Independence Day weekend 125 years after that Dvořák summer, I went to Spillville, to a city park not far from the white oak stump on which the composer had sat. The town has a population of approximately 350—almost exactly that of 1893—and some residents are the great-great-grandchildren of those who heard Dvořák play the organ at St. Wenceslaus. Most still have Czech names. Their neighbors no longer consider them suspicious. On the day of my visit, hundreds of people from the region had descended upon the town, spreading blankets on the grassy part of a baseball field, eating ice cream, and watching their children chase each other around the evening shadows, while waiting for the start of what I'd heard was the best fireworks show in northeast Iowa.

It had been an uneasy year in this part of the state, especially when it came to the subject of immigration. Young children at the U.S.-Mexico border were being separated from their asylum-seeking parents, and many in Iowa worried that—after a long period of easing tensions—federal agents were going to once again raid the state's meat-processing plants, which employed foreign laborers. Anxiety over immigration was also threatening to spill into the upcoming congressional election between the incumbent Rod Blum, a sixty-three-year-old Republican millionaire with roots in the Tea Party, and Abby Finkenauer, the twenty-nine-year-old daughter of a union pipe fitter and welder and a rising star in the Democratic Party.

I drank a beer with Randy Ferrie, a fifty-nine-year-old supervisor for a company that makes horse trailers in the nearby town of Cresco, and asked him about the election. He told me he didn't like the new closed-door attitude of the United States.

"It wasn't like this when I was younger," he told me. "A lot of people in this country are indeed very generous, but to be honest, we've gotten selfish and stuck-up. Now it's about, 'If new people coming here doesn't benefit me, why would I want to help?' The American Dream is eroding, and it is scary."

Ferrie said that although business was good, he was having a hard time finding qualified laborers. The answer, he said, was simply to make coming here easier. "If we want to have business or manufacturing, then we need to have bodies."

The fireworks began, and we paused to watch the red, green, and purple flashes exploding in the summer sky, reflecting off hundreds of upturned faces. A recorded medley of Van Halen, Lee Greenwood, and a Kate Smith imitator singing "God Bless America" boomed from a set of outdoor speakers while the fireworks fizzed off from three battle stations on the lip of a nearby sewer lagoon. A lightbulb display flashed military iconography: a jet, some tanks, clustered soldiers lifting a flag Iwo Jima–style. Then there was the inevitable finale of multicolored cannonade, which left the air fragrant with sulfur.

Most people folded their blankets, trashed their ice cream wrappers, and joined the scrum of cars inching for the exit at U.S. Highway 325, but about three dozen hardcores stayed to drink more beer inside the Inwood Ballroom, a wood-framed dance hall built in the early 1920s that had been expanded and lovingly restored over the years. Bobby Goldsboro, Louis Armstrong, Glenn Miller, and Lawrence Welk all played here on their tours through Corn Country. Tonight's act was a band called Yukon, featuring the mayor of Spillville, Mike Klimesh, on lead guitar. He wore his blond hair in a large swoop on top of his head with buzz-cut sides and a red plaid button-down over a T-shirt that said I'M A BADASS.

Klimesh is a direct descendant of one of the six Czech families that founded Spillville in the nineteenth century, and he has a pragmatic view of his mayoral post, which he has held for nearly two decades. "I'm like a plumber," he told me. "When they flush the toilet, they want to know the shit stays gone." As the mayor's band launched into a cover of "Copperhead Road," I stood next to a farmer with a baseball cap and a Czech last name. He swayed gently back and forth and told me he would vote for the incumbent president even though the recently announced tariffs on soybeans would cost him thousands of dollars. "It's going to hurt, but we have to get through it," he said. "We have to shake things up. We have to make things right again."

The state that novelist and short story writer T. C. Boyle once called "the Mesopotamia of the Midwest, the glorious, farinaceous, black-loamed hogbutt of the nation" is often held up as a bellwether for the collective American mood, which has a lot to do with Iowa's outsized role in electing presidents.

Its quadrennial January caucus takes place not in the solitude of the voting booth but inside school gymnasiums, living rooms, church basements, or anywhere that neighbors can gather, politely talk among themselves, and cast their votes to steer our national destiny in ways that resemble a lithograph of old-style, face-to-face democracy. The formal ritual started before the Civil War but took on its modern importance during the Democratic primary of 1976 when a southern governor named Jimmy Carter traveled extensively through the state and went door to door in dozens of towns to build an early lead for himself that proved unstoppable. The national political correspondent R. W. "Johnny" Apple elevated Carter's corn-pone charm with favorable stories that helped open donors' wallets.

Aspirants to national office are expected to court favor in Iowa in the same ponderous way: by buttonholing those of voting age at county fairs or on the street and eating enough dinners in the reserved back room of the local Golden Corral to double their diastolic blood pressure. As an old local joke goes, a farmer is asked if he's going to vote for a particular famous presidential candidate. "Don't know," he answers. "I haven't met him yet." This civic privilege might be on the way out. A series of management flubs in the 2020 Democratic primary—combined with observations that Iowa's largely white and aging population is unrepresentative of a heterodox nation—cast serious doubts on the caucus's continued prominence.

The U.S. representative of the district that includes Spillville, Rod Blum, supported a ban on travel to the United States by residents of seven predominantly Muslim countries. He told me in an email that although he wants to improve the visa program for farmworkers, "the massive influx in illegal immigration is driving down wages and making jobs less lucrative for those here legally. This must end."

His opponent, Abby Finkenauer, had beat out a crowded Democratic pack in part with a campaign video in which she held up her father's welding sweatshirt, covered in burn marks. "I'm running for Congress so families like mine have a champion in D.C.," she said. But immigration didn't figure into her message. No statement about her position appeared on her website until deep into the summer, and even then, it largely rested on platitudes.

I went to hear her speak at the opening of a Democratic Party office in the city of Decorah, and the crowd was so big that the event was moved to a larger space next door. After the customary thank yous and warm-up speeches from local office seekers, Finkenauer got up and spoke in the flat-vowel accent particular to the Upper Midwest. "This does the heart good to see this," she said. "Folks in Iowa care about others. That's who we are. We are not a country or a state that grows out of fear and division. We grow out of hope. That's what's on the line—hope. The future of our state is on the line here."

It wasn't a bad five-minute stump speech, though it was devoid of specifics. I edged out to the sidewalk in hopes of asking her a question on immigration. Several emails to her campaign had previously gone unanswered. When I had visited her Dubuque office, her staff promised me callbacks that I never received.

I introduced myself, and she smiled, but when I mentioned the word *immigration* in connection with the race, an unhappy look crossed her face. "We need commonsense immigration reform that treats everyone fairly," she muttered, barely above a speaking voice, and moved away quickly down the sidewalk, as if embarrassed.

Her campaign also went mum about a notorious incident on the western side of the district—the arrest of a migrant from Mexico in connection with the murder of twenty-year-old college student Mollie Tibbetts. National conservative media jumped all over the story as supposed evidence of an immigrant crime spree. Blum used the incident to rail against "sanctuary cities." Finkenauer offered prayers to the Tibbetts family over Twitter and said little else.

A longtime observer of the Iowa political scene, who could not speak on the record because of his job, told me that the sine qua non of state politics is the quality of neighborliness. Does a politician seem likely to help a stranger out of a jam? To listen to country music and drink a Budweiser with you? To solve a problem in a practical way while looking you in the eye? The last Democrat to have held this seat, Bruce Braley, lost his race for the U.S. Senate in 2014 at least in part because of a public mistake he made when a neighbor's chickens had strayed onto his vacation property. He threatened legal action—a brazen violation of rural protocol.

Being neighborly, however, can get complicated when the neighbors happen to be immigrants. Iowa's conflicted legacy on immigration can be traced back to 1975, when the state's Republican governor, Robert Ray, bucked elements of his party to accept more than one thousand refugees from Southeast Asia. In recent years, in addition to immigrants from Mexico and other parts of Latin America, small clusters of Bosnians, Liberians, and Congolese have arrived in Iowa.

"We're very cautious about it," the observer told me. "It's the toughest issue anyone faces. The polling numbers are not good. Immigrants save Main Streets, they save these little towns, but there's so much frenzy around the issue."

"I was raised in an atmosphere of struggle and endeavor," Dvořák liked to tell his music students. He was the son of a butcher, and it was expected of him that he would go into his father's trade. But he was spared the life of the block and the cleaver when his aptitude for music persuaded his father to allow him to pursue it as a career. He learned the violin, then later the piano and organ, which he played during church services as a teenager while living with his uncle in the Bohemian town of Zlonice.

His rise to international prominence as a composer was gradual, though by the time he arrived in the U.S., he was an eminent figure, admired for his symphonies, concertos, and chamber music. No matter how welcome the move must have been, leaving New York for the vast expanses of northeast Iowa surely caused something of a shock.

"It is very strange," Dvořák wrote to a friend back in Bohemia, describing the open spaces that he found at once intoxicating and alienating.

> Few people and a great deal of empty space. A farmer's nearest neighbor is often four miles off. Especially in the prairies (I call them the Sahara), there are only endless acres of field and meadow and that is all. You are glad to see in the woods and meadows the huge herds of cattle which, summer and winter, are out to pasture in the broad fields. And so it is very "wild" here and sometimes very sad—sad to despair. But habit is everything.

Spillville is on the edge of the physically lovely Driftless Area, which was spared the flattening impact of the glaciers during the last ice age and is thus characterized by dramatic hills and ridges that can remind a viewer of Provence. Vistas extend across twenty miles of small groves, hayfields, tidy farmhouses, and lonely silos. Corn is the big crop here, almost all of it meant for livestock feed, and it is planted in robotically precise configurations by mechanized planters guided by GPS technology.

Open space between two towns in the Driftless Area is dominated by an unbroken tableau of broad corn leaves waving in the breeze, but every now and then, a traveler passes a hog barn with big exhaust vents. Somebody has to feed the hogs, change the heat setting, shovel the manure, and move the hogs to processing, and this industry is the source of a good percentage of Iowa's subterranean workforce that few want to talk about. The laborers live discreetly, often in basic housing on the farm itself. According to a recent study by three Iowa State University econo-mists, U.S. pig farmers spent more than $837 million on temporary labor in 2012, paying out increasing sums of money for low-status jobs that few Americans will take.

The more visible concentration of immigrants is within the slaugh-tering facilities of major meat-packers—places that Dvořák might have recognized from the smells and sights in his father's butcher shop. About twenty miles down the road from Spillville is the larger town of Postville, which has a sign on the edge of U.S. Highway 18 proclaiming it to be the HOMETOWN TO THE WORLD. Not long after that, you pass the reason why: a processing plant called Agri Star Meat & Poultry.

In many ways, Postville is arranged—literally and economically—like a perfect company town in which every dollar flows from the factory gates. Such towns are often brutal, but they have a rawness and honesty about them that the immigrants of Dvořák's time would have recognized instantly. Loyalty equals survival: loyalty to the bonds of work, company, family, and ethnicity.

In this sense, Postville has changed very little, even as its racial demo-graphics have shifted, something its neighbors regard with a mild sense of alarm. Where else in the midwestern Corn Belt will you find, on an ordinary downtown street, African men wearing flowing Islamic robes, black-suited Orthodox Jews with curly *peyos*, and a Mexican evangelist preaching the risen Christ through a loudspeaker?

The transformation of Postville into an immigrant-heavy Iowa town began in the 1980s with a hunch by a Brooklyn butcher named Aaron Rubashkin, who specialized in custom kosher meat for the borough's growing population of ultra-Orthodox and Hasidic Jews. But transport-ing cattle to New York for slaughter under rabbinical supervision was ex-pensive. Could industrial livestock slaughter—a specialty of the Midwest since the days of the nineteenth-century Chicago feedlots—be married to a regimen of rabbinical oversight? And could a new market be developed among younger Jews who wanted to broaden their religious life by way of the kitchen table? Rubashkin wanted to find out.

According to Stephen G. Bloom in his book *Postville: A Clash of Cultures in Heartland America*, Rubashkin bought Postville's old HyGrade plant, renamed it Agriprocessors, and persuaded a staff of rabbis to move out to rural Iowa to certify that steers and chickens were killed according to kashruth standards, then developed methods for vacuum sealing and shrink-wrapping that kept the meat fresh for weeks. His business sense proved correct: sales were immediately strong, and annual revenues eventually reached $250 million. But Rubashkin and his son Sholom also developed a reputation in Iowa as bad neighbors who stiffed creditors on their bills, dumped effluent in streams, harassed union organizers, and started arguments among rabbis over what some considered sloppy and unnecessarily cruel practices on the kill floor.

The end of their reign came on May 12, 2008, when U.S. Immigration and Customs Enforcement agents raided the plant and arrested 389 people for various immigration-related offenses. Buses took the arrestees to the city of Waterloo, where inside an improvised federal "courtroom" located in a cattle fairgrounds hall, most were sentenced to five months in prison and later deported. Sholom Rubashkin denied knowledge of the illegal workers, but he was eventually charged with violations of child labor laws. He was found not guilty but received a twenty-seven-year federal sentence for financial crimes (his sentence was commuted in 2017). Postville lost a quarter of its population practically overnight, and Agriprocessors went bankrupt within six months.

Pledging to operate a more ethical business, a new set of Jewish owners bought the Agriprocessors plant in 2009. They renamed it Agri Star Meat & Poultry, repainted the water tower, spent $7.5 million in renovations, and brought in a crew of legalized Somalian refugees who had been living in Minnesota and Wisconsin. Guatemalans and Mexicans also started to come back, and today the factory is once again paying an average of nine dollars per hour to approximately 350 workers who kill, disembowel, and partition livestock.

On a bright morning in July, I met Nathan Thompson, a young employee of the Northeast Iowa Resource Conservation & Development office, who took me on a walk around Postville that I will never forget.

He first pointed to an old two-story, redbrick hall next to his office. "That's the Turner Hall," he said. "There were lots of these in German American communities all over the Midwest. They were like a gymnasium, an opera hall, and a social service agency all in one. Kind of like a YMCA. The German roots of this place go pretty deep: the Mass at the Lutheran church was said in German up until the 1950s."

We then crossed Lawler Street and went into a combined restaurant and *carnicería* named El Pariente, run by a man in his fifties named Ricardo Garcia. By any measure, Garcia is an American success story. Born in Aguascalientes, Mexico, he crossed the border and took a job in a slaughterhouse in Glendale, Arizona—work he didn't enjoy. But he was known as a charismatic man with functioning English, Spanish, and Chinese who could round up a lot of employees on short notice. One day he got a call from the owners of Agriprocessors, who offered him a job as a supervisor on the condition that he bring dozens of Mexican and Central American laborers with him.

"I told them that I'd need them to guarantee there would be places for these guys to live," Garcia said, "some cash deposits on housing, and a little food money before they got their first paychecks. Otherwise, don't waste your time dealing with me." The owners came through, and they had their workers within six weeks. The new arrivals soon bore the telltale signs of work in an abattoir: bent fingers and scars on their lower arms.

"I don't really like being here," Garcia told me. "But I love the business opportunities." Too many people in town do drugs, he said, and many of the white residents give subtle and overt snubs to the Latinos. But he does not offer any back talk. "When I was younger, I fought all the time. Ruined a lot of relationships. Now I just let it go in one ear and out the other. It will one day be a good town. We're not there yet."

Thompson and I then went around the corner and found a group of black men in long robes and short rounded caps called *taqiyah*, sitting in plastic chairs and gossiping in Somali. In a different time in Iowa, in Dvořák's time, they might have been old German farmers in overalls, cracking jokes and complaining about the weather. Thompson pushed the door into what is now called the Juba Grocery & Halal Market and introduced me to Ibrahim Sharif, a slender man wearing a purple button-down shirt and business slacks. Originally from Somalia, he worked at Agri Star for five years but had since gone into business as a seller of basic household goods and the occasional delicacy of camel meat. He tells me he closes the store three times a day for Muslim prayers. His competitor in North African goods across the street shares a wall with a synagogue, the Congregation Degel Machane Yehuda Stretin, which itself stands near the Iglesia Apostólica de Cristo and a nameless storefront mosque with sheets taped up in the windows.

A few doors down from the Juba grocery is the simply and elegantly named Kosher Market. Racks of tinned borscht, crackers, candy, and other goods with Hebrew labeling stand in front of glass-doored coolers containing beef products bearing the labels Aaron's Best and Shor Habor—the big national brands used by Agri Star, which is just down the street.

I talked with Yaakov Yitzak, a native of Israel with roots in Argentina, who wore a baseball cap emblazoned with the Brazilian flag. "Around the world, there are problems between Muslims and Jews, for sure," he said over the counter. "But when somebody is right in front of you, they are your friend. We didn't create the world, we only live in it, and we have to accept it."

He was articulating the basic rule of Postville, Iowa, which functions in the classic state of cultural détente known to multiethnic cities such as Beirut, Montreal, Dubai, and Hong Kong, all founded on keeping the peace among different races and religions in the name of a liberal capitalism that accepts anybody willing to work.

Today's strivers in northeast Iowa usually pass through Dubuque, one of Iowa's handsomest cities and one that also has a difficult relationship with newcomers who don't look like they belong there.

Settled by German Catholics in the 1850s, Dubuque boasts a status as the "first city" of the state, a jumping-off point for wagon trains and a city of opportunity for those who wanted to build a life in the cosmopolitan atmosphere of a Mississippi River town. Graceful homes cling to limestone cliffs, descending to a shabbier central city and blocks of three-story brick warehouses and millworks that now house tony steak restaurants and clothing boutiques. The waterfront itself is still active in chemical and coal traffic, but also boasts a casino, luxury hotel, and riverboat museum. The big industrial money is in the John Deere plant, which makes the 1050K Crawler Dozer, especially popular among overseas buyers.

Dubuque can be clubby and insular; family connections and friendships go back more than a century, and newcomers sometimes complain sardonically about being "Dubuqued"—that is, frozen out of social gatherings. An old legend holds that seventeen families run the place; everyone else is incidental. This isn't entirely true. Dubuque began its life within the banking and railroad orbit of Chicago, and in some ways, it still functions as a distant outpost. After the razing of some of Chicago's most notorious high-rise projects like Cabrini–Green and the Robert Taylor Homes, officials from U.S. Housing and Urban Development encouraged poor black families to use their Section 8 vouchers elsewhere, and several landlords on the north side of Dubuque stepped up with cheap apartments that once housed German American dockworkers and tractor-builders. HUD later complained that the city was discriminating against voucher applicants from "out-of-state," generally understood to mean "black from Chicago." In 2016, somebody burned two crosses on a downtown street, which summoned unpleasant memories of a 1992 riot that started after four hundred members of a local chapter of the Ku Klux Klan held a rally in Washington Park, then got heckled and shouted down by a much larger group of counterprotestors.

Immigrants keep a low profile in Dubuque. Those who want to learn English often make their way to the basement of the old Carr, Adams & Collier mill, which manufactured doors and windows at the turn of the century. Now called the Schmid Innovation Center, the old mill has a slick new interior that includes a coffeehouse, an art gallery, and several nonprofits including the Presentation Lantern Center, a drop-in center managed by an order of Catholic nuns. When I visited, the executive director, Sarah Gieseke, was getting ready to give a talk to her clients on a new Iowa law that had frightened many of them. She wore large green corduroy earrings the size of beverage coasters and sat at a conference table bearing cranberry muffins and cups of tea in the midst of six new Iowans from, respectively, Peru, Saudi Arabia, Iraq, Sierra Leone, Syria, and Guatemala.

Gieseke explained how Senate File 481, not yet law, would require local police to help federal immigration officials detain those in the country illegally—a measure similar to the anti-sanctuary bills touted by conservative commentators. "I know this is not an easy time," Gieseke said. "But know that we are here to keep you informed." As the group broke up, I asked the man from Sierra Leone—a native speaker of British-style English—if he felt like America had been generous to him.

"It's fifty-fifty," he told me. "A few people have asked me if people sleep in trees where I come from. Or if they have enough food to eat. They are watching you 24/7, especially when they know you come from a different continent. But they are not bad-spirited. They are just ignorant and naïve about what happens on the world stage. They have not traveled outside the Midwest."

He works as a teacher in a school for autistic children and needs the math skills to advance to a supervisory level. And for him, the ability to work at a non-farm job was the benevolent side of Iowa. "I love the opportunity here. That's why I say America is 'generous,' but in quoted form. If you don't work, it's a different America. With hard work, anyone will succeed."

Back in Spillville, at the Farr Side bar, a farmer named Jerry, on his third Calvert whiskey sour of the night, held forth on the peril facing the country. "What good do these immigrants do us?" he said to a small crowd gathered near his stool. "All they want is to take our welfare and send it back to their home country to make bombs. And then breed with our women, so their kids can be citizens. They learned it from that Kenyan. He wasn't born here—that birth certificate is a fake. You know it and I know it."

Sitting next to him was Lisa Costello, a dental assistant who also voted Republican. She has gotten to know several Mexican migrants and their children through her practice, and she offered some mild pushback. "They are hard workers, Jerry. They are here to make the most for their families. But I agree with you that this has to be straightened out."

"They don't know how to work," Jerry roared back. "We can't have these SOBs crossing the Mexican border without being a citizen. It's against the Constitution. They have to be here the *right way.*"

Listening to the tumult without getting involved was Mark Kuhn, a member of the county board of supervisors. "Very few cows get milked around here without an immigrant," he told me in a low voice after Jerry had migrated to another part of the bar. "Your average hog farmer out here? He hires immigrants to shovel the manure."

"How did this happen?" he wondered, sipping a beer. "When did we become such a closed nation?" It's a question that even reluctant politicians must address. That November, Abby Finkenauer defeated Rod Blum by a convincing margin of more than sixteen thousand votes. And even though she had hardly made immigration a cornerstone of her campaign, Republicans immediately predicted that she'd be a prime target for unseating in the next election because of this anxiety. As a headline on Breitbart put it on the evening of the election: "Mollie Tibbets' District: Pro-Amnesty, Pro-Sanctuary City Democrat Wins."

The Farr Side bar is two blocks from where Dvořák lived. In the months before he came to Spillville, while living in New York, he had invited several black performers to sing tunes for him that had their origin in the plantations of the South, and he incorporated parts of these songs into his *New World* Symphony. Dvořák knew that there could be no consideration of the folk music of America without first paying homage to the Negro spiritual; moreover, he believed that American composers had an obligation to draw from this material, just as he had worked rural Bohemian melodies into his own symphonic and chamber works.

While in Spillville, Dvořák indulged his fascination with America's indigenous people. He went to see a traveling medicine show put on by the Kickapoo tribe, who played drums and sang in a way he had never heard—the ensemble included two black Americans who incorporated

Native American musical elements into their performances on banjo and guitar. He took a side trip to Minneapolis to see the waterfall mentioned in Henry Wadsworth Longfellow's poem *Song of Hiawatha*. He later wrote an article for *Harper's* that expounded on the specific style of American music he felt was emerging. "It matters little whether the inspiration for the coming folk songs of America is derived from the Negro melodies, the songs of the creoles, the red man's chant, or the plaintive ditties of the homesick German or Norwegian," he wrote. "Undoubtedly the germs of the best in music lie hidden among all the races that are commingled in this great country."

Within a week of his arrival in Spillville, Dvořák finished the first sketches for his String Quartet in F Major, op. 96, now known as the *American*. "Thank God!" he wrote at the bottom of the score. "I am content. It was fast." The piece was first performed in private at the home of Jan Kovařik, the town schoolmaster and the father of Dvořák's secretary.

Music critics have since read all manner of native sounds into the *American* Quartet. Dvořák was a notoriously democratic sampler, and he never made it clear whether the third movement was supposed to channel a songbird, or if the second movement did indeed incorporate one of the African American spiritual hymns that he loved. Others have discerned within it the rumble of the *Chicago Express* train that took him to the Midwest, or the delighted laughter of friends mingling in a country tavern, or a Stephen Foster melody, or the ritual drums of the Kickapoo Tribe. It all blends together without a firm answer. This *American* Quartet yields whatever its listeners want to hear within it.

The National Road

President Thomas Jefferson authorized the construction of a highway on March 26, 1806, putting the federal government into the business of laying down roads to unify the eastern port cities with the fields of the interior. The all-weather road of crushed stone extended in a southwestern arrow from Cumberland, Maryland, into then-exotic lands like Ohio and Indiana.

Where a road goes, commerce will follow. Brick taverns quickly sprung up along the right-of-way, offering warm fires, liquor, and newspapers for travelers of the new national turnpike. "The signboards were elevated upon high and heavy posts," wrote lawyer Thomas B. Searight, "and their golden letters winking in the sun ogled the wayfarer from the hot road-bed and gave promise of good cheer."

Construction on the wagon road terminated at Vandalia, Illinois, when the funding ran out, and the road has long since been superseded by railroads and asphalt highways—commerce also leans inexorably in the direction of technological efficiencies and ever-larger markets—but portions of the old highway are still listed as "National Road" in their legal addresses. A retired nurse named Charlotte Fogarty lives in a two-story house down a long driveway off the road to the west of Springfield, Ohio. One morning in 2017, she went out into her yard and saw a cluster of hazmat trucks at a nearby trailer park. *This can't be good*, she thought.

Fogarty made some phone calls and learned that the crews were clearing the site—which included a defunct candy store—of underground oil tanks to make way for a new Dollar General store. Fogarty was familiar with the discount chain store with a yellow-and-black logo that had become a ubiquitous presence in small towns across the Midwest and South. There were already twelve of them within an easy drive of her home.

In the custom of citizen orneriness, which is often the only way things can get done in this country, Fogarty took it on herself to knock on the doors of fifty of her neighbors around the rural patch of country known formally as Bethel Township. She asked them if they wanted the store. Just two of them—a pair of elderly women—said yes. The rest were upset about the specter of traffic, noise, accidents, and the armed robberies that were semi-routine occurrences at the other Dollar Generals ringing Springfield. "This was all done under the radar," said Fogarty. "And this is all about money."

Dollar General is, in fact, a fantastically profitable company and it got that way by targeting forgotten segments of the American economy tucked away in places like Bethel Township and colonizing them with "little-box" stores that supply basic household needs like soap, toilet paper, and dog food at prices a few pennies below the local grocery store or even Walmart. The company likes to build its stores in clusters, which can be more easily serviced by distribution trucks and can share a staffing pool. Once land is acquired by the company, it can erect a cinder-block box about the size of a large tract home for as little as a quarter million dollars.

A stroll through one Dollar General is like walking into a colorful explosion of name-brand confetti: packages of Crayola, Viva paper towels, Dixie cups, Gain detergent, Energizer batteries, Fructis shampoo, and yellow bursts of cardboard announcing prices typically a fraction cheaper than usual and in smaller packages. The visual mosaic calms into a subtle and logical progression toward the cash register. An average store—as small as it seems—holds well over ten thousand products.

There are now more Dollar Generals in the U.S. than there are McDonalds, which also grew its business in a distinct way in the 1960s when founder Ray Kroc chartered helicopters for an aerial view of where the suburbs were likely to grow next. He made franchising decisions based on how he read the street patterns.

The Dollar General method is the curious inverse of the Ray Kroc method, seeking not growth but decline. "They are not waiting to see where a city is expanding," said Alexander Lowry, professor of finance at Gordon College in Wenham, Massachusetts, who has studied the industry. "They are looking for contractions, reading the tea leaves in an opposite direction. This is the opposite of Ray Kroc's technique. And that's realistic. The trend is not upwards. The economy in rural America is getting worse."

The new national road of dollar stores also passes through the village of Nice, California, whose name is pronounced "Neece," like the city on the French Riviera. But Nice's economy is the opposite of prosperous. This was resort country during the Gilded Age, but tourists are scarce these days and the surrounding county is now the poorest in the state when measured by median income. A perfect place, in other words, for a cinder-block Dollar General store, which now straddles

U.S. Highway 20, a two-minute walk from the gazebo that marks the village center, on a strip of land wedged dramatically between steep hills and the shores of Clear Lake.

When the Dollar General store opened back in 2015, some locals worried it was yet another symbol of civic decline. But for Dean Schneider, it was nothing but a blessing. The sixty-nine-year-old retired commercial fisherman with a self-described "authority problem" now had a place to go for basic household items such as dish soap, tuna fish, bread, and Coors Light. "This gave us some options," said Schneider, who lives on a fixed income.

Lake County, where Nice is located, has given the chain a mixed reception. Three stores received approval from the board of supervisors, but two others were rejected under pressure from residents who feared the same consequences as Charlotte Fogarty had back in Ohio: increased traffic, incongruous design, bad symbolism, lights, noise. Even the customary civic boosters were ambivalent. "I try to be objective, but Dollar General doesn't pay well and they don't hire many people," said Melissa Fulton, the chief executive of the Lake County Chamber of Commerce. "I'm looking down at the construction site for one of them right now." And, indeed, her office window has a view of the rebar and poured concrete of what would soon be the new Dollar General serving Lakeport, the seat of a county where the median annual household income is $36,132, about half of the California median. About a quarter of the population is on some form of public income assistance, and the Nice store makes it clear from posters in the front window that it welcomes electronic benefit transfers from CalFresh, the state's food stamp program.

Its presence has also come close to driving away just about every other retail business in town. At the Nice Market, co-owner Pinda Kaur says that most of her regular customers have vanished and that she cannot offer better prices to compete. She and her husband are contemplating closing up shop after thirteen years selling basic foodstuffs. "These are poor people who live here and they need to find the bargains," she said. "To spend $200 in food stamps in one grocery run is nothing."

She takes the biggest hit on milk. On a recent summer afternoon, the Dollar General just down U.S. Highway 20 was offering a gallon of Clover Sonoma 2 percent milk for $3.35, whereas the cheapest that Kaur was able to sell it was $5.99, thanks to the costs of her distributor. "How do they sell it for that?" she wondered. "Is it from cows that don't eat?"

The answer lies in Dollar General's business model. Beyond its low labor costs and distribution efficiencies, it is able to negotiate volume deals directly with manufacturers. It employs about one-third of the staff of an average hometown grocery, and the payroll is lean: the average annual salary for an assistant manager is just over $28,000. In a presentation to investors, Dollar General executive vice president Jim Thorpe identified the American underclass as the company's "best friends forever."

The chief characteristics of the loyalists, he said, included "living paycheck to paycheck" and "relies on government assistance." Thorpe predicted the growing customer demographic—generally white people with household income lower than $40,000 a year—would shortly expand to include large numbers of African Americans and millennials. The average Dollar General shopper is among the last "to feel the effects of improving economic conditions."

Lake County seemed an ideally decrepit place. The rough topography of the area meant the railroad never found it profitable to build tracks here. Nor could petroleum companies justify a natural gas pipeline. The passing of the "taking the waters" fad during the 1950s and the availability of cheap airfare to travel farther spelled the end of the glamorous hot springs resorts, leaving Clear Lake with a lot of emptying motor courts and cabins around its 102-mile shoreline.

As nearby wine country counties like Napa and Sonoma grew less affordable, Lake County's abundance of housing—a two-bedroom house can go for as little as $600 a month—helped make it an attractive place for people without a lot of money and without a need to travel for work. The volcanic ridgelines make it impossible to get in from the west or the south without going over a corkscrewing two-lane road that appears as tight squiggles on the map. A large proportion of the one out of four people who live below the poverty line are disabled or elderly.

Dollar General representatives were therefore surprised when residents of Kelseyville—a more affluent town to the south—pushed back against the company's plans to extend the footprint of stores into their town. "The big stores are going to drive us out," said Vijay Sharma, co-owner of Kelseyville Market and Liquor. "This isn't just me saying this. They are wrong for this area." Resistance also sprang up in Middletown, where Dollar General tried to plant an outpost on a lot across the street from a church near the edge of the St. Helena River and a vineyard where the grapes are planted in rows as precise as tombstones in a military cemetery. Most of the objections centered on aesthetics.

"None of us liked the look of the Dollar General stores," said Monica Rosenthal, who owns a local vineyard. "We were like, 'Oh my God!' They are more concerned with maintaining their corporate identity than our unique country charm and diversity."

Nothing makes people flood into a council chamber like a land-use issue. The board of supervisors denied the company a permit in a closely watched 3–2 vote after the planning department wrote that the squat Dollar General design was in contrast to the overall look of Middletown: "The proposed structure consists primarily of box elements, only somewhat softened by applied design elements such as faux shutters." This was, in fact, the same generic design common to Dollar Generals across most of the U.S.

The decision didn't sit well with those in the poorer parts of Lake County, who felt that there was an element of classism and snobbery to the objections and that the design complaints were a fig leaf for deeper-set worries about building a monument to poverty in the midst of grapevines.

"I can safely say I've never set foot in a Dollar General. But this is someone trying to invest in this county," said Claude Brown, the second-in-command at Westgate Petroleum, which supplies local gas stations with fuel, and the former head of a Middletown advisory board. He sat at the edge of the Hidden Valley Lake Golf Course drinking an iced tea. "But some people are protectionist. The name Dollar General represents 'poor.' Well, we've got 24 percent of people on government assistance. This county fits their model."

And so did the countryside around Springfield, Ohio, which had first prospered from traffic on the National Road and then the later gift of American industrialization before falling into gentle economic decline.

With its famously generic name—one of thirty-three Springfields across the nation—the city's moniker may well stand for Anywhere, U.S.A., though it has its own unique markings. A school superintendent here named Albert Graham started a popular boys and girls agricultural club that became nationally known as 4-H. A network of factories connected on the city's interurban streetcar system churned out farm implements and road graders under trusted brands like International Harvester and Buffalo-Springfield. A publicity tool for this trade, a magazine named *Farm & Fireside*, soon grew into the giant Crowell-Collier publishing plant downtown that ran off millions of copies of *Collier's* and *Woman's Home Companion* magazines, as well as encyclopedia sets, editions of Harvard Classics, and bestselling books by Margaret Mitchell, Winston Churchill, and Jack London. "The roll of the presses in Crowell-Collier's Springfield plant is like the throb of a giant heart," said the company in a promotional brochure.

The managerial and ownership class of Springfield built a row of competitive mansions on High Street, and their children rode tall bicycles known as penny-farthings. Groceries flowered on the bourgeois corners, their names in an old city directory a lexicon of family-owned commerce and a portrait of the English German ancestry of the shopkeepers: J. C. Laybourn and Sons, D. E. Moore and Co., Myers and Lafferty, Swonger and Fenstermacher, Roth Brothers, Kearns Brothers, Theodore Trouper. The stores sold goods on credit, and most customers kept accounts.

But in 1902, a threat to this system emerged. The grocery chain A&P opened its first location in Springfield at 26 Fountain Street and immediately siphoned away business from the competition through volume deals, low prices, and national brands like Jane Parker pastries and Eight O'Clock coffee. Within a decade, the chain introduced the "A&P economy" model with a strategy of appealing to lower-class consumers, and the mom and pops of Springfield and elsewhere started to fail. The conglomerate, which was owned by the Hartford brothers and had started in lower Manhattan as the Great Atlantic & Pacific Tea Company, was soon handling the biggest share of food in the country, with a small empire of warehouses, trucks, and confectionary factories behind the scenes.

The Hartfords were working from a certain pattern, as American towns had already seen the creative destruction of their local apothecaries and hardware stores. On June 21, 1879, Frank Woolworth had opened his Great Five Cent Store in Lancaster, Pennsylvania, and had sold nearly 30 percent of his inventory on the first day. His formula of offering an unpredictable explosion of cheap goods proved a hit with the public. The five-and-dime fad spread quickly through the U.S.

Woolworth's business model bore a striking resemblance to those of the dollar stores of a later generation. He dealt directly with manufacturers to negotiate rock-bottom invoice prices and studied demographic data to find out where the poorest Americans were living and shopping. He squeezed profits on tiny markups, sparked visual delight through carefully arranged shelves, and spent almost nothing on publicity, knowing that the physical fact of the store in a prominent location—combined with word of mouth—would generate its own buzz.

At some points in Woolworth's history, customer enthusiasm for the store rivaled that of any modern Black Friday event. In the hours before a location opened on Fulton Avenue in Brooklyn in 1895, the anxious crowd "threatened several times to go through the big plate glass windows in front of the store," reported the *Brooklyn Times.*

"The millions who daily go shopping and adventuring in these stores are not lured by advertising or other modern methods of salesmanship," wrote Woolworth biographer John K. Winkler in 1951. "They come because they know their every need can be satisfied quickly, conveniently—but most of all because of the sheer wonder of what their nickels and dimes will buy."

Woolworth's success generated a fleet of competitors: Ben Franklin, Kresge, McCrory, McLellan's. A&P saw its own set of well-capitalized rivals emerge in Safeway and Kroger. In 1962, Sam Walton opened his first Walmart in Rogers, Arkansas, the first of another wave of mass-merchandise discount stores that would plant outposts in small towns and make business difficult, if not impossible, for anyone trying to compete without the vast distribution networks and "private brands" that permanently fixed the idea of quality inside a customer's mind.

Dollar General emerged from the same era as Walmart, though with a Woolworthian hook: J. L. Turner opened his first Dollar General store in Springfield, Kentucky—another Springfield—in 1955 with the explicit guarantee that none of the merchandise would cost more than one dollar. By 1968, the chain had expanded out of the mid-South and was generating more than $40 million a year in sales. The truly spectacular period of growth, however, happened in the recession of 2008 when the chain let go of the one-dollar price limit and started acting as a semi-substitute for the grocery stores that were withering away from small towns too far for a convenient Walmart trip.

The company's philosophy of minimum staffing took another page from Frank Woolworth, who believed that clerks shouldn't have the job of fetching goods from a storeroom or from behind the counter and that customers would derive an addictive sort of entertainment from browsing the shelves themselves. Each Dollar General needs only a skeleton crew of about five permanent employees—a manager, an assistant manager, and three associates—to unload trucks, stock shelves, patrol for shoplifting, and run the register. This hiring practice is part of what allows Dollar General to keep prices low and enable even its most impoverished customers to enjoy small luxuries.

"While you might be driving out poor Mr. Jones, he doesn't offer the same prices the dollar stores offer," said Elizabeth Racine, a professor of public health at the University of North Carolina who has studied the effect of dollar stores on struggling communities. "People want the good price and they will drive for them. You need to understand how stressful the lives of these poor people are before you start with narratives about driving people out of business."

What they get with the good price, however, is terrible food that can't help but create obesity and disease. Only the most determined customer could assemble a dinner that isn't heavy in the sugar, salt, and fat that define ready-to-eat processed foods. "Economically, it doesn't make sense for them to have a lot of fresh food," said Racine. "They sell whatever their contracted agreements say with Coca-Cola and Frito-Lay when it comes to shelf space." In the food deserts of America, that's what you get. Dollar General has fitted out some of its stores with coolers for fruit and vegetables, but the temptations of cheap processed food are great for those struggling to pay the bills. "Why would they buy a two-dollar bunch of celery when they can get four bags of chips for fifty cents each?" said Michael Cooper, the public information officer for Clark County, Ohio, where Springfield is the county seat.

Cooper's office is one block from where the downtown Woolworth's used to stand before it went out of business in 1974 and was torn down to make way for a park. The city is still hanging on to a remnant of its industrial past in the form of the Navistar factory, which employs eighteen hundred people and manufactures trucks under the GM and International labels. Two hospitals, the public school district, and a Lutheran college are the other big job providers. Shuttered blue-collar taverns brood on corners, and the Upper Valley Mall in the western suburbs officially became one of the nation's many anchorless "dead malls" when it lost its Sears in 2018. Dollar General has six locations around Springfield, and at least two of them are frequent targets of shoplifting and armed robbery by people with severe addictions struggling to feed themselves and pay off their dealers.

The over-prescription of opioid painkillers in the early decades of the twenty-first century hit Springfield harder than many other midwestern cities—at one point, the regional medical center was treating an average of one overdose per hour. High schools began keeping supplies of the revival drug Narcan on hand to prevent addicted students from dying. The week I visited, the *News-Sun* ran a story about a man with a history of drug use lying amid burned garbage in a dumpster. He had almost gone through a compactor before another man driving a front-end loader spotted him. "Springfield man saved from trash said he was set on fire," said the headline.

The residents of Bethel Township worried that a new Dollar General would attract similar chaos on the National Road, and they point to the nearby exit on Interstate 70 as a likely escape route for anyone wanting to knock it over. The rural western margin of Springfield also has a historic character the locals fear would be blighted by parking lot lights and a big yellow-and-black plastic sign broadcasting guaranteed deals. Two miles down the hill is the site of the Shawnee settlement of Piqua where the indigenous leader Tecumseh was born, and where in 1780, the Revolutionary War general George Rogers Clark poured artillery fire into the village before burning it down and erasing it from the map.

The Clark County Board of Commissioners nevertheless voted to rezone the old penny candy emporium called the Fort Tecumseh Old Fashun Store at 5550 West National Road, clearing the way for the building to be bulldozed for the newest location of Dollar General. People in the neighboring trailer park were told they would have to find a new place to live, before the site's architects discovered a nasty surprise. Many of the trailers came equipped with underground fuel tanks that had leaked into the soil. All construction halted. The company said nothing publicly, but residents were told the subterranean mess was too expensive to clean.

Gary Cox, a retired General Motors employee, said he didn't think anything as trifling as an oil spill would ultimately stop Dollar General from putting up the next of its locations somewhere down the block from him. It was only a matter of time. "They'd like one on every corner, if they could do it," he told me. The National Road does not sleep.

The Whole Hoop
of the World

I've got at least four hours of sunlight left as I exit Interstate 81 at the
town of Chilhowie, Virginia, and start up the road threading through
the spruce-fir of George Washington and Jefferson National Forests. If I
time it right and don't linger, I can bag the peak and be down with the
light still in the sky. It's just nine miles in and out. Prudence would say
forget it, another time, but I'm not sure when I'll next be nearby. Now
seems like a good opportunity to knock off the state's highest natural
point.

I'm on a quest to climb the tallest mountains in all fifty states for reasons that I cannot really explain. At this writing, I have done forty-four
of them, with only five really difficult ones out west—plus Florida's Brit-
ton Hill (elev. 345 feet)—still outstanding.

Can I make it to all of them? I'm not sure. Denali (elev. 20,146 feet)
in Alaska takes an average three weeks of effort and thousands of dollars
paid out to an expedition company. Even then a climber must accept a

fifty-fifty chance of summiting. An official plug-pulling for weather reasons is always a possibility. I lost my nerve on the edge of a glacier about three-quarters of the way up Mount Hood (elev. 11,249 feet) in Oregon, turned back from the forty-foot drop on both sides of a jagged wall made of ice, and haven't looked at that mountain since, except from the window of an airplane. I dread the inevitable second attempt, but I may not be able to stop myself. Collections always strive for completion.

Now I'm pretty sure I'll have no trouble whatsoever with Mount Rogers (elev. 5,729 feet), a moderate highpoint in a part of Virginia far removed from its tobacco colony settlements on the Atlantic and without much of a human imprint, though carrying a respectable backstory. William Barton Rogers taught geology at the University of Virginia and authored a survey of the entire state in the 1830s that helped explain why Appalachian coal burned hotter and longer than varieties mined elsewhere. He later became the first president of the Massachusetts Institute of Technology, and his fellow Virginians named the peak for him in 1883. I lock the car and start up a hill that looks like a meadow in Northern Ireland. The trail soon leads directly into a thick forest, and I settle in for the steady four-mile slog upward.

These rooftops of the states do not always require a physical struggle. In the Deep South and on the Great Plains, you can pretty much drive up close to all of them and get the climb done in less than an hour. But in the West, they are invariably atop peaks—some of them fearsomely remote, windblown, snow-coated, and difficult to climb. The rest are a scattering of Appalachian-scaled hillocks, prairie swales, and barely discernable bumps. Delaware's highest peak, for example, is marked with a metal disc called the Ebright Azimuth (elev. 448 feet) embedded in a sidewalk in suburban Wilmington. Indiana's Hoosier Hill (elev. 1,257 feet) is a hickory grove on a gentle pimple of farmland just west of the border of Ohio, which itself can brag of a worn-down glacial moraine on the grounds of a job-training center. Connecticut's Mount Frissell (elev. 2,454 feet) is a spot on the slope of a high hill that lies mainly across the Massachusetts border—you actually have to hike *down* to reach it. Maryland's otherwise beautiful Backbone Mountain (elev. 3,360 feet) features a view of a smoke-chuffing power plant in the distance. And then there's Jerimoth Hill (elev. 812 feet), an otherwise forgettable and unfarmable lift of earth within the political borders of Rhode Island, not far from the home of a curmudgeonly music teacher named Henry Richardson. He threw up a few No Trespassing signs, yelled at highpoint pilgrims, and threatened to shoot anyone he caught trying to access the summit by stealth. After he died, a more cooperative family donated the land to the state. Now walking to Jerimoth Hill is about as physically difficult as walking back to your car in a Walmart parking lot, and only slightly more scenic. It sees thousands of visitors a year.

This quest started for me with an impulse in a dull moment when I had a day off from my job at a newspaper in Cheyenne, Wyoming. I looked at the Rand McNally Road Atlas and saw a black triangle icon in neighboring Nebraska. In the usual typescript, mountains were hollow triangles. This was different, filled-in, black. *Panorama Point. Highest point in Nebraska* (elev. 5,429 feet). Quirky.

Without anything better to do that day, I drove the hundred miles or so to see it. Asphalt gave way to some dirt farm roads, which gave way to an unplowed path up a big swell of grassland with a stone marker— looking like a cemetery headstone—keeping sentinel. From here you could see at least a mile to yet another marker that denoted the geometric oddity of where Nebraska, Colorado, and Wyoming came together at right angles. Standing here was like existing in two dimensions, a parallel world of sterile mathematics: limitless plain and invisible lines. And at that moment, I was the most elevated person in Nebraska.

I experienced a moment of pure fascination that has never entirely departed. "Nebraska" was a purely coincidental political entity: a trans-Mississippi free state creation of Congress as a failed compromise to head off the Civil War. Had the western border been set a few more miles to the west of the 104th meridian, into present-day Colorado, this pasture would have no special meaning. But now it was like the entire state—cornfields, football, rivers, houses, telephone wires, grocery stores, big skies—had been concentrated into one tight ball: almost *one dimensional*. A metonymy for the whole.

As I grew more serious about mountain climbing, the summits got more challenging. Boundary Peak (elev. 13,147 feet) in Nevada lies just inside the state line. The trek up its exposed cone took all day long, but not nearly as long as California's Mount Whitney (elev. 14,505 feet)—the highest in the lower contiguous states, requiring a punishing eighteen-hour march. The last half mile seemed like a ramp into a burning indigo sky; the trip down made my knees turn gelatinous. The most frightening thus far was Idaho's Borah Peak (elev. 12,662 feet) and its infamous Chicken Out Ridge, where I lost a hat to the wind and the sole of my boot to the rocks. My happiness at arriving to the summit was significantly dimmed by the knowledge that I'd soon have to once more walk across a narrow beam covered with ice with fatal drops on both sides.

The most unexpectedly beautiful of them, strangely, were the ones without such obvious topographic drama. In the far western edge of Oklahoma's panhandle, a lengthy dugway of basaltic lava called Black Mesa (elev. 4,973 feet) rises to greet the border of New Mexico; just a few yards short of the line is a pink monument erected on the barely discernable highest spot that still lies within the boundaries of what used to be called the Cimarron Territory before it was ceded to Oklahoma in 1890. Paleontologists discovered a lode of dinosaur remains from the Triassic and Jurassic periods in the mesa and have removed at least eighteen tons of bones over the years. I did the hike at sunset and had the place entirely to myself. The trail wound through tough prickly pear, swarms of stinkbugs, and grasshoppers of many colors. I kept hearing a funny roar, but when I stopped to listen, I could hear only silence and the whoosh of blood in my ears.

Louisiana's Driskill Mountain (elev. 535 feet) is a mound of red earth inside a private logging preserve in the piney woods. I spent the night at its trailhead on the grounds just outside the Mount Zion Presbyterian Church, which in its name pays tribute to the equally diminutive hill on the edge of Jerusalem that came to embody the collective hope—both corporeal and spiritual—of the ancestral Israelites. "By the waters of Babylon, there we sat down and wept, when we remembered Zion," it says in Psalm 137:1. This mound tucked into the azaleas and dogwoods—not even as far above sea level as the One Shell Square petroleum tower in downtown New Orleans—had an odd serenity about it the morning I visited. All was still; not even the mosquitos were out. Its base of quartz sand may have been the most geologically flimsy of any of the country's summits, but it felt caught in time, and timeless. I didn't want to leave.

The romance between America and its own mountains—preserved in the Hudson River School paintings of the frontier—owes even more to the poets and critics of the nineteenth century in Europe, whose descriptions of the Alps and England's Lake District influenced a generation of their peers on both sides of the Atlantic. The art critic John Ruskin introduced the power of metaphor in landscape writing that is today almost inescapable: because the grandeur of a mountain can never be captured in ordinary speech, vivid comparatives must be used along with the copious use of "like" and "as." He compared the alpine heights to "the skeleton arch of an unfinished bridge," "an island out of a sea," and "the bones of the earth." Percy Bysshe Shelley went further outside the usual patterns of speech, equating a peak in Switzerland with a transcendent higher authority—the eternal living fountain of intelligence that radiated traces of "a remoter world" in its snowy folds. He wrote the poem in a frenzy, having experienced "a sentiment of ecstatic wonder, not unallied to madness" upon his first look at Mont Blanc (elev. 15,774 feet), western Europe's highest point.

> Mont Blanc yet gleams on high: — the power is there,
> The still and solemn power of many sights,
> And many sounds, and much of life and death.

Shelley got a return argument, of sorts, from the later alpine traveler Sir Leslie Stephen, the freethinking father of Virginia Woolf, who was not persuaded by any of the spiritual rhapsodies of the Romantic poets when it came to mountains, and thought that standing on top of one brought nobody any closer to heaven's door. But in a revealing passage, Stephen experienced a sensation at the summit of Mont Blanc that he claimed was too complex for "a few black marks on white paper," such as is all writing, that could ever do it justice.

> Why that should be so, and by what strange threads of association the reds and blues of a gorgeous sunset, the fantastic shapes of clouds and shadows at that dizzy height, and the dramatic changes that sweep over the boundless region beneath your feet should stir you like mysterious music, or indeed, why music itself should have such power, I leave to philosophers to explain.

He seemed to have been aiming at what Albert Camus would later observe about beauty—that at the heart of it lies something inhuman.

That inhuman romance is often best perceived at American highpoints that present surprising figuration in regions that don't seem to promise a lot of geologic theater. Though Texas is dominated by flat pine woods, gentle hills, and brambly plains for most of its considerable bulk, the far west is relieved by a series of dry mesas and peaks that mark the former edge of the supercontinent called Pangea. The highest spot of what used to be a seaside fossil reef is Guadalupe Peak (elev. 8,751 feet), whose trail snakes up a side canyon filled with Douglas fir and gray oak. At the top is a commemorative steel pyramid, looking like an alien sentinel, bearing a tribute to the Pony Express on one side and the winged logo of American Airlines on another. Around it, the lone and level sands of the Chihuahuan Desert stretch far away in Shelleyan vistas.

New Jersey's highest peak is a proud wedge of quartz called— prosaically enough—High Point (elev. 1,803 feet), flying like a stone wing at the north end of the mummy-like Kittatinny Mountain with views of rolling farmland off to the north and hemlock groves down at the Delaware River. A marker at the top looks like a poor rendition of the Washington Monument and ought to be ignored, as it only robs from what the earth already offers. But it insists upon your attention and takes the eye hostage. The 1920s were an era when local governments and veterans groups felt compelled to throw around promiscuous amounts of marble and polished granite, and this rocket-tall obelisk was put up at the end of the decade as a war memorial. The sons of Frederick Law Olmsted designed a preserve around it, in a style reminiscent of European gardens but with democratic openness.

Massachusetts, however, totally botched its summit at Mount Greylock (elev. 3,849 feet), which suffers a worse emanation of early twentieth-century hubris. The Veterans War Memorial Tower is shaped like the pawn from a chess set, with a spherical electric beacon at the top. The scene is further corrupted by a road that takes tourists to a small hotel called Bascom Lodge, meaning the summit is mobbed by those who can drive right up.

While I'm not necessarily morally superior to the highpoint motorists, I have different ideas and parked the car near the base to hike up at least two symbolic miles on a drizzly afternoon through pine forests. Herman Melville used to look at this mountain from the window of his house in nearby Pittsfield; he was said to have perceived a whale in its lumpy form. His friend, the witch-haunted Nathaniel Hawthorne, walked here at night, and he once saw a fire in a lime kiln that inspired him to write a short story he first called "The Unpardonable Sin." Thousands of other New England dreamers and seekers have been drawn to this hump; it may be the most oil-painted of all the state roofbeams. At the summit, slick with rain, I wanted to touch the monument—just a symbolic tap—but it was protected with a ring of construction fence. The rest of the tourist detritus up there might have made Hawthorne turn red under his three-day beard.

Alabama's Cheaha Mountain (elev. 2,413 feet) and Arkansas's Mount Magazine (elev. 2,753 feet) have also been transformed into profit centers with chintzy resort hotels and made dull in the process. And a state so richly blessed, cursed, and defined by mountains as West Virginia— enough so that the Latin motto of the state, *Montani Semper Liberi*, means "mountaineers are always free"—has capped its highpoint at Spruce Knob (elev. 4,863 feet) with a parking lot and stone platforms that bring dishonor and banality to what ought to be a noble wintry dome.

These are known as the "drive-ups," the otherwise beautiful summits, generally in the East and South, that the road-building armies of the American century had conquered long before the rest of us could have a say. The absolute worst highpoint in the country belongs to Kentucky, a state with a profusion of beautiful mountains, but the combined forces of heaven, the United States Congress, and the fossil fuels industry have conspired to give it the dismal inheritance of Black Mountain (elev. 4,139 feet), which is off a dirt road from Route 160 and not far from a stupendously ugly gash left by mountaintop-removal coal mining. Mercifully enough, you can't see anything from the summit except a high-voltage tower serving the mine. Tens of millions of dollars of coal lies directly underneath, giving Kentucky the possession of the most financially valuable of all the highpoints, but also the most impoverished.

The beautifully rugged state of Tennessee is also cursed on the roof, but by a different form of human perfidy. Its peak of Clingman's Dome (elev. 6,643 feet) carries the informal sobriquet "Old Smoky," as in the child's song, as its brow is often covered with fog on even sunny days. The road to a short but steep asphalt trail to its top became a sad inevitability after the 1934 creation of Great Smoky Mountains National Park, the most visited park in the system. One of the worst towns in the United States happens to lie just outside its gates: the abominable honky-tonk hellhole of Gatlinburg, stuffed to its retail innards with T-shirt shops, neon come-ons, restaurants serving "drippy meals" (in the words of Bill Bryson), go-kart tracks, minigolf, hotels with fake Swiss styling, and cheap geegaws of every description on sale in every direction—a Daytona Beach with no saltwater relief. The thoughtless architects of the park at Clingman's Dome decided that if God were going to create a flat-topped mountain coated with inconvenient fir trees, they would assist Him by erecting a strange viewing platform that looks like what would happen if Albert Speer ever designed a landing pad for *The Jetsons*. You walk up a curving ramp to gaze over the nearby peaks unobstructed by the trees, most of which are rotting from within because of an invasion of wingless insects called balsam woolly adelgids. Between the cascading waves of gray fog, the brutalist concrete platform, and the ghost forests rotting away in the quiet death of climate change, the overall effect is disquieting.

As if this wasn't the worst example of highpoint arrogance, the surveying of this mountain bears a heavy history. Thomas Clingman explored the area in the 1850s, and before leaving for military service in the

Confederate Army, he spent a lot of time trying to convince settlers to move there. He also got into a bitter argument with one of his old professors at the University of North Carolina named Elisha Mitchell over whether the mountain everyone then called "Smoky Top" was higher than a rival over in North Carolina. Mitchell wanted to prove his student Clingman wrong, so he conducted extensive measurements, and while out on one of his expeditions, he fell to his death at a waterfall on June 2, 1857. But Mitchell was right—the North Carolina mountain *was* higher, and today it is named Mount Mitchell (elev. 6,684 feet), the highest point in that state and also in the entire eastern United States. Which makes it all the more terrible that this peak is also a drive-up with an ugly concrete platform near the tomb of Elisha Mitchell, who occupies his namesake mountain on a long-term residential basis.

Touching these tops is a peculiar kind of hobby among a type of traveler with a fondness for mountains and a compulsion to collect them like stamps. The ultimate prize, of course, is to bag all fifty and become semi-royalty in the Highpointer Club, an organization in Golden, Colorado, founded in 1986 by a conservationist with the wonderfully appropriate name of Jack Longacre. The group now has more than one thousand members, a board of directors, a website, an annual conference, and a related foundation to care for the landscape at some of the spots that typically sit on out-of-the-way corners of their respective states. About a fifth of these spots are on privately owned land, but most of them now have benches or signposts with the Highpointers' logo attached.

The president of the club is an amiable electrical engineer in his midsixties named Alan Ritter, a longtime devotee of the Boy Scouts of America whose posts have included Eagle Scout, troop leader, and administrator ("I'm a has-been," he told me. "I *has been* a lot of things."). The typical member of the club, he said, is an outdoor enthusiast who climbs a state highpoint as a non-deliberate act, learns its significance, then gets hooked, sometimes through the intellectual thrill of the topographical distinction, other times from meeting a fellow hiker on the trail out to boost their own numbers. "A lot of it has to do with people who are list-driven," said Ritter, who himself has climbed forty-eight.

Highpointers, it should be said, are temperamentally exempt from a philosophical rift that exists among some mountaineers as to whether the summit is of any real value. There are those who view with contempt the sport of "peakbagging"—climbing for the sake of summit-attainment—believing instead that the journey toward the goal and the experience of walking through nature should be reward enough. A few fundamentalists of this school will even climb a mountain to within an eighth mile of the very top, then turn around in a conspicuous display of holy abstinence. The obsessive focus on the goal ruins everything, they believe, and this difference in belief is as unbridgeable as that of the old soteriological divide between Protestants and Catholics over the role of faith versus good works. Highpointers have no such moral agonies; they will *always* summit.

That is not to disparage the journey. A surprisingly hard one to claim is Charles Mound (elev. 1,235 feet) on the farm of the Wuebbels family, just inside the Illinois state line from Wisconsin. To limit foot traffic on the working farm, the Wuebbels open up the property to visitors four weekends per summer and close it tightly at all other times. I timed a business trip to bag the peak right before the Fourth of July, and I walked the path down a lane of trees and past a red barn with a tennis coach at a New England prep school who was on his thirty-eighth highpoint. Within ten minutes, we arrived at a small clearing with two lawn chairs and a wooden sign. WELCOME TO CHARLES MOUND, HIGHEST POINT IN ILLINOIS. WAYNE AND JEAN WUEBBELS, OWNERS, PRAISE OUR LORD JESUS CHRIST, IN HIM WE HAVE ETERNAL LIFE. The tennis coach stayed three minutes, but I sat in one of the chairs and looked over a sunlit field of soybeans into Wisconsin for a half hour before an engineer for Hewlett-Packard from Colorado sauntered up in a fleece vest to join me. He was sick of climbing the fourteener peaks in his home state, he told me, and wanted to see parts of the country he hadn't seen before.

"This really gets you out," he said. "I'd *never* come to a place like this otherwise."

To engage in this odd pursuit is to drive obscure rural roads far away from interstates, eat in small-town diners, sleep in rarely visited forests and motels, and see quotidian parts of the nation where only the locals and a flock of eccentric alpinists regularly venture. State highpoints are a way of attempting to imbibe the experience of the nation in distilled form: fifty individual symbols for the United States in all of its natural beauty, hubris, greed, nobility, and urge to conserve, memorialize, and sanctify. One of the most dramatic thunderstorms I ever saw at night was in a deserted logging reserve in the Upper Peninsula of Michigan near the summit of Mount Arvon (elev. 1,979 feet). The next morning, I did there what I did at all highpoints, a cornball ritual in the final seconds before approaching a summit, a pause to consider the state itself: what I've seen of it, what I like about it, what it may be known for. I thought of Detroit factories, both working and abandoned; I thought of melancholy lakes with hunting cabins; I thought of cherry farms. Before creeping up the last few yards to the summit of New Mexico's Wheeler Peak (elev. 13,161 feet), I tried to think of piñon pine campfires, red and green enchiladas, the wind-filled grasses next to the road near the town of Santa Rosa, the flyspecked Dairy Queen in the sad little railroad town of Deming on the other side of the state. On Minnesota's serene Eagle Mountain (elev. 2,301 feet), a loaf of granite and quartz on the edge of the Boundary Waters, I thought of church potlucks and the bridges over the streets of the Twin Cities; South Carolina's Sassafras Mountain (elev. 3,563 feet) conjured a vision of low-country boils, palmetto trees, and golf courses humid with predawn dew. Gasping for air on top of Colorado's Mount Elbert (elev. 14,439), I had a peerless view of the country that Walt Whitman called "the vertebrae or backbone of our hemisphere" and dwelt instead on what I remembered of attending kindergarten in suburban Denver, the spires of the chapel at the Air Force Academy, and how the prairies outside Greeley smell pleasantly of cow manure. This mental exercise in iconography recalls nothing so much as a grade school wall map, or the children's educational tool "Game of the States," in which the shapes of our fifty political entities came festooned with little rebuses signifying their economic or cultural importance: Independence Hall for Pennsylvania, an ear of corn for Nebraska, a Lincoln silhouette for Illinois, a Space Needle for Washington. These signifying images are like highpoints themselves, a concentrated essence of the whole.

And there is another concentration sitting on every highpoint: a round metal disc about the size of a tea saucer, shaped like an outsized thumbtack and set in a small bed of concrete. These metal discs are called benchmarks and are placed as permanent surveying markers by both the U.S. Geological Survey and the National Geodetic Survey in their semi-competitive quest to create a comprehensive topographical map of the entire nation, but mainly as a guide to settling disputes over mining claims.

The popular sentiment of our era has been unkind to bureaucracies, but a look at one of the benchmarks in an improbable place should inspire a measure of respect for the truly badass work done by the nameless field officials who blazed up inclines with survey sticks, metal spikes, sledgehammers, and dry-mix concrete on their backs. Nearly every spot of rural prominence is tagged with a benchmark, and—oddly—no list exists of their numbers. The total number of these brass spikes nailed down on the national roof since 1898 may be higher than one million. They're not loquacious. A typical one is ringed with the legend: FOR

INFORMATION WRITE THE DIRECTOR, WASHINGTON, D.C. with a simple triangle symbol and the number of feet above sea level stamped into the middle.

This important calculation is what determines a state highpoint, and the science behind it is as old as Pythagoras. A surveyor uses a level—the device with a bubble of air trapped in liquid—to find two perfectly flat pieces of ground under the chosen precipice, measures the distance between them with a chain or rope, and then uses a telescopic device called a theodolite to determine the angle between the two flat spots and the top of the mountain. Knowing those two angles tells you what the third must be—and with it, the height—because they all must add up to 180 degrees.

This method got a valuable supplement in the 1650s when French scientists discovered that mercury in a tube steadily compressed at higher elevations because of barometric pressure. But this technique was considered less precise; the mercury could fluctuate at different times of the day. The elevation number on the old metal spike, usually scuffed with age, is the human element of the ceremony—along with perhaps a dented ammo box containing spiral notebooks where previous hikers have registered their names, signs that you're not the first, nor the last. I always make sure to touch the spike and sign my name. A clue to the age of these spikes can be seen at North Dakota's highest point, on a chalky reef called White Butte (elev. 3,508 feet) on which the pale earth around the shaft has eroded several inches, thanks to years of rain and wind.

When the new western states were trying to survey their high country and determine elevations in the mid-nineteenth century, a Yale man named Clarence King joined the California Geological Survey. He developed a method called "rapid triangulation," which involved using fixed spots to measure distance, creating new triangles from preexisting ones and drawing changes in terrain with cross-hatching. He named many of the features of the Sierra Nevada himself, and while he was a scientific disciple through and through, he yearned for the rapture of animism within the mountains. "It is hard not to invest these great dominating peaks with consciousness," he wrote, "difficult to realize that, sitting thus for ages in presence of all that nature can work, no inner spirit has kindled, nor throb of granite heart once responded, no Buddhistic nirvana-life even has brooded in eternal calm within these sphinx-like breasts of stone." He, too, was rebuking Percy Shelley.

One of his favorite ranges was the High Uintas, a solemn and isolated march of basalt prows that had once been taller even than the Himalayas before a relentless set of glaciers wore them down. The tallest of these is named Kings Peak (elev. 13,528 feet) in his honor, and it marks the most elevated spot in Utah. I set out for it on an August day with three days' worth of supplies for the trek, which led through a park-like valley lined with gray bluffs resembling Soma blocks or terrifying urban cubes designed by Le Corbusier, striated with bands of snow thousands of feet above the valley floor. Clarence King had insisted the mountains he surveyed had no mystical inner life, but he must have been tempted to think otherwise by this view in the summer of 1869. Lakes full of glacial runoff presented themselves one by one between the pointed pines. The trail switchbacked up a ridge called Gunsight Pass and opened a view of Painter's Valley: a startlingly wide yawn of lichen, grass, and mountain slopes that extended twenty miles.

I walked in a few more miles and got my first look at Kings Peak at four o'clock in the afternoon—a mammoth wedge of tan rock that looked like the hull of a battleship looming about five thousand feet overhead. I would be up at first light for a summit attempt. Now there was nothing to do but set up camp, which took about ten minutes. I'll never forget the anxiety that descended when I realized that I had forgotten to pack a book and there was still about six hours of daylight left before I could credibly go to sleep. There was *nothing to do*. My customary escape from stillness was foreclosed: I had to conserve power in my cell phone, and there was no reception out here, anyway. And I did not want to contemplate Kings Peak at all.

So I walked to the edge of a bluff and looked at Painter's Valley until my eyes hurt. I scribbled story ideas in a notebook, remembered the faces of old friends, played mental word games, climbed higher up the bluff, tried meditating. An hour inched by. The silence grew even more oppressive; the emptiness became loathsome; my mind cried for focus but my hands could find no purchase on slippery walls. I could not be alone with myself. With no other options and daylight still pouring into the valley-prison and exposing every feature, I headed back over toward Gunsight Pass, and after about ten minutes, spotted smoke rising from a fire between two vinyl tents.

This sign of other humans a half mile away was like a pond of clear water after a spell in the desert. A pair of guys about my age bid me to sit at the fire: Mark and Derek had been companions on their Mormon Church mission to Germany and stayed friends, even as one went on to manage investments and the other to deal Subarus. Their climb up Kings Peak was a brief vacation from their families. I have no recollection of what we talked about for the next ninety minutes as the sun made its exodus, only that I was intensely grateful for it.

The next morning's ascent took only about three hours, and it amounted to a boulder scramble. Mark and Derek were picking their way down at nine o'clock in the morning as I was still climbing—they had started hours earlier in the predawn. We exchanged pleasantries, they left, and I scampered up the rest of the peak to find a small wooden sign, the NGS disc, and a registry at the very top, which was no wider than an average dining room table. I was twelve miles and four thousand vertical feet from the trailhead, alone, and with no way to call for assistance in case of a mishap like that I experienced on Idaho's Borah Peak. But none of that was frightening; what was much more troubling was my dreadful evening of solitude under the mountain.

Another moment at a highpoint that approached this level of intellectual terror was, of all places, in Kansas at Mount Sunflower (elev. 4,039 feet), which I came to long after midnight and with the lights of transcontinental jetliners far overhead, pointing vaguely to Denver and San Francisco. To any passenger looking down, this spot on the high plains would have been lost in a velvet black covering. I had only vague directions from the last Kansas exit off the interstate and down a series of dirt ranch roads, and it took almost an hour before the words on a directional sign, MOUNT SUNFLOWER—a hyperbolic joke, as it constitutes an unremarkable prairie swale just over the Colorado line—swam into the cone of my headlights.

I cannot fully explain the urge I had then to turn back and forget the whole thing, despite the trouble it had taken to get there. Treading on this ground suddenly seemed wrong, like inviting damnation and death, even though this was not exactly the Holy of Holies, only a topographical quirk given importance because of a slope of windblown silt and the act of Congress in 1859 that fixed the border at the twenty-fifth meridian. Yet the gigantic midnight sky, the bluestem grass steady in the headlights, the stark letters of the sign, the wire fence ringing a wrought-iron sculpture at the spot itself, all of it seemed primitive and ominous. I was glad to leave. And yet, when I think of my favorite highpoint, I always come back to this one in its modesty and unexpected terror.

Religions the world over have venerated high spots on the earth and the revelations they bestow; the holy anchorite at the summit is a staple of sacred literature. The Tahoma people call Washington's Mount Rainier (elev. 14,411 feet) "The Mountain That Used to Be God," a snow-covered remnant of a more numinous world. The Navajo revere and refuse to climb the four peaks in the Southwest that mark the boundaries of their lands, a policy shared by the traditional indigenous owners of Hawaii's highest spot, Mauna Kea (elev. 13,803 feet), where a sign requests climbers not ascend the last half mile to what amounts to the tallest mountain in the world when measured from its volcanic base that lies far beneath the floor of the Pacific. All mountains resist complete perception; this one especially so.

There are secrets lying here that cannot be expressed in vernacular speech. "As for mountains," wrote the thirteenth-century Zen monk Dōgen Kigen in his most famous sutra, "there are mountains hidden in jewels; there are mountains hidden in marshes, mountains hidden in the sky; there are mountains hidden in mountains. There is a study of mountains hidden in hiddenness." The first time I read the enigmatic section of the gospel of St. Matthew when the devil tempts Jesus and takes him to "a very high mountain and show[s] him all the kingdoms of the world and their splendor," I was sitting on a couch listening to the B-minor chords of Beethoven's *Emperor* concerto, and felt exulted and frightened.

Perhaps it has to do with the sweep of the visible world, and the awareness that even this is a pitiful fraction of the reality that lies outside the realm of perception and that would drive us into insanity or death to behold its totality. My friend Greg McNamee has written that the sharp rise of the Santa Catalinas near his home in Tucson is a reminder to humanity "to yield again to tininess, even to terror, and to the ever-expanding universe that lies in the ranges beyond."

Mountains are ultimately striking because of what is missing. That is to say, all the ground that should be there—and isn't. The upthrust is only what used to lie level and of one substance with its surroundings in the Eden of geological time. The peaks of the earth are visible remnants of a lost whole, a cosmic unity that is evoked in the wonderful Taoist phrase "the uncarved block."

The highest mountain in South Dakota, Black Elk Peak (elev. 7,242 feet), used to be called Harney Peak after a U.S. Cavalry officer who ordered massacres during the Indian Wars, but it is now named for the Sioux medicine man who experienced a moment of insight when he stood atop it: "Round about beneath me was the whole hoop of the world. And while I stood there I saw more than I can tell and I understood more than I saw; for I was seeing in a sacred manner the shapes of all things in the spirit, and the shape of all shapes as they must live together like one being."

The most remarkable part of mountains, and what I believe really assaults the conscience, is not the ordinary mass of metamorphic stone at their heart but how their prominence breaks the emptiness in all directions and sweeps the land out of sight. Perhaps it is a direct metaphor for the terrifying emptiness we suspect lies outside the buzz of our own thoughts and the moment of unwilling submission to the state of listening to what in Sanskrit is called *sunyata*, or the void. On top of mountains, we see what lies out there. It does not always make us comfortable.

Henry David Thoreau experienced a profound intellectual shock in 1846 when he attempted to climb Mount Katahdin (elev. 5,267 feet), the highest point in Maine. He talked with a Penobscot elder who advised him to leave a bottle of rum at the base as an offering to the guardian spirit, who might otherwise be displeased that people were crawling up where people shouldn't be going. When Thoreau had finished scrambling up the granite boulders that skirted the thousand-acre plateau at approximately forty-six hundred feet that leads up to the final approach, he reflected on what he had been told. "The tops of mountains are among the unfinished parts of the globe, whither it is a slight insult to the gods to climb and pry into their secrets and try their effect on humanity." The winds howled and made strange patterns of dark gray clouds and brief patches of sun, and he watched clouds forming on the rocks before worrying he would have to spend the night in such an eldritch place. And on the way back to the warmth and rationality of his cabin, he and his companions passed through a plain called "the Burnt Lands" that seemed to strip away all of humanity's illusions and shove Thoreau into the face of the void—what he called in another place the otherwise nameless "IT" of reality that is always present but never truly touchable, the same way that ancient Israelites refused to write or pronounce the name of God.

"This was that Earth of which we have heard, made out of Chaos and Old Night," he wrote, invoking John Milton's dour description of an unredeemed world. "Here was no man's garden, but the unhandselled globe. It was not lawn, nor pasture, nor mead, nor woodland, nor lea, nor arable, nor wasteland ... Man was not to be associated with it. It was Matter, vast, terrific ... rocks, trees, wind on our cheeks! the *solid* earth! the *actual* world! the *common sense! Contact! Contact!*" He seemed to have temporarily lost his mind.

The day I climbed Katahdin was a day like Thoreau's, moody and threatening storms, but I made it to the top in visibility that extended fifteen feet. On the way down, I knelt and drank like a dog from the spring at the plateau named for Thoreau, but saw nothing of the Burnt Lands he described and received nothing of the existential fear that burst through him and that I had briefly glimpsed in Utah and Kansas—that terrifying "wholeness" that defies all attempts at eyewitness description and even language itself. Such moments of perception cannot be forced. The elemental hostility of the IT melts away quickly into the drunkenness and deception of everyday thought, though its overweening presence still casts a shadow on our language. "It's the 'it' when we say: 'It's raining,'" observed the critic John P. O'Grady.

And what is to distinguish a highpoint from any other point of land? Thoreau came to the same conclusion that travel writers throughout the centuries have also realized: the road outward is really the road inward. "What a fool he must be who thinks that his El Dorado is anywhere but where he lives!" You have aimed yourself at a shelf of earth or stone that has been beatified only by geologic uplift and the long-ago property squabbles that flung imaginary human lines around it—and, in the United States, they don't even have the fences, checkpoints, or gravity of international boundaries. They're just made-up lines that create internal jurisdictions, and they arguably are more important these days for sentimental reasons than legal ones.

You will sweat and struggle, often for hours. And then it is eventually upon you, sometimes granting a splendid view, sometimes only a ring of trees. You drink from your water bottle, maybe eat an apple from your pack. Take a few photos for social media. And then what?

I have never left a highpoint without a pang of regret—a sense of skipping a crucial thought or deed, a nagging feeling *that I still have not ascended*, even though I have signed the register, tapped the metal disc, contemplated the state around it, did everything that I was supposed to do. But we cannot own the peak, though we want to trap and possess feelings that cannot linger, like the ecstasy of being in love, the thrill of accomplishment, or the shiver of orgasm. In such experiences, we glimpse a version of *forever* that quickly recedes from our grasp. The top of the mountain presents a chance to force everything in the world into a portable moment, like the unfathomably dense coins of matter that are said to lie in the center of black holes, or inside the tiny singularity that existed before the Big Bang scattered all creation in every direction. Buddhist monks talk of a practice called *samatha*, or one-pointedness—that is, focusing the mind on a singleness of concentration. It is not hard to believe that instinctual happiness mimics an original deep state of existence—the unvaried, unchanging wholeness that eludes capture, though we spend decades chasing the contentment that will not flee. Renters here only; not owners.

So it goes with highpoints. The summit is not yours. Neither is the romantic love, the accomplishment, the dwelling, even your own life. These possessions are not possessions—they pass through you the same as water pouring through fingers or a bird fluttering through a cottage with open windows. Though we try to slam every door shut, the bird never stays. Mountains provide us those tantalizing visions of forever, and an average brain the size of a softball is a poor receptacle indeed for such immensity. But there is the long slog back to the car, dull and painful, which you had better find a way to enjoy or at least tolerate.

The trail up to the summit of Mount Rogers is a pleasantly representative slice of Appalachia: mixed oak and hickory, slabs of rhyolite on the open patches, then a flattened branch path of about a mile that leads to a small clearing at the summit hemmed in by spruce-fir, which affords no view whatsoever of anything else in Virginia. I tap the brass disc, think about tobacco fields and Thomas Jefferson, and sit on a rock. For a few minutes, I'm the most elevated landbound person in the Old Dominion.

The shadows in the emerald-green grove have grown darker and deeper in the half hour I've spent off the main trail, and I reach for the pouch that contains my flashlight only to discover it missing. I have left it in the glove compartment. Perhaps an hour and a half of daylight remains, and I've got a six-mile descent. At a brisk walking speed, it should be no problem. But on the way back, I make a costly mistake and get diverted down the wrong path on an open meadow called Milburn Ridge and I'm at the fence of a neighboring wilderness area before I catch the error. Now I've got to backtrack, and I've lost a half hour. The sun is gone and I'm working in twilight as I get back into the embrace of the oak-hickory that shrouds virtually the entire last four miles, and I start to trot, then run, trying to balance speed with the avoidance of stumbling over the roots that I can now barely discern underfoot. Tonight's overcast sky will give nothing of the waning moon. Losing the trail here would entail a night in these woods with my pack for a pillow. I run until the last of the light makes it impossible to run without foolish injury, focusing instead on the dim bases of the trees and trying not to lose the two-foot gap between them that signifies the way out.

Lucky tonight: I emerge from the woods in full-scale darkness, and the final clearing before the parking lot at Elk Garden is on top of a bald knob where I flop out under the clouds blowing overhead, my heart slowing and my sweat drying. Another highpoint: the thirty-ninth. This one was messy, but I never have to do it again. I linger there for ten more minutes, then descend once more to the car and to matters more easily understandable.

Late City Final

The owners of the *Appleton Post-Crescent* opened their new headquarters on Superior Street on June 27, 1932, with a special edition and a flourish. The mayor sent congratulations on what he called "the most beautiful as well as modern newspaper building in the middle west." The new headquarters included a spacious newsroom, indoor climate controls, a composing room with eleven linotype machines, stairs made of veined marble, mezzanine executive offices clad in dark walnut by the same decorators that had paneled the Waldorf Astoria, lacquered nickel door handles, and cream-colored piers of Kasota stone festooned with wrought aluminum on the outside, giving the news plant in this northeastern Wisconsin city the stature of an Egyptian temple.

"The new building of the *Post-Crescent* is the outcome of the investment of money and labor that reaches into the spruce forests, the mines, the jungles, the flax fields, the turpentine swamps and the plains of the whole world," wrote an anonymous correspondent in that day's edition.

"If your evening paper, smelling fresh of ink, had qualities of a pho-
nograph record you might hold it to your ear and hear the axes on the
spruce in many lands."

The visual centerpiece lay behind a two-story showcase window:
a new electric Duplex Tubular printing press manufactured in Battle
Creek, Michigan, that consumed sixty tons of paper every month and
could print thirty thousand newspapers in an hour. Pedestrians on Superior Street could watch the papers come off the giant rolls at 3:45 p.m.—a
metaphor for democratic transparency. But the press on display could
also be read as a boast, or even intimidation. *Look what we've got! Look
what we can do!*

By the time I arrived at the *Post-Crescent* as a twenty-one-year-old
intern, the Duplex Tubular was gone and the building had been expanded twice, but the *Post-Crescent* still showed off its crown jewel—a
Goss-Metro press—through a huge picture window. The floor of the
newsroom shook perceptibly as the presses attained full speed an hour
after deadline, and the amaroidal stench of fresh ink pervaded the halls.
Words written in studied frenzy at 10:00 a.m. would be inside a fleet
of trucks by 2:00 p.m. The newsroom was stuffed with reporters who
brought their lunches to work in Playmate coolers, swore like minor poets, and wrote dependable prose with astonishing speed. One figure of
legend was known as "Windy" for his ability to squeeze forty paragraphs
out of a meeting of the regional sewer board.

The only one who ever wore a tie was the managing editor, a reti-
cent Swede named Bill Knutson, who would grin like a little boy when
he heard chatter coming out of the Bearcat police scanner fixed in the
middle of the room like a plastic oracle that promised unusual morning
events: a fire in a paper mill, a jackknifed truck, a bank robbery. He was
prohibited from joining the union, and didn't receive one of the colored
lollipops from the Local 4621 shop steward tied with a slip of paper: *We*

won't settle for a sucker contract! Knutson had hired me to back up the morning police reporter as he chased the addresses on the scanner, wise-cracking with the cops over the yellow tape before coming back to the stone palace to write it up. Knutson eventually set me loose—to cover a model airplane show, the closure of an old locals' tavern on the river, an angry public meeting about subsidized housing, and one glorious feature about summertime heat lightning that ran above the fold on the Sunday front page. It was an inoffensive ten-minute read from an off-the-grid town in the Upper Midwest, but to me that day, my lightning story felt like the announcement of the liberation of Paris in *Le Monde*. By the next afternoon, it was gone.

So many words slung out from newspaper temples all across the country—zinging words, dull words, manipulative words, defensive words, beautiful words, incisive words, wrong words, right words. At that time, there were 1,611 daily newspapers in the United States pro-ducing an average combined daily output of 33,831,000 words. That was thirty-eight times the lifetime literary output of William Shakespeare each day; a book that would have dwarfed the King James Bible by a factor of forty-three. And this is not even counting the wire services, the weekly news magazines, or the country weeklies and biweeklies. All those fingers working all those keyboards in cities from coast to coast, knitting for the country a massive skein of words that spoke to us ev-ery day through a banquet of trivialities (sewer boards, model airplane contests, fires, elections) who we were. There seemed more words in the excited babble of newsprint than stars in the firmament, and even then, those words signaled only a fraction of the potential stories that could be told.

After that summer at the *Post-Crescent*, I knew for certain what I wanted to do for the next fifty years. I wanted to pour a trickle of words onto the flimsy pages of newsprint and help cover America. It seemed like the best job ever created. But I didn't know that I was standing just inside the last generation to have known what the good times were like.

Bursting with ambition after my *Post-Crescent* summer, but unable to find a job on even a medium-sized paper, I read about David Halberstam traveling to Mississippi after his Harvard graduation to ask for a job at the tiny West Point *Times-Leader* so he could get an unparalleled view of the civil rights movement. I had no such fancy credentials and was too blinkered to see a clear good versus evil narrative roaring through the country in the 1990s, but I liked the idea of apprenticing at a tiny paper far off the interstate.

After washing out of a construction job in Denver, and with cold weather on the way, I drove east along the Platte River through Nebraska and stopped in to cold-knock at a series of daily newspapers to ask for a job. Only two editors came out to witness this novelty from off the highway, and both regarded me with bemusement. And then at the *Express*, in the little town of Superior (pop. 2,435), editor Bill Blauvelt listened to my spiel at the front counter, regarded me with a cocked head, and said, "Well, I guess I could take you on for a bit." Behind his cluttered office was a composing room where the paper was assembled with wax, tape, and knives. And in a nearby room the size and dimension of a small bowling alley was a delightful green monster: a Goss Community offset press redolent with ink. I was content.

Bill helped me find an upstairs apartment on Main Street—*Main Street!*—with a stinky gas space heater. For three months, I went to city council and school board meetings for Bill and typed up the essentials in prose that went down like oatmeal: literal and nutritious. The big controversy that winter was whether the city should pay $15,000 for a corrugated irrigation tube under the public tennis court. When I called up a council member to inquire his reasons for the no vote on this particular issue, he screamed *None of your business!* and slammed down the phone. That was just how it went in the story. When I picked up the paper the next day, I saw Bill had changed my words to "declined an opportunity to speak about the subject." It peeved me, but I couldn't fault him. Bill was one of the most respected men in town and picking needless fights was not his style. His father had owned the gas station on the banks of the Republican River, and he knew more secrets than he would ever be able to tell. It confirmed a rule: the two people likely to know where the figurative bodies are buried in a small town are its librarian and its editor.

Bill reacted with customary sangfroid when I told him in December that I'd gotten a job offer from the *Wyoming Tribune and Eagle*—a daily paper, where I always wanted to be. The city editor there sent me to the capital for legislative news, to Yellowstone National Park to write about the reintroduction of wolves, to talk to people who had never learned to read, to listen to cranks fighting city hall, and to professional bull riders flocking into the annual Frontier Days rodeo, the biggest in the nation. My starting salary was $22,000, with which I rented a room with a pull-out bed in a Tudor-style house and felt very, very rich, a little like Tom Wolfe, who accepted a job on the *Springfield Union-Leader* and sang all the way back home: "Oh I am a member of the working press!" At an awkward little church gathering one night, a guy next to me asked if my bosses at the newspaper let me write articles "from a Christian perspective." *Truth* is a Christian perspective, pal—I wanted to tell him. My love for the profession already bordered on the obnoxious. I told people that when I got up for the flag during the anthem at baseball games, what I was really standing for was the Freedom of Information Act of 1967, which made almost every government document public—theoretically, at least. Ours was the only private occupation explicitly named in the

Constitution, right at the top of the Bill of Rights at the point of freedom's spear. The daily newspaper to me was a marvelously shifting window on world events and a keyhole into local power structures. Though I never worked for the Scripps-Howard chain, I admired its lighthouse logo with the triangular beam and the epigrammatic saying borrowed from Dante Alighieri: "Give light and people will find their own way." Does this sound demi-religious, and more than a little annoying? I plead guilty.

The reporter's cloak fit effortlessly over my basic self, calling me out of my native shyness and giving me an excuse to ask questions of strangers. I was never more in a timeless flow-state than when staring into a monitor at the words floating there in green just before a 10:00 a.m. deadline for the afternoon *Tribune*. I loved the flash of a public argument, and the delegated role of crystalizing the daily controversy into a competent summary for the city of Cheyenne, a nebulous sea of folks who I pictured as a vague kind of amoeba just past the glass of the smoky second-floor windows. Journalism was a way to be subversive and respectable at the same time. The big money interests were letting you play with their presses, and you could occasionally puncture official lies. And it all contained an element of word-wizardry; creativity within certain boundaries. As a 1947 handbook put it, in terms fragrant with the era's gender politics: "The lead of the story—the first paragraph—is a sort of come-on. Like a woman's eyes or a barker's line, the lead must invite and interest or the suitors and the customers may turn away. The best is usually the shortest one that reads well and sparkles a bit and is still truthful."

Holding the morning *Eagle* still damp from the presses, especially if some of my words were in it, made me remember the magical and eternal look of the English Clerkenwell flag over papers like *The Arizona Daily Star*, a high-culture image my childhood pal Greg Cullison and I had tried to imitate in a mimeographed sheet we called *The Sixth Grade*

Times. Now I had a press badge and a salary. Here was a magnificent old dream made real.

For a trade dedicated to the pursuit of truth and the discovery of uncomfortable facts, the newspaper business missed one hell of a story flying right at its face.

The first bulletin board services with dial-up modems arrived in 1978, and when the World Wide Web made it easy for nonexperts to navigate a constellation of free websites—everyone now in possession of a Deluxe Tubular—*The New York Times*'s Max Frankel urged the national paper of record to relinquish its hold on the ancient profit model of subscriptions and display ads and reposition itself squarely as the gatekeeper for computerized classified ads. "The future belongs to free and universal listings on the Web, complete with pictures of the available houses, their neighborhoods and floor plans and probably a chance to bid with the click of a mouse," he wrote in 1997. His Cassandra insight was ignored at the exact time it would have mattered most.

Newspapers had thwarted the technological challenge of radio seventy years before by doubling down on editorial quality and, in many cases, buying stations themselves. But they didn't know what to do with the computer wave. In one early but misfired attempt at adaption, the Knight-Ridder chain invested in a service called Viewtron that let modem users with special equipment read news on their screens. But they shut it down after it failed to turn a profit in two years and when they discovered—and did not understand—a key piece of information: users were even more interested in talking and arguing with each other than they were in the news. This early missed chance to invent Facebook before Mark Zuckerberg left the industry gun-shy about newfangled gadgetry, and clinging even harder to the ethic of information monopoly of the sort the *Post-Crescent* had framed in its plate-glass window.

Creeping monopolization had already made us lazy. Those afternoon papers that I used to work for had already been folded into the regional chains that owned them: they were "independent" only in name. With complacence and dominance came an expectation of annual profit margins as high as 40 percent, without having to bother with innovation, reinvestment, or worries that technological thieves in the night could steal the customer base. "Simply put," wrote the business columnist Jon Talton, "the model involved sending miniskirted saleswomen out to sell ads at confiscatory rates to lecherous old car dealers and appliance-store owners." If anyone wanted to show a lawnmower, a cleaning service, a horse, hothouse tomatoes, or insurance to a wider public by doing more than dragging it out to the curb and putting a For Sale sign on it, they had to come to the newspaper and pay up. Don't like the rates? Tough.

The rhythms of heavy manufacturing had kept afternoon papers aloft for years. With deadlines at 10:00 a.m. or later, they could get that morning's national news off the telegraph and the local news off the streets and have a digest to hand to the shift worker at the gates while the sun was still out. Most papers—like the *Post-Crescent*—had multiple editions updated with fresh wire stories or new discoveries by the local news staff; the last of the day was customarily known as the "late city final," an urgent noirish term reminiscent of trains with names like the Broadway Limited or the telegrams labeled "rush." The afternoon papers were less staid than their morning cousins; they were a little splashier, racier. But then the television news and the twilight of American factories forced the afternoon papers into mergers, morning publication, or untimely death: *Washington Star, Philadelphia Bulletin, Spokesman Chronicle, Milwaukee Sentinel, The Los Angeles Herald-Examiner, Dallas Times-Herald, The Wyoming State Tribune, Savannah Evening Press.* All gone. When I worked for those last two newspapers during the 1990s, they already felt like poorly attended museums. And when the 135-year-old *San Francisco Examiner* published its last afternoon edition, I went out to the tired presses on Cesar Chavez Street and watched the conveyor belt of editions bearing the apocalypse headline "GOODBYE!" Standing next to me was a venerable cop reporter named Malcolm Glover who had once been a teenage gardener at William Randolph Hearst's estate and been personally brought into the newsroom by the old chief. His broad and bespectacled face gave away nothing.

At *The Arizona Republic*, employees were ordered to sit by their phones after a merger with the afternoon counterpart. If yours rang, it was a summons to HR to have your keycard stripped. Around the same time, a programmer from New Jersey named Craig Newmark was finding an audience of millions with free searchable classified ads. Here was a truly catastrophic threat, but newspapers did not respond in kind. "The Internet will strut an hour upon the stage, and then take its place in the ranks of the lesser media," proclaimed the editor of the London *Times*, riffing on *All's Well That Ends Well*, and speaking for hundreds of his dithering American counterparts. They failed to acquire Yahoo or partner with Facebook or try to beat Craigslist to the notch in the valley where the tollbooth stands.

"How did you go bankrupt?" a character asks in *The Sun Also Rises*. "Two ways," comes the answer. "Gradually. And then suddenly." Forcibly weaned from the reliable cash infusion from classifieds, newspaper ad revenue went from $80 billion to $20 billion within two decades. The physical empire necessary to run a newspaper—all the ink barrels, paper spools, offset presses, diesel trucks, querulous unionized employees—seemed like a giant anachronism, an army rushing into a modern drone war with cavalry and plate mail. The solidity embodied by the *Post-Crescent's* temple had become a strangling liability in a new information game that called for nimbleness. Big morning papers began to fail like their afternoon counterparts had, as certain as the collapse of the Tsarist lines in the Russian Revolution. Among the first of the big old war-horses to go under was *The Rocky Mountain News*, Colorado's oldest operating business, whose first issues were printed for gold miners on a press hauled in by oxcart. Then came the fall of *The Tampa Tribune*, *The Kansas City Kansan*, *The Lime Springs Herald* in Iowa (circ. 600), and more than eighteen hundred others, as total national readership dropped by half between 2004 and 2019. The tallest mountain on the west side of Tucson is named for the frontier-era editor of the *Citizen*; an executive from the Gannett Corp. casually shuttered the paper for good on his way to play in a Palm Springs golf tournament.

The survivors labored under harsh quarterly expectations from their NYSE-listed companies or private equity firms squeezing what they could out of an exhausted orange. The need to radically change the business plan hit a wall of opposition: a continued expectation of the fat margins of the twentieth century when owning a Deluxe Tubular was a license to print money. Jay Rosen of New York University termed this strategy "profitable demise," noting acidly: "They won't stop the gravy train even though the engine is broken. How does such a thing eventually stop? It crashes."

Most newspapers went the slow-suicide route of cutting their way out of the mess, which bought time but destroyed quality. Display ads began to sprout like weeds on once-sacred front pages. Empty desks spread through newsrooms like blight through a cornfield; a walk through the grand old Spring Street headquarters of the *Los Angeles Times* was a journey through a lich's tomb. *The Cleveland Plain Dealer*—a name Winston Churchill once called "the best newspaper name of any in the world"—shrunk to just fourteen editorial employees from 340 and was on the verge of extinction in the spring of 2020. Papers that had been substantial and lively became pamphlets, disappointing readers and hastening the spiral. Coin op racks became scarce and papers shrank their circulation areas, becoming ghosts.

Aggregator sites like BuzzFeed sprouted up, the crude memes spread on Facebook, and the around-the-clock harangues of cable news channels flowed like gray water loosed from a sanitary lagoon into the emptiness of the country's news deserts. A significant portion of the raw informational material still emerged from traditional newsrooms, but users found it easy to rip off the painstakingly gathered information for free and spin it to whatever purpose. "Newspaper companies completely misunderstood the openness inherent in the Internet and stubbornly tried to force a control-based publishing model into a platform that fundamentally was designed to operate without central control," wrote media analyst Keith L. Herndon.

In the midst of the weakening, a more malicious threat emerged. It had long been fashionable in hard-right circles to slam the press for what was perceived as an excessive sympathy to liberal causes. At rallies around the country, journalists stood in cordoned pens and took abuse from whipped-up crowds. *Fake News! Liars! Socialists!* "You should be arrested, traitors!" a man with a ponytail yelled at reporters at a Pennsylvania rally. He spoke for many departed readers who had been trained to hate the institutions that had once given texture and flavor to their towns, and whose disappearance came in tandem with the unprecedented spread of lies in high places.

What I didn't know during my newspaper career—what I had never been taught—was that I was robotically performing an assembly-line skill that had emerged as a compromise answer to a philosophical crisis.

The ancestors of bourgeois local institutions like the *Post-Crescent* grew up in the boisterous 1830s of new railroads, public education, mushrooming big cities, and a revolt against the elites by the rough-edged president Andrew Jackson. With an army of newsboys on the street, the biggest papers sold tens of thousands of copies, fresh off the steam-powered presses and spouting partisan diatribes without apology. Nobody blinked; such rhetoric was expected of them. In the coming years, the well-capitalized sheets like *The Baltimore Sun*, the *Chicago Tribune*, and the *New York Herald* ran dispatches from Europe and employed a staff of correspondents to ferret out news closer to home. With the proper Victorian literary flourish and enough swash in their buckle, a writer could become a celebrity: Richard Harding Davis, Henry Morton Stanley, Jacob Riis, and Ida Tarbell all made their reputations in their own days though a colorful epistolary style that still finds a home in today's magazines.

The rise of scientific rationalism near the turn of the century—with new methods of rigorous analysis trained on social ills as well as factory production—caused a generation of owners to rethink the splashy approach that led to headlines like "Actress grew and the bodices didn't fit" and "Stabbed by a stranger on stairs of theatre." *The New York Times*, led by polymath managing editor Carr Van Anda, helped standardize the terse summary first paragraph—already growing as a convention because of the telegraph—as well as prioritize the calm voice of interpretation that made the reporter more dignified than a stenographer or a frustrated novelist. And the *Times* elevated the paper itself out of the partisan mud bath and into the role of civic grown-up. The *Times*, said its owner Adolph Ochs, "does not soil the breakfast cloth" with tawdry stories and seeks out high-quality information "in concise and attractive form." His more bawdy-minded rivals were at first stunned to see financial success in this model, and then began to copy it. Now the reporter—a figure once considered little better than a spy by Union generals and a sneaky little cur by the general public—would be the ultimate referee of proper thinking, the guardian of reliable discourse, and the trustee of what was gamely called "objectivity."

This ethic had its pitfalls, of course. Newsrooms were almost exclusively white and male with a heavy emphasis on upper-class values, especially in the more prestigious newsrooms like the *Post-Dispatch* in St. Louis and the *Globe* in Boston. The columnist Walter Lippmann helped define the journalist-as-expert in grim fashion: he believed the average citizen was too incompetent and easily flustered to make proper decisions in a democratic society, necessitating "men with a new training and outlook" to make a careful presentation of the facts before any debate even started. If he had had his way, as he suggested in his long essay "Liberty and the News," a central government agency would have put out newspapers carrying all the pizzazz and romance of sociology textbooks. What Lippmann wanted most was news that supported the establishment's status quo.

He never discussed what Benedict Anderson later said about the emotional experience of reading the daily newspaper: that it bred unconscious conformity to the prevailing views of a society too big to govern through the brute forces of the police or military. Or as *The New Yorker* writer A. J. Liebling put it, he had gobbled news items like cookies as a child and went to college believing that "the country would be forever prosperous if we let prosperous-looking people run it." The hypnotic power of newspapers to establish a version of public morality left readers thinking—innocently—they had discovered these truths on their own.

Newspapers were doing something even more important: birthing a renewed national mentality. In his thick and extremely German prose, Martin Heidegger argued that language creates its own reality and becomes "a house of Being"—that we literally speak the whole world into existence each day through a set of prior understandings imprisoned within words. The unapproachable center of reality that we call "objectivity" is almost irrelevant. The very structure of a news story creates its own set of embedded assumptions: that truth is quantifiable, that governments are legitimate, that public officials should be accountable, that "news" itself is a specific event in which differing interests are in conflict and for which dueling quotes counts as balance. It is a formula as reliable as Aristotle's *Poetics*, and one that leaves much of the real story untold.

But people still have to know. They *needed* to know. That was my

lodestar, what stiffened my back in a hundred confrontational encounters
with various cops or petty civic officials trying to hold back information
that was likely not critical to the continuing functioning of the republic
but which seemed to me at the time to be on par with the formula for the
bubonic plague antidote.

One night during a thunderstorm when I was working the night
police beat at *The Salt Lake Tribune*, the power went off across downtown
and the power company was unable to tell us when the lights would
come back on. We had no reserve generators and the press foreman called
up to the newsroom at around 11:00 p.m. to tell us they were planning to
put the run on hold indefinitely. It was the hour of the night when every
other news staffer had gone home and the managing editor had told me:
"Your judgment is the judgment of the *Tribune*."

The copy desk editors and I sat muttering with a set of distributed
flashlights, and the possibility arose—first as a sardonic joke and then as a
real possibility—that the next day could be the first time since 1868 that
the *Tribune* failed to publish. The paper had started as an anti-Mormon
scandal sheet and a mining digest when Brigham Young was still alive
to denounce it, and then grown up through the twentieth century into
probably the best daily newspaper in the entire Rocky Mountain West.
That it might falter in its core mission as I sat helpless to do anything
seemed unimaginable; it would be as if the entire state of Utah would
disappear if the paper didn't come out.

Had we been doing it wrong all that time? Did we in the newsroom have
a blind spot just as big as the people on the floors above us who were
supposed to have been fiercely guarding the business side?

One of our worst flaws was that we were, too often, boring. Certain stories about policy or government process are irredeemably thus,

and can be no other way. But perhaps too many of them came delivered in the same package, with the ontological arrogance that made readers' eyes slide past yet another recap of property tax scuffles or leaking landfills. We didn't make the paper interesting enough on too many days to justify the cover price. After a few years on the *Springfield Union-Leader*, the paper that he had been so ecstatic to join, Tom Wolfe became convinced that the British-toned omniscience that infused the language of workaday American journalism was tiresome to his readers. "When they came upon that pale beige tone, it began to signal them, unconsciously, that a known bore was here again, 'the journalist,' a pedestrian mind, a phlegmatic spirit, a faded personality, and there was no way to get rid of the pallid little troll, short of ceasing to read."

Well, he got his way. A pair of devastating blows shattered the jaw of the Lippmann consensus within the space of a generation—the lack of a comprehensive response to the new Internet business model, and the narcissistic Big Lie aimed from the White House at half the country that "what you're seeing and what you're reading is not what's happening." Today's free-fire zone of the Internet gives Wolfian poets more room than ever to go deeper into the truth of events beyond what dry newspaperese could have conveyed. But what is lost is the sense of place that a local paper can provide. They were always at their best when they reflected a sense of their own geography—when a reader would put it down feeling like she learned something about the place she lived and thought she already knew. An unusual fact, maybe, or the origin story of a familiar sight. A profile of somebody who pulls the levers of power, especially in a hidden way. An explanation of what makes their town special, and an acknowledgment of the inevitable passing of time. Almost nothing I ever read in *The Albuquerque Journal* angered me as much as their brief and limp obituary on the death of Ralph Edwards, who had offered to broadcast his game show *Truth or Consequences* live to the first town to rename itself after the show.

In March of 1950, the town of Hot Springs, New Mexico, did just that, and has been Truth or Consequences ever since. Edwards went back every May for a parade, even after he was well into his nineties. When he died in 2005, the state's biggest news outlet yawned and scratched and did a disgraceful half-assed job of remembering him.

Complaints like this about the failings of the newspaper—its syntax errors, its rhetorical excesses, its over-coverage of crime—was a national pastime long before "Fake News" became a brainless chant. Lincoln Steffens told the story of how he single-handedly created a public belief in a "crime wave" via the *New York Evening Post* in 1892 by writing about all the routine items in the police station blotter that usually never got reported. Americans have bitched about their media like the British have made a spectator sport of dumping on their passenger trains. You can see it in the funny names locals bestowed their dailies: *The Denver Post-Mortem, The Substandard Exaggerator, San Francisco Comical, The Atlanta Urinal-Constipation.* Wiseasses in Appleton used to call the *Post-Crescent* the *Roast Pheasant.* Long before the *Columbia Journalism Review* branded the hopelessly inept *Daily Oklahoman* as "The Worst Newspaper in America," residents of that city had tagged it as *The Daily Zero.* But it was like making fun of an uncle at a family reunion; affectionate bile. You might get torqued at a wrongheaded editorial or a story and cancel your subscription, but you'd climb back on after a while because a part of you enjoyed being pissed off. Even as zealous a press-basher as A. J. Liebling admitted that he was so tough on the dailies because he loved them so much, and expected consistent excellence of them. "A good newspaper is never quite good enough," wrote Garrison Keillor, "but a bad newspaper is a joy forever."

Is it because we were "biased"? The term has now lost almost all of its meaning, entangled as it is in partisan yelling. In my decade-long career as a daily reporter, I never once experienced a case of being told to arrange or eliminate information to help a given party. While some don't love the way they're quoted or portrayed in the narrative of a complex issue, the root cause of the discontent is mostly in the limited space they're given to explain themselves or a make a point. Journalism is simply not equipped to let every character in a story ramble endlessly; compression is the soul of the art. If readers had endless patience and time, there might be a way to use more than two lines from an hour-long conversation. Language itself is also a restrictive technology, and the frustration many may feel at not seeing the totality of a situation is understandable. But it isn't the paper's fault. An encyclopedia-length volume might be written about an oak tree next to the sidewalk that still never touches the heart of that oak tree.

The social historian Matthew Pressman has argued that the "liberal bias" that disgruntled readers began to complain about during the Vietnam War—a grievance turned into performative genius by the administration of Richard Nixon—was really a necessary transformation away from the deferential stenography given to authority figures, a practice that benefitted demagogues and helped usher in the fact-free chaos of the McCarthy era. What came in its place was a movement not necessarily toward political liberalism but what Pressman called "liberal values"—skepticism, critical thinking, a multiplicity of voices, a greater weight placed on previously marginalized people. When I was working as the political reporter on *The Savannah Morning News*, a former mayor named John Rousakis—an old-school urban majordomo trying to recapture his old office—called to chew me out over how I had portrayed his campaign proposal to overhaul the city's parking division. "Back when I was mayor, reporters didn't do this," he barked. "They wrote down what the guy said, and that was it. That's your job."

Well, no it isn't. Anyone who joined the business after the 1960s was trained not to let official pronouncements get in front of the public without at least a little analysis—the old Lippmann prerogative reasserting itself. "Interpretation replaced transmission," wrote Pressman, "and adversarialism replaced deference."

The strongest bias I ever saw was in deference to established interests—especially of the fiduciary kind. For as much as I loved my first daily job at the *Wyoming Tribune and Eagle*, it was a thoroughly pusillanimous booster rag when it came to anything that might offend local business interests. When a shady credit card security company moved its headquarters to Cheyenne from Fort Lauderdale to take advantage of a more "pro-business climate," we used that happy euphemism in print and were proscribed from explaining that it really meant paying call-center workers a lot less. A colleague of mine was effectively fired from the *Albany Herald* in Georgia for pushing a never-published story showing a clear pattern of racial discrimination in lending by the biggest bank in town. "This story is not for us," the editor told him. Lawsuits cost big money, after all, even the spurious ones. What's the point in inviting them during a stage of profitable demise? I knew my clock at *The Arizona Republic*—and my reporting career—was winding down on the day the managing editor leaned forward from his high-backed leather chair and stabbed his finger down on the printout of the fifth rewrite of a story documenting mid-level graft at Phoenix City Hall. "You're making this guy look like he did something *wrong*," he told me. Well, yes. And that was another story that never ran.

We missed a lot more important stuff almost routinely, especially the stories staring us in the face for which we had no vision. We were stuck in a template that recognized "news" as the emanation of officialdom: a public meeting, a police report, a speech, a petition, the stamp of approval. The deeper movements of society—even the private war of individual human hearts—were often the truest story, and they might as well have been invisible to the supposedly vigilant eyes of the town watchdog. We weren't equipped with the proper language; we didn't know how to categorize fuzzy non-"news" realities in ways that didn't carry the insect-repellent stench of sentimentality. Or maybe straying from the Lippmannian template was just too much of a mental struggle on busy days. The official narrative is often as good as it gets for comprehending the primary lay of the land and should not be a target of constant suspicion; the nation would crumple without basic faith in institutions. But nothing can ever tell the whole story. Language itself is but a shot glass of salt water that, pitifully, stands for the ocean. As the gospel of St. John said about the unknown works of divinity, the world could never hold enough room for all the books that could be written.

I knocked it out of the park one night on a Salt Lake City homicide. This story had it all—gripping lead paragraph, scene details, victim's family interview, leaked investigation detail—and I got to take it above twenty-five column inches. A superb job of dictation, and a nice existential chill for the morning's readership. What we called "a talker." The managing editor was going to be pleased. *Nothing gets by me*, I remember thinking as my masterpiece sailed through the edit. Around midnight, I headed for home and caught the second traffic light on Main Street, where a group of the city's throwaway kids were clustered in a semicircle in the median, ages ranging from about seventeen to twelve; they were pierced, inky, and dressed mainly in dark colors. I only knew vaguely about this community. Runaways from abusive homes mingled with the children of the hardcore homeless who hung together in a collective unit, sharing drugs and companionship.

I pressed the gas when the light turned green but wondered what did I know about that life? Not one useful thing. I was an alleged public safety reporter, and I had never once talked with these kids. But I sure knew how to take down the official cop narrative. Probably the only way we ever would have written about this small street culture is if one of the kids had gotten in trouble, creating a pinpoint of civic meaning, and there was some sort of agency-based discourse—an arrest report, an indictment, a peer-reviewed study, an expert quote—we could use to establish a frame of reality. Because portraying life as it is actually lived demands proof to stand upon. The rambles of a would-be poet on the median didn't fit into the established table of contents. "Journalism," said the Chicago sports promoter Bill Veeck, "prefers simon-pure mediocrity to a touch of tarnished genius."

When he worked for *Newsday* in the 1960s, Robert Caro believed himself to be a ruthless bird dog of bills in the New York legislature that would affect traffic on Long Island. He filed reams of stories on how a particular bridge at Oyster Bay was never going to get built, but then got taken by surprise when a clandestine visit to the capitol by Parks Commissioner Robert Moses suddenly flipped the opposition into a majority. "So I thought I was accomplishing my purpose, which was to explain political power to my readers," recollected Caro to an interviewer. "But driving home from Albany to Roslyn that night, all the way I kept thinking, Everything you've been writing is bullshit, because everything you've been writing is based on the belief that political power comes from the ballot box, from being elected." Telling the real contextual story required an almost unimaginable number of hours—impossible to do when a chaotic and ever-moving city has a hundred thousand emergent stories rolling at any given time, not to mention the slow-moving narratives. An average newspaper can select twenty of them at most to fit into the late city final.

Is there any sight in a household more laden with pathos than a stack of last week's newspapers near the door? "Read me," they beg, their only remaining function. But pulp is static and doesn't have the dynamism of the electronic screen; it's locked in place forever and can't change. A mayfly lives longer. No surprise that the reason so many readers gave for canceled subscriptions, even before the present unwinding, was that too many back issues were piling up and becoming clutter. Perhaps guilt more than cleanliness was the motivator—we knew we should read them, but didn't.

Journalists know a thing or two about institutionalized guilt. Many joined the profession, especially during the "liberal values" era defined by Pressman, to make a difference, or change the world, or whatever old-shoe phrase defines the revolutionary impulse that writhes to some degree within all of us, especially when we are young. Reality cooperates with notable stinginess. The public pressure and embarrassment fired up by a local paper can indeed bend the course of events in a beneficial direction—a bad idea dropped, a criminal arrested, a person's life enriched by seeing the right story—but direct cause-and-effect on the moving hand of history is impossible to chart in the long term. Mostly we just wondered if any of our labors did any good. "It's all chalk on the sidewalk," my colleague Judy Nichols once told me. "Gone in the next hard rain."

Perhaps we worked so hard on certain stories—insisted on their importance—as penance for all the ones we knew in our hearts we overlooked. I never turned the car around to talk to the homeless kids on the median, for example, and I left Salt Lake City a year later without ever writing about them. And when I left my career behind with a sigh in 2003, walking out of *The Arizona Republic* knowing I would never be going back, I did so burdened with a long mental list of stories that I wish I had found the time to write. This was true of everyone I ever met in a newsroom.

What we were doing with all those shorter items we slammed into the paper, however imperfectly, was logging a record of events into the permanent memory of the nation. Crack open any civic history at the bibliography, and odds are excellent that most of the details are sourced from the local paper. If we didn't publish it, it might as well have never happened, so far as a future consciousness is concerned. Now that a daily record of happenings is vanishing from America's towns and cities, so with it will come amnesia. The stack of newspapers that mattered most, and which we spent almost no time thinking about, was delivered to the library archives. Future urban historians will come across an abundance of detail about virtually every town and city in the U.S. up until the first decade of the twenty-first century, when the record starts to trail off and the permanent record of what happened across America begins to disappear like brain cells under attack. How far this new Dark Age will last is, as yet, unknown. The COVID-19 lockdown and recession tore through an already feeble business, killing dozens of newspapers that had served their towns for more than a hundred years and leaving the civic lights dimmed, perhaps permanently.

Academics of the future are also likely to note a correlation that may not be coincidental: the era of America's greatest world influence; the time when it expanded the most rights than it ever had before to its minority citizens and began to surrender the exclusively white male grip on the levers of power, when it lurched away from a Gilded Age of corruption and toward a general expectation of public honesty and probity. However flawed, halting, and unfinished that one hundred years of forward motion may have been, it all happened when the decentralized power of far-flung newspapering was at its greatest democratic reach, and career professionals in every city and town were working every day to make a record of American doings. All history is first made of publicity, and newspapers were the foundation.

Our bards of technological optimism promised us that the ease of digitized information would bring the country to unheralded levels of transparency and knowledge. None of the utopians foresaw that the disruption of the dead-tree business model would also mean the death of the ethic of fairness that stood on top of it as a superstructure, or that the computerized age of hot takes and a million choices might actually starve us of news about ourselves.

On June 28, 2018, a disgruntled reader of the Annapolis *Capital-Gazette* shot his way into the newsroom and murdered five staff members before his capture by police. He had been fixated on the paper ever since they published a crime story about his conviction for harassing a woman online seven years before. In the strange national atmosphere of hatred toward journalistic "enemies of the people," coming from the highest levels of government, it is impossible to say how much the dialogue might have ricocheted around the gunman's mind as he contemplated his takedown.

I watched the television coverage, horrified, knowing the victims could have easily been colleagues I knew, their blood spattering the monitor screens of half-finished stories. But one strange visual detail stood out. The offices of the *Capital-Gazette*, which traces its roots to 1727, were in a characterless business park in the suburbs. Whatever historic real estate they had once occupied in the center of town was long gone. American newspapers deliberately built their offices as close as possible to city hall or the capitol, a physical metaphor for their role as guardians of good policy and the conspicuous prestige that entailed. But now most were banished to remote cul-de-sacs where nobody could see them, the profits from the sale or lease of their beautiful buildings gone to plug up the wound in their dwindling finances. The *Los Angeles Times* and Ohio's *Springfield News-Sun* are now condos. *The Chicago Sun-Times*'s riverfront perch became the site of a hotel branded with the name of an obnoxious politician. The *Daily Breeze* in Torrance is a cancer center, the *Miami Herald* will become a casino, the art deco *Seattle Times* offices belong to Amazon, the *Denver Post* was banished to an industrial neighborhood near the freeway. Employees of the *Pottstown Mercury* were simply told to work from home. *The Salt Lake Tribune*, where I sweated out many nights, used to stand defiantly a few blocks from the world headquarters of its archnemesis, the Mormon Church. It is now hidden on the top floor of a struggling shopping mall west of downtown, and its new owner— the vampirical hedge fund Alden Global Capital—sold off its share in the printing press for $23 million and simply trousered the money.

What happened next, however, offers a clue into how the local newspapering trade will likely stay afloat for a few more years. The local philanthropist Carl Huntsman, heir to a chemical fortune, picked up *The Salt Lake Tribune* from Alden in 2016 and eased down the cost-cutting as part of a strategy to transform it into a nonprofit similar to other civic features, like a symphony, a ballet, or a museum, that cater to occasional customers, not regular ones. Already some of the best investigative talent in the country has migrated to online-only nonprofit entities like the *Texas Tribune, Vermont Digger, Colorado Independent, Tucson Sentinel, MinnPost*, and *ProPublica*, which routinely break stories that used to be the provenance of local dailies. National prestige brands like *The New York Times, The Washington Post*, and *The Wall Street Journal* have found renewed life and bigger readership in the political unrest of the age.

The smallest papers, too, have put up a good fight against the dying of the light. When I went to go see my first boss, Bill Blauvelt, in the cluttered offices of *The Superior Express* in the summer of 2019, he was still putting out a weekly paper stuffed full of community news and buying enough barrels of ink from a Kansas supplier to make him the fifth biggest user in the state. But the same vigor isn't present within the weakening firmament of medium-sized dailies that narrated the middle of the country. The physical *whereness* of newspapers is fading into the ethereal *nowhere-and-everywhere* character of the Internet, as if they had experienced a corporeal death and been transformed into a spirit with white robes, an Obi-Wan Kenobi of the modern information era.

There's a cosmic joke in all this. The ephemerality of newspapers mirrors the physical insubstantiality of the thin paper on which they're printed, as well as the nature of the business itself. Nothing is staler than yesterday's news, goes the saying, and to live as a reporter is to live in the eternal present, alive only in the passing moment, like a figure in an existential fable. Time makes the product instantly obsolete. And yet there was an electric pleasure in living that way; in caring only about what was happening that very day, and inserting oneself with authority into the civic gyroscope at will and exiting it shortly thereafter. In ten years of that life, I talked with more people than I can ever recall, up and down the social ladder, and forgot with brutal efficiency what it ever meant to be introverted. Others had better adventures and saw worse horrors, but I had a few modest ones available nowhere else for such meager salary: I got yelled at by Evel Knievel, counted votes at political conventions, watched murder trials, trudged through slums, did interviews in prisons and jails, watched the twentieth century tick down its last seconds from the hills above Jerusalem, got doors slammed on me, listened to clandestine audiotapes, witnessed a man die in the Georgia electric chair, endured the drone of public meetings, chased congressmen down the street, dined with polygamist outlaws, walked up to plane crashes, rode in small airplanes and huge ocean freighters, and once had the exquisite privilege of accepting leaked documents in a deserted parking garage (that holy Woodwardian geography) and then confronting the head of a San Francisco charity about using donations for the poor for his Botox treatments. "As I look back over a misspent life I find myself more and more convinced that I had more fun doing news reporting than in any other enterprise," wrote H. L. Mencken, who started his career at *The Baltimore Sun*. "It is really the life of kings." But it is fundamentally temporal; it yellows even quicker than the cheap paper on which the flood of words is poured. As another old chestnut of the business goes, a reporter is a confidant of the powerful, a friend to the poor, an interpreter of the truth, a trusted finder of fact; he walks among kings and paupers alike; he is magnetic and accessible; he dispenses trustworthy analysis; people hang on his written words. And when he is gone, people remember him for maybe a day.

Newspapers aren't the only totem of an older America laid waste by the Internet and changing consumer tastes. Travel agencies, indoor shopping malls, stock brokerages, car dealerships, record companies, taxi fleets: all of them took repeated blows that sent many longtime family businesses to the grave and left those still standing shadows of what they had been. But newspapers have a different animating spirit than the rest. Most of them have been voices in their communities for more than a century and a half, and some on the East Coast are older than the republic itself. They had personalities and style. They influenced history, even as they documented it. The columnist Bob Greene wrote that the only time he cried covering a story was when he was there for the production of the last edition of the *Columbus Citizen-Journal*, where he had gotten his start as a teenager. Newspapers are an American romance as old as the musket and the plow. But just as the biological body sometimes wastes away before the brain is ready to go, a paper needs circulation to keep the words coming. "The function of a press in society is to inform," said Liebling, "but its role is to make money."

The Goss-Metro presses no longer roll behind a showcase window at the *Post-Crescent* in Appleton. The corporate owner, Gannett, sold them off and shifted all printing of the thinned-out daily newspaper to a plant in Milwaukee in April 2018. The following year, the paper sold its cream-colored temple on Superior Street to a development group calling itself Crescent Lofts-Appleton LLC, which had plans to make it into hipster apartments. I was in Appleton for a visit around that time, and before it occurred to me to buy a copy of the paper, I had already left town.

Villages

The restaurants cast yellow light onto the side blocks off Columbus Avenue, and I used to go into them even though I had no intention of eating. I couldn't afford to spend the money, but I liked to be inside for just a minute. Their tables were typically jammed with young people about my age, looking polished and chatty. Feigning customerhood, I would either go use the bathroom in the rear or ask the host if I could "see the menu," pretend to evaluate the thirty-dollar pork chop for its suitability for my nonexistent future visit, then thank them and ghost back out onto the sidewalk. This was my first winter in New York City.

I had moved there from Savannah, Georgia, with the intention of writing a novel, but after three months, my money was nearly gone. Moving to the city had once seemed almost a patriotic act. An idea had been knocking around—a novel about an elderly music teacher in Nebraska—and what better place to write it all out than the city where a long line of Americans had gone to pour their art on the page: Mark

Twain, Willa Cather, Ralph Ellison, thousands of others whose names I
didn't know. So what if New York wasn't on the midwestern plains where
the novel was set? Through an ad in the *Village Voice*, I found a room on
the twenty-fifth floor of a tower at 95 West Ninety-Fifth Street, a condo
with disco-era shag carpeting owned by a Jamaican legal secretary named
Faye, who had served in the U.S. Marine Corps. She dressed in flowing
fabrics and high boots, and her bed was covered with leopard-print velvet. When I walked onto the balcony and saw the colored diadem of
midtown glowing peacefully three miles to the south, I knew this was
where I had to be. I set up my computer on a gunmetal desk borrowed
from Faye and got to work on the novel I was calling *Spring Concert*,
plunging into a story I barely understood. My usual lunch was a can of
lima beans—sixty-nine cents at the Key Food—with hot sauce. Because
I had no real money and no clue where to go at night, I didn't join my
peers as they waited in line for nightclubs in Chelsea and Tribeca.

Those first few months as winter drew near, my occasional evening
splurge was on a bottle of bourbon. I would drink an iced glass of it while
listening to jazz on the radio, lying propped on my twin bed reading
one novel or another whose style I was trying to imitate. My window
faced north and I could see three bridges—the George Washington, the
Whitestone, and the Throgs Neck—with blinking lights on their cables
and the big orange-and-green neon sign for Newport cigarettes on the
Harlem River over hundreds of jeweled towers and brownstones. Rain
and fog washed the view in November, and the radio would give half-
hour reports from the National Weather Service lending further reas-
surance to my decision to stay inside. If I felt lonely, I would walk down
Columbus Avenue and duck into warm restaurants for a few minutes.

On the many days when the words weren't coming, I shrugged into
a denim jacket and went over to the A-C-E station on Central Park
West and got on the subway, aiming for a random destination near

one of its 424 stations. On different days, I picked Jackson Avenue in the Bronx, 205th Street in Inwood, Astoria Boulevard, Flushing Main Street, Far Rockaway, Lorimer Street, Utica Avenue, Kingston-Throop, or Hoyt-Schermerhorn, names that smelled of asphalt, lead paint, frying onions, and forgotten men in bowler hats. I walked underneath the iron bridges that held up the tracks, peered into shops owned by recent immigrants, had coffee in bodegas where cashiers called me *papi*, ate lunch in a place I would likely never see again, and wandered down residential blocks with striped metal awnings over small porches.

"No one can know Brooklyn because Brooklyn is the world," Arthur Miller once said, and he could have been speaking for the other four boroughs as well, in which more than eight hundred languages are spoken, with English and Spanish topping the list and generous helpings of French Creole, Urdu, Hindi, Russian, Korean, Tagalog, Mandarin, and Swahili. To live in New York was to forever give up on the idea that you could have detailed knowledge of so vast a geography. These streets had known chuffing horses dying in the snow, lovers kissing in doorways, police beatings, cons, gang fights, Dutch soldiers looking warily toward the shore, and Lenape hunters stalking game. Who was anybody in this immense design?

My daylong walks still made me feel less alone, even as I became aware that I couldn't understand New York City any more than I could understand a fictional sixty-nine-year-old music teacher. I had been a reporter in Savannah, another complicated Atlantic city with a clipper-ship past, but I imagined that I had a grasp on it because I could get the mayor on the phone, I knew where the streets went, and I knew who donated money to what cause. But what did I really know about the place? What does anybody really know about a place they weren't born? Henry David Thoreau said he "traveled a good deal in Concord" and learned almost everything he knew about human nature from watching the inhabitants of his little Massachusetts village. That would never be possible in New York City. My presence here was that of a drifting ember. I would not change the metropolis one iota; it would not notice when I left.

The physical lostness eventually felt comforting. "And when one inhabits a city, even a city as rigorous and logically constructed as Manhattan, one starts by getting lost," wrote Olivia Liang in a book called *The Lonely City*. "Sometimes as I walked, roaming under the stanchions of the Williamsburg Bridge or following the East River all the way to the silvery hulk of the U.N., I could forget my sorry self, becoming instead as porous and borderless as the mist, pleasurably adrift on the currents of the city." I was eventually able to predict what lay around almost every corner of Manhattan below 125th Street because I had already walked it dozens of times.

This couldn't go on forever. Snow came, turned quickly to dirty slush, and my walks got less frequent. Con Edison mounted orange plastic towers over the steam vents on the streets. By February, I had a half-finished unruly blob of a novel and no money. That spelled only one thing: *job*.

I signed up with a temp agency on East Fifty-Sixth Street that sent me out on fifteen-dollar-an-hour gigs dressed in discount Hagar slacks and generic ties. At one shady marketing company, I sat at a tall reception desk that fronted a locked door and was told to open it for no one. My only role was to answer the phone, say the desired person was "unavailable," and take a message. A single call came through in a week. Another time, I was sent to move furniture at an ad agency near the Worldwide Plaza in Hell's Kitchen. An account manager about my age, in possession of a very nice suit, a wedding ring, and far better life choices, came out of his office and we collided accidentally. He glanced at me sweating through my cheap shirt and walked away without a word.

Then came good fortune: a relatively long-term assignment at HarperCollins Publishers, which occupied a sleek headquarters on East Fifty-Third Street with an obelisk out front and a lobby display of first editions of famous authors with whom they'd done business: Twain, Melville, the Brontë sisters. My job as editorial assistant to a cookbook editor involved not just answering the phone but sending sales figures updates to authors and writing jacket copy ("savory," "sunshine," and "crisp" were go-to words). Then a science fiction editor upstairs asked me to reject her slush pile of unsolicited spaceship manuscripts and I tried to inject hopeful shadings into the rejection notes even as those for *Spring Concert*—which I had managed to finish—began rolling in. I saved all my rejections in a thickening manila folder and wondered if the rejected sci-fi authors were also saving my handiwork: "Dear Mr. Baker, While we enjoyed the depiction of planetary civil war on Malunga and felt your characters were well-developed, we ultimately felt it was not right for our list. We wish you the best of luck in finding a home for it."

At the photocopier one afternoon, I started talking with a woman about my age from the business books side. She was also a temp, she told me, and was being let go that week. I liked her eyes and her smile, but was too shy to do anything more. Then she left a charming note on the desk of my cubicle asking me out, with her number at the bottom. In those days, such a punch to the nose was what it took for me to grasp that somebody liked me. Our first date lasted until dawn the next morning, beginning with pints of beer at an ancient bar in the West Village called Chumley's, then proceeding to a carnival in front of St. Anthony of Padua Catholic Church on Houston Street where hesitantly, shyly, we kissed on the upward rotation of the Ferris wheel. We spent the next ten hours wandering the streets of lower Manhattan together, telling stories to each other in darkened doorways. Her hand fit nicely into mine, and she apologized for its smallness, quoting e. e. cummings: *not even the rain has such small hands*. I was poleaxed with infatuation. When the sky began to lighten, we were in Washington Square Park and I fell into a doze with her on a bench underneath the statue of Giuseppe Garibaldi.

New York started to make sense, at least for a little while. We drank in SoHo bars with big couches and house music. I had never eaten sushi before she took me. The Village south of NYU had always seemed to me like a place whose moment in the cultural sun had departed along with Bob Dylan in 1964, but she made it my favorite neighborhood. An Italian restaurant near Sixth Avenue served up cheap pasta and let you bring your own bottle of wine. We tumbled around most nights on her bed, which was next to a window on the top floor of a walk-up on Sullivan Street, and I grew accustomed to catching the C train at the West Fourth Street stop in the gray of morning. She had studied poetry at a fancy Massachusetts college, but worried she wasn't living up to expectations and fretted about her career, which had been as aimless and poorly planned as mine.

One day we walked across the Brooklyn Bridge and kept walking all the way to the docks at Red Hook. I was going on about some half-assed theory about how Brooklyn was beautiful because of its visible economic wreckage, and she paused, looking straight ahead at the harbor water. "I understand why you like me now," she said. "Because I'm like Brooklyn. A glorious wreckage."

She wasn't the only one thinking that way. My time at HarperCollins ended, and *Spring Concert* was still ice cold, despite a complete rewrite. I wondered how much I understood—if anything—about the motivations of a Nebraska music teacher and those secondary characters around him. Did I really *get* human nature? Did I have anything worth saying? Fiction was supposed to be about reimagining the ungovernable cosmos and narrating it in a sensible way; probably the same brand of creative equilibrium required to navigate a place like New York City on a long-term basis.

Perhaps this is why no nonfiction book has ever really been able to portray the city in all its heartbreaking extravagance. It is left instead to novels—*Motherless Brooklyn, Bonfire of the Vanities, The Age of Innocence, Winter's Tale, The Invisible Man, Breakfast at Tiffany's, Lush Life, Open City*—to tell the emotional truth about New York City, and with it, approach the enigma of life itself. *Time* magazine had once said that Thornton Wilder, a great chronicler of village truth, was in possession of an "interplanetary mind." Looking from my room at the three bridges winking over the carpet of northern Manhattan Island, I understood I would never have that capability to conjure a fictional world on a page.

As I came up on my one-year anniversary of living in the city, I had a failed novel, no job, almost no money, and a relationship with the woman from the photocopier that had succumbed to disappointments and tears. The jazz station that I listened to played a regular commercial for an electronics store and the jingle went: *Going down, down, down, down / Lower prices here / Going down, down, down, down.* I sat on my bed and stared at the three bridges, knowing that I, too, was going down unless I took new action.

That spelled only one thing: *leaving New York*. I accepted a reporting job in Utah without telling the woman from the photocopier and broke the news only when it was a fait accompli. This was a dishonorable move on my part. But she stayed with me until the day when I woke at dawn, took the subway up to the northern tip of Manhattan, and walked thirteen miles all the way to Battery Park—a valedictory meander through the place that had eluded me. The next morning I drove a borrowed car out through the Holland Tunnel. Our nation is a collection of villages, and I was only exchanging one that I could never understand for another that I possibly could.

But it would not be my last go-around with America's biggest village. Seven years later, I quit another newspaper job and moved back with a little more confidence and a reduced scope of an idea. Fiction was not going to be my path; I would no longer be chasing abstractions or trying to paint the sky with big cosmic equations. But I could write about manageable slices of the world from real life instead of the imagined kind. "It is not a bad thing," wrote Walker Percy, "to settle for the Little Way, not the big search for the big happiness but the sad little happiness of drinks and kisses, a good little car and a warm deep thigh."

Beyond all the songs and postcards and implausible movies, there turns out to be nothing particularly spectacular about Manhattan oxygen. The dollar is legal tender there, the beer is mainly domestic, the people are as alternatingly dull and charming as they are in Topeka, and the grocery stores have carts. You may live in rough proximity to some extremely rich people in doorman buildings, but it is no Quivira. And neither is it hell. I found a third-floor room on the Lower East Side with two roommates and a view of a coin laundry. Then I got lucky. A nonfiction book sold. Then another, then another. I could pay rent for a while. New friends appeared. I threw parties, went to concerts, danced in clubs, went out with women I would have been previously terrified to approach, ate with groups of friends at the same restaurants off Columbus Avenue that I had once slunk through like a wraith. New York City became less of a supernova mystery and more of just a plausible American place to live, albeit with more street noise and slightly more expensive toothpaste.

I surrendered the goal of mastering even a fraction of it. But the city would never again be as sharp or as magnificent to me as it was during that first year of loneliness, insolvency, and defeat.

The Valley

Silvia Saige twirls a plastic wedding ring around her finger with a bemused expression on her face as she waits for her male costar to finish toweling off and the production assistant to readjust the boom mike. Then the scene—and the sex—can continue.

They're in the smallest bedroom of a gated mansion in the western part of the San Fernando Valley for the one-day shoot of a hardcore pornographic film entitled *Different Wives, Different Lives*. The bedspread is the color of pumpkin candy, the walls are painted baby blue, and the throw pillows are embroidered with golden sparkly hearts. A large box of Huggies Natural Care baby wipes is on a stool nearby.

The shoot is running on schedule and the four-person crew is relaxed enough to joke about whether tea-tree oil should ever be used to treat genital warts, but the room has grown stuffy enough to be uncomfortable and the director Jacky St. James fans herself with a file folder containing the script, in which Silvia plays an ambitious real estate agent and the male star Marcus London plays her conniving boss.

The scene they're filming reads this way in the twenty-page script:

MARCUS
There's a vacant property we've got for sale - right across the way. Wanna check it out with me?

SILVIA
You're so bad.

INT. VACANT PROPERTY ROOM—DAY

SEX SCENE SILVIA AND MARCUS.

The shade on the window isn't drawn, but nobody is worried about intruders. The walls facing the street are taller than seven feet, and the driveway gates are locked. This sprawling 1955 house with a Spanish tile roof is one of the six mansions in the Los Angeles metropolitan area rented out by their owners for films like this—what amounts to a clandestine geography particular to the pornographic trade. Few people except the director, the crew, and the performers know where these houses are, but these residences receive constant use and require constant redecoration to keep the backgrounds looking fresh and ever-changing for heavy viewers of the genre.

No part of this house looks like any other; each room has a different scheme. The living room features a tall Chinese vase, a fireplace with fake logs, tiled floors, and a painting of two pigs in a grassy field. The backyard has a swimming pool, a ramada sheltering a barbeque, and mature olive trees casting patches of shade. This part of the Valley was walnut-farming country a century ago, and the spacious lots retain a rural feel. In the far part of the backyard is a square villa built in the Tuscan style, with a fake classroom on the first floor that can also be converted into a locker room or a doctor's office, depending on the erotic biddings of the script. On the blackboard is a chalked equation: $x^2 - 12x + 36 = (x-6)2$.

The homeowner—who lives here with his wife—is a man in his early sixties who says the adult house rental business runs on trust. "You be nice to them and vice versa. I have definitely had disrespectful crews that never get invited back." He wears scuffed boots and canvas pants spattered with paint, and he has the weary look of a general contractor who has seen it all. He stays away from the shoots, keeping busy on another part of the property, but he has seen the various rooms of his house as the background in the sex films when he watches them. He notices the handiwork he put into the interior. "I'm proud—like seeing your kid walk across stage at graduation," he tells me.

Among his rules is the insistence that crews park their cars in the yard inside the locked gate. Street parking would attract the attention of the neighbors and possibly lead to a police investigation. "And then," he said, "it would all come crashing down."

In 2012, L.A. County voters approved Measure B, which requires the use of condoms on porn sets. Enforcement by state inspectors is poorly funded, and the law is widely flouted. To this homeowner's mind though, there is no sense to put Measure B to the test and risk losing a source of passive income. The going rate for shoots like this is $100 per hour, and shooting days typically last fourteen hours, so it's an easy $1,400 for doing nothing.

The touchy subject of prophylactics comes up in the blue bedroom during a shooting break. A wholly naked Marcus London, a former barkeep with a British accent and a missing canine tooth, is telling the story of a recent date who told him he didn't need to use a condom.

"Who has sex in their personal lives?" Silvia wanted to know.

"I do," said Marcus. "Lots! Always wear a condom out there. Always."

A common thought within the trade—where all performers are legally required to have a certified STD test conducted within two weeks of the shoot—is that sex with outsiders, "civilians," is more dangerous.

"I mean, how *stupid* can people be?" London wonders out loud as he hovers over Sylvia, ready to go again.

From the kitchen wafts the smell of frying bacon—lunch for the hungry crew, as soon as this scene is over.

The assistant director, Mike Quasar, hefts his Canon C300. "All right," he says. "Three, two, one, fornicate."

This upmarket house in the Valley represents a seismic change in a business known as "The Other Hollywood," which is constructed around the reproductive urge and selling its visual wares mainly to men.

Annual revenue figures are squishy—estimates range wildly from $2.6 to $15 billion—but the reach of the product into the American subconscious has grown exponentially in the last decade through free Internet sites, social media, and a gradual lowering of cultural standards. The old *Boogie Nights* business model of making VHS tapes for rent behind beaded curtains at the video store has succumbed to an ocean of clickable "content" catering to every describable kink, often shot by hobbyists who don't waste time with a plot or the semblance of phony frisson leading to the main event.

Producers who wanted to distinguish their films from the rest were forced to spend even more money on locations with a lot of windows featuring natural midday California sunlight—which is kinder to the naked human form than mounted key lights—and gaudy interior styling. The days of shooting in soundstages behind warehouse walls are over, as competition forced directors to look more upscale in their scenarios. Sex has long been associated with glamour in American culture; now even more so in the new spatial map of adult films shot within the zip codes of the 1 percent top income earners.

"At the end of the day, pornography is the fantasy creation business," said Dan Miller, an editor with the trade publication *Adult Video News*. "It calls for an ideal setting in which someone might imagine themselves. These locations symbolize wealth and success. That all adds to the atmosphere of the sex acts. Why does it matter where you're 'at'? Well, it does. It's part of the overall experience."

The drive to use what director Joanna Angel called "the six magic houses" of the Valley and the Hollywood Hills was driven not so much by taste but by psychology and raw economic logic. When any product loses a price tag and becomes free, it becomes inherently less interesting. Production companies that survived the onslaught of free Internet porn made a conscious choice to double down on the importance of location and emphasize the illusion of luxury as a value-added proposition. The owner of the Vixen Media Group started paying airfare for his actors to shoot in Parisian apartments on snow-white sheets with the Eiffel Tower clearly visible in the background.

"We had a huge decision to make," said Angel. "If I want to breathe and stay alive, I have to make my highest quality shit ever. This is survival of the fittest. There were all these companies just shitting out scenes and now all of them are gone—they weren't doing anything memorable."

If an identifiable location has been used so many times that it becomes recognizable, it becomes "shot out," in the parlance of the business. So the six houses that do regular business with companies like Sweet Sinner and Mile High Media require periodic restaging with new furniture and wall hangings so as to maintain the illusion of variety. "It's like a soap opera or a *Saturday Night Live* skit—one little set constantly redrawn," said a production assistant. The wealthy owners of these houses started making deals with porn directors after the economic recession of 2008. And while the caretakers of other Hollywood Hills mansions might occasionally be slipped $500 to allow a day of shooting unbeknownst to the absentee owner off in the Bahamas or Guangzhou, the more conventional practice is to do a deal aboveboard. "People are tired of seeing sex in a windowless room," said producer Jules Jordan. "They want to see an ocean out the window. Twenty-five years ago, you could shoot cheap and people would still buy it. Not any longer."

Pornography already involves the depiction of a predictable and repetitive act in which there can only be so many kinetic variations. Eventual boredom is guaranteed. To ensure repeated consumption, there has to be at least the remnant of the initial thrill of newness. But stuck to the same rooms of monotonous glamour—most of the six houses have a white room with a white couch, for example—directors have to improvise. Jib cameras can make a room look bigger or smaller. Angles can emphasize different windows. Plot scenarios are often written around whatever house is available that week. A line of throwaway dialogue is usually sufficient.

"If I'm writing a college picture, I have to justify why students are living in a multimillion-dollar mansion," said St. James. Her fictional characters have also been bumped down the socioeconomic spectrum. She still is regretful that one of her favorite films, a *Fifty Shades of Grey* knockoff called *The Submission of Emma Marx*, had to be reformulated when her shoot at a Hollywood Hills house, complete with a curved staircase and a piano in the foyer, was canceled with a day's notice. The shoot moved to a horse property in the valley, scenes were rewritten on the fly, and the BDSM billionaire character instantly dropped several tax brackets. "This is an industry and a world where you really have to be flexible and you can't be firm in your artistic choices," she said.

St. James—an earnest redheaded woman with the aspect of a bubbly soccer mom—comes from a Catholic family in northern Virginia. She moved to L.A. when she was twenty-seven and worked in online advertising before submitting a script aimed at female consumers called *Dear Abby* to a company that produced it as part of their "Romance Series." St. James always had a taste for the product, even during the beaded curtain days of the 1990s, and she soon made a full-time career for herself behind the camera. The worst part, she said, is dealing with neighbors of the designated houses who find out what's going on inside.

Parking turns out to be the biggest giveaway—all those cars piled up for long days—which is why she prefers to rent locales with locking gates and big front yards. Once she had to give up on a "beautiful mansion" in Newbury Park after she found her car smeared with dog feces by a local moralist. "They lump us all into one category—they think we work in a dirty, disgusting business," she said.

The United States leads the world in the production and consumption of pornography, which has existed in a semi-outlaw geography long since before the founding of the republic. The word itself is a portmanteau of the Greek words *pornea*, for fornication, and *graphos*, for writing.

Racy French postcards and "educational" Victorian novelettes of debauchery with far more emphasis on the sin than the redemption were in private circulation long before a scandalized postmaster named Anthony Comstock founded the New York Society for the Suppression of Vice and succeeded in getting a series of anti-obscenity bills passed into federal law in the 1870s.

Then came the motion picture and the fullest demonstration of the historian Joseph Slade's observation that "whenever one person invents a technology, another person will invent a sexual use for it." Depictions of real intercourse on camera are commonly dated to a nine-minute silent short filmed in 1915 titled "A Grass Sandwich," said to be the earliest American porn flick, in which a tubby mustachioed man in a touring car picks up two female hitchhikers and cavorts with them in a meadow. It was never shown in theaters, but circulated as a bootleg among collectors for showings at stag parties and clubs—a forerunner of the "blue movies" later produced on the sly and meant for private audiences. In its brief length, unlikely premise, straightforward appeal to the male gaze, and fantastical depiction of no-strings-attached sex, "A Grass Sandwich" anticipated tens of millions of Internet clips a century later.

Porn is different from other types of cinema in multiple ways—not least of which is that it breaks an important taboo of the species. Humans are the only form of life who mate in private. Almost every society in the world metes out punishment for public exposure and gratification of the genitalia: the statist form of Sigmund Freud's parental figure who rushes to thwart the four-year-old child from self-pleasure. Pornography breaks that ancient egg open and shows what lies inside. Its visuals are a farrago of the repulsive, beautiful, hypnotic, and profoundly alienating. This act is where we came from, after all, and it lives uneasily within all of us as a craving at the heart of the temporal lobe. The memoirist Donald Miller writes of the time when he happened upon a skin magazine next to some railroad tracks when he was twelve and saw his first image of a naked woman. "I felt that I was being shown a secret, a secret that everybody in the world had always known and had kept from me."

The word *secret* is a curious one when applied to fornication's depiction, as it is a literal uncovering and publication of what is fundamentally secret—"the secret parts of fortune," as Hamlet called a vagina in act 2, scene 2. Pornography is most always filmed in secret; the paranoia surrounding the six mansions is not for nothing. It is also consumed in secret. Its experienced users know how to clean their browsers of evidence of this most private of habits that nevertheless has a tripwire into our basic programming—"both the taboo and the altar of Western culture," in the wonderful phrase of historian Paul Thompson.

The hidden geography of American porn took on dizzying new ironies with the Internet. Sex itself is a localized spatial activity, of course, a geography of tabs and slots that represents the closest union between human beings—its base biological purpose to knit strands of DNA together into a new entity. Porn exposes the surfaces of this "insideness" to outsiders, casting it onto wide waters. Its pleasures may now be a subject of mediated participation by strangers. It puts out an illusion of intimacy but instead promotes solitude. Like the Internet itself, pornography is everywhere and nowhere at the same time. Sex is a particular exploration of place whose thrill comes from the specialness of the terrain; porn throws open the gates for public inspection.

But for all of its deceit and counterfeiting, a kernel of honesty glows at the heart of pornography. We seek to conceal our ordinary daytime lusts with clothing and propriety and shelter, but this burning river of mystery flows inside all of us, this frightening animal portion of humanity that we try to grasp, tame, and use but never fully comprehend. To conquer it is to conquer our bestial natures. But porn shows us for twenty minutes what lies beneath; it is by turns hypnotic and deeply uncomfortable.

The nihilistic honesty of hardcore pornography has another dimension: it is a variety of "acting" that has an indisputably genuine element: the sex itself.

Film actors have used method techniques for generations to mimic tears, laughter, disappointment, ecstasy, the full range of experience, and Hollywood technicians spend tens of millions of dollars each month to fake homicides, car crashes, structure fires, explosions, and all manner of mayhem. But hardcore pornography does not fake its most essential element. The characters are in actual sexual congress, the alpha and the omega of the genre. The indispensable end of a scene, the so-called "money shot," is carefully framed and valorized as the ceremonial close, inevitable as a wedding in act 5 of a Shakespeare comedy.

Porn has always had an odd relationship to "story." Plot is famously one of the hokiest concepts in this tasteless genre, with its pizza deliveries and voluptuous nurses. Two people appear. They converse (or not), and the action commences; the individuals reduced only to hungry pistoning parts; the established mileposts of the act in harmony with the left-hand slope of Freytag's Pyramid of dramatic structure: introduction, rising action, climax. But that's where the scene always cuts. Everything ends. The two people fade back into meaninglessness. We have learned nothing. The people emerge from nowhere and return to nowhere having told their twenty-minute "story"—albeit one of the most important biological stories humanity can tell itself. "Birth, copulation, death," said T. S. Eliot. "That's all the facts when you come to the brass tacks."

This unapologetic stripping-down—both literally and intellectually—is part of why the Freudian literary theorist Linda Williams calls pornography "a confessional moment of truth" in a search for the ultimate Real that invariably concludes in the sexual surrender of cardboard characters. There isn't much else there yet it is repeated endlessly. "That the 'solutions' to the problem of sex are most often constructed from the dominant power knowledge of male subjectivity should come as no surprise," Williams notes dryly. The story goes on; it never ends. By one estimate, a new pornographic film is shot in the United States every thirty-eight seconds.

The ease of digital piracy means that a ninety-minute movie that cost $36,000 to make will likely be chopped up scene by scene and posted around the tube sites within weeks. But a narrow window exists in which money can still be squeezed from DVD sales and licensing the softcore version—i.e., an "everything-but" version for cable channels.

A single company, MindGeek of Montreal, Quebec, has nearly cornered the market on the video clip trade through ownership of a half-dozen production studios as well as the most well-known warehouses for free online content: PornHub, YouPorn, Redtube, and the like. The money comes in through advertisements for a cornucopia of bottom-barrel products: erection pills, sex toys, cam-girl sessions, and more. With an average of 207,405 videos being viewed every minute by 115 million daily visitors—an estimated 10 percent of the world's data streaming at any given second—porn companies are able to get a peephole into the global libido by observing which videos get the most clicks. That information is then fed back to the production companies. Such data mining of searches like "ripped yoga pants" or "my sister's friend" is responsible for the rise of specifically formulated scenarios.

"A lot of it comes down to analytics: the combination of the performers, the color of the couch, a maroon bikini does better than a blue one. They take these results and replicate them," said Tommy Gunn, a longtime performer who started in the business at the age of thirty-six and still gets work at the age of fifty-two. He has a New Jersey tough-guy accent that makes him sound like a Martin Scorsese street thug when he wants to play it up, but he's soft-voiced and almost shy as he sits on a white couch waiting for his afternoon scene in *Different Lives, Different Wives*. Both his advancing age and shrinking paychecks are working against him; the average scene for a male performer pays $700 before taxes.

"I've had every blue-collar job under the sun," he says. "Construction, plumbing, motorcycle repair. When I was in my twenties, I got into bodybuilding and some of the guys at that gym were part of the Chippendales. I started doing male erotic dancing. The segue from that into this wasn't that difficult. I'm blessed I can do this, but I know it won't last forever. Then I'm ready for something else. Welding, fabricating, I can do anything."

Gender roles in heterosexual porn, despite a veneer of liberation, still carry a certain Victorian formality, along with a particular set of economics and manners. The women on the high end of the trade typically make twice as much as the men and can make as much as $2,000 per scene for especially humiliating or uncomfortable gymnastic acts. But the real payday comes through exposure on social media sites, which then leads to charging money for custom acts on Snapchat. The men in an actress's legion of fans thereby have an ongoing relationship with her that mimics that of a real-life bond, except they will never meet her in real life unless they pay to go to a convention in Las Vegas, where they may share, at most, a few minutes of awkward conversation at a booth. She does one fundamental trick for them on film, at an extreme distance. In this way, the widespread piracy on the tube sites works in an actress's favor as it provides free advertising. Full-length movies like *Different Wives, Different Lives* have become a loss leader, not the profit center. "Girls who are good at this are making more than they ever did in the golden days," said Quasar.

He's a middle-aged Canadian with a weary look who favors Vans surf shoes and AC/DC T-shirts and likes to play up the "reluctant pornographer" mien, complaining that he never gets a day off, that gazing at copulation through a camera only makes his back hurt, and that he wonders why he bothers trying to put quality into a feature film when it will only be ripped off, dismembered, and scattered through the MindGeek digital empire within an hour of going live. He once tweeted: "Everything about porn makes me so uncomfortable. Strange that I'm responsible for so much of it."

He hasn't dived into the other way to make money in the new skin economy, which is to make bespoke fetish videos for customers with strange predilections. A look at the online catalogs is a glimpse into American paraphilia, and perhaps the ghosts floating around some deeply carved neural trenches left over from childhood. Many of these videos don't feature any nudity. An anonymous client engaged the Pittsburgh director Nate Liquor to film a five-minute, forty-nine second film called "Mustard Bra," in which an angry mother-like figure berates the camera. "I'm going to march you to your class and make you take off your shirt so that all of your classmates can see that you're wearing a bra," she yells. "And then, I'm going to take out my mustard and fill your bra with it so you can be humiliated in front of all your classmates spending all day at school wearing a bra full of mustard!" Other offerings include mud baths, pies in the face, women painted with gold, and medical exams, bearing out the Internet maxim known as Rule 34. "If it exists, there is porn of it."

For these and other reasons, Mike Quasar predicts that he'll be out of a job soon. "The traditional business is going away. In five to seven years, there won't be any more Porn Valley."

Breaking down the studios that sustained "The Other Hollywood" has been a longtime goal of anti-porn advocates, who watched with dismay as the widespread availability of VCRs in the early 1980s took blue flicks out of raincoat theaters and moved them into living rooms. The anti-porn backers point to a multitude of sins: the business shields international sex traffickers, conceals myriad physical abuses, spreads a toxic ethic of male entitlement, uses and discards its performers, and jeopardizes any future careers its actors may have in schools, hospitals, and other institutions that frown on prior associations with a disreputable trade.

The end of a hegemonic era also means the emergence of a hundred thousand smaller operators who can film in apartments and upload within minutes. This is a much harder economic activity to monitor. Not surprisingly, analytics show at least three-quarters of the viewership is male. Porn has become ubiquitous among boys as a part of growing up in America. One recent study indicated that 93 percent of college-aged men had viewed pornography at some point in their adolescence.

Luke Ford was among the most exhaustive chroniclers of the trade before he had a crisis of conscience and got out before the rise of the six magic houses. He is from a suburb of Sydney, Australia, and is the son of a charismatic Seventh-Day Adventist preacher. He enacted his own peculiar form of rebellion by moving to a small Los Angeles apartment and setting up shop as a graphomaniac blogger, running hundreds of verbatim Q&As with performers and cinematographers that went off into odd directions, and holding forth in stentorian tones on AIDS, sex trafficking, dishonorable business practices, mafia influence, and pedophilia.

He spat regular contempt for his subjects and himself, confessed to what he called "erotic rage," terming porn "lowbrow hard-on fuel," and yet could not seem to stop himself from writing about it most hours of the day. The manuscript of a book he wrote about the history of the business ran over one thousand pages.

Ford has since renounced this life. He converted to Orthodox Judaism and now wears a *kippah* head covering and a prayer shawl wherever he goes. He also cut all his associations with anyone in the porn industry, several of whom expressed a desire to kill him at various points. "When I was growing up, Los Angeles was a sexual utopia, as pictured on MTV," he said, while sitting in a West L.A. coffee shop. "Then I moved here and thought that porn women were going to be the ultimate, the whipped cream on the smoothie. It's like reading *Penthouse* in quest of knowledge. I wanted to taste it, I wanted to understand it, I wanted to know it. But it's not easy to access God at Dodger Stadium. You're going to be put into a place where you're not going to access God. You're going to see a lot of mud. This is a sewer."

He came to that conclusion after visiting hundreds of sets to watch the filming before the rise of expensive mansion shoots. He found the sex lacking in the mystical knowledge he was seeking—it even got boring after a while. The entire porn empire was built around an idea that it never actually embodied. "If there's one thing you'll never see on a porn set," he told me, "it's love."

The six mansions of porn lie within or at the foot of the hills at the southern edge of the San Fernando Valley, the giant frying pan of land annexed by the city of Los Angeles in 1915 when water diverted from the Owens River guaranteed a residential explosion in what had been fields of lima beans, walnuts, and oranges. Movie executives soon discovered its virtues, and Carl Laemmle opened up the lot of Universal Studios at the mountain pass that led into the city proper.

Wherever an industry giant locates, a cluster of technology and talent is certain to grow nearby and branch out, and with the advent of home video in the early 1980s, "The Other Hollywood" was a steady source of employment for camera operators, electricians, and set designers who were prepared to accept the potential scorn of being associated with a trade that still operates in semi-darkness. Measure B, the condom law, chased some of the production companies away to Las Vegas and

Miami, but L.A.'s peerless cluster of ready-to-work film professionals, plus the number of good-looking young people who constantly flock here in search of an entertainment career, means that the Valley is still the national capital of pornography, even though it has no visible markers.

An oblivious traveler could pass an active porn shoot behind high walls or see a female performer in the grocery store line, unrecognizable without her makeup, and never know the business was there. A trade that traffics in the ultimate exposure is itself almost invisible. Another paradox of porn geography: this dull-as-dishwater swath of the Valley is the avatar of an imagined "California" for consumers all across the nation buying their sensual goods at a thousand Lion's Den adult emporiums off the rural freeway exits, every bit as humdrum as the undistinguished reality of the northern edges of urbanized Los Angeles County. Such is the power of film on the libidinal imagination.

The author of the twenty-page script of *Different Wives, Different Lives* prefers to do his writing in a coffee shop in one of the innumerable strip malls that anchor major intersections. He's a lapsed Catholic from small-town Texas named Shawn Alff, a handsome blonde guy with sharp facial features who reads intellectually difficult books about atheism and used to pen a love and sex column for an alternative weekly newspaper in Tampa. He has never been filmed *in flagrante delicto* and never wants to be.

"I've got that Woody Allen in my head," he said. "Performing on camera is dissolving the ego, where you just feel. Turn off all the noise and just perform. But I need someone to *like* me."

The secret to a pornography script, he says, is the same formula of Aristotelian tension that drives most classical drama: a character wants something and must overcome obstacles to get it. In this industry, that translates to an initially reluctant character, and another's attempt to seduce them. In heterosexual porn, the woman most often plays the aggressor with the man as the one who must be convinced—another nod to the fantasies of consumers. The "story" lies between the first line of dialogue and the inevitable fornication.

"There's always a motive beyond sex, which is true of the act in real life," said Alff. "The best scenes depict the newness of a relationship. So much is in the first encounter. The tension builds. There's a selection, a choice. There's a factor of 'I can't believe she likes me.' We use the same tropes over and over again. A boss using his or her power to get what they want—using sex to get something else." Such a dynamic was at work in the adultery-themed *Different Wives, Different Lives*—every character harbored a desire outside the sex. Marcus wanted to build his business; Silvia wanted a promotion; Tommy wanted to live a surfing life.

But few consumers watch a plotted movie like this in one sitting. Data analytics show the average users' visit to a porn site lasts about ten minutes—an allotment of time assumed necessary for a no-frills auto-erotic experience. The users who spend more than eleven minutes watching are mainly in the Deep South, where politics and religion both run conservative. The top five states for extended viewing of pornography are Mississippi, Alabama, South Carolina, Louisiana, and Arkansas.

Just as characters in plotted porn are chasing a specific goal, so are its consumers. Alff likened it to junk food: a way to satisfy a short-term desire, "a treat, like a candy bar. You don't want it to become a staple. It's giving you an emotional catharsis, a release. We can get the thrill of a bank robbery through a movie without having to experience the consequences. Same with porn. It's not going to hurt your heart, or get you pregnant, or give you an STD, or beat you up, or steal your cat."

There are echoes here of a more critical observation made in 1956 by the Oxford literature professor C. S. Lewis, a skeptic of conventional male fantasies. "For the harem is always accessible, always subservient, calls for no sacrifices or adjustments, and can be endowed with erotic and psychological attractions which no woman can rival," he wrote. Or as the Catholic convert Malcolm Muggeridge once said: "The orgasm has re-placed the Cross as the focus of longing and the image of fulfillment"—a modern magisterium.

In the middle of one work session at the coffee shop, Shawn was joined by his friend Silvia Saige, who had played the ambitious real estate agent in *Different Wives, Different Lives.* She hosts a comedic podcast on the side and runs a lively Instagram feed, and they often collaborate on writing projects. Later that day she would be picking up a pair of brother-and-sister white shorthair kittens she had already named Bonnie and Clyde.

Saige grew up in public housing in a suburb of Kansas City, Mis-souri, and worked as an X-ray technician before moving to L.A. to be-come a stand-up comedian. But that proved no way to pay the bills in a recession, nor did bartending or doing the books for a construction company. For a time, she was homeless and living on a series of friends' couches. The loneliness and depression pushed her, at the age of twenty-four, to attempt suicide by drinking bleach and trying to slit her wrists before having a change of heart and calling 911. "I was saying, 'Please love me, please pick me up and hold me.'"

A friend convinced her to try adult films to pay the bills, which she's been doing steadily since the age of thirty-one. She has acted in 160 movies, including *Cougar Orgy, Babysitter 12*, and *Please Bang My Wife.* Saige's parents have mixed feelings: her father claims to enjoy the fact that she's found a way to monetize hedonism, though her mother disap-proves and would not accept a trip to Hawaii from Silvia because it was paid for with money earned through pornography.

Though Saige had done a convincing acting job in her scene with Marcus London, she describes her own coital pleasure as "null and void" when cameras and a crew are present, and she's being told by directors to arch her body in unrealistic ways. A litany running constantly through her head during shooting is whether she looks attractive from a particular angle and where her long hair is falling. Losing self-consciousness is impossible in these circumstances. As one maxim of the business purports: if it feels good, you're doing it wrong. It's like being poked with a wand full of novocain.

"I get nothing," she said. "I'd sooner do it in the kitchen with a paper bag over my head, eating a burrito."

But pleasure was never the point. "For me it was all about the funding," said Saige, leaning forward and covering her face in sheepishness. "Women are paid for the stigma. You have the scarlet letter. People will scorn you and look down on you, but they're all consuming the product. That's the most frustrating thing."

Different Wives, Different Lives was released on DVD a few weeks later. The promotional copy on the box read: "And while Marcus and Silvia are trying to forge a fitting business relationship, their spouses are making plans of their own." That there even *was* a DVD—as antique as a Victrola today—provided a marker of what passed for old-style legitimacy in an empire still operating in the semi-shadows and drowning in amateur content. A thin plot glues five sex scenes together, and there was surface resemblance to the presentation of a mainstream movie: credits, adequate lighting, a brief soundtrack, billing of mid-level stars. A makeup artist had been at the shoot, there was a little costume jewelry, including the plastic wedding ring she wore, and the house was a vision of tidy bourgeoisie America—not the "dirty and dingy" apartment sets of the old Valley that Saige has seen in her career.

"Context matters," she said. "I like to know that I'm being taken seriously. I'm not just there to be thrown around."

Welcome to Dirtytown

The city of Calverton Park consists of barely thirteen city blocks scrupulously patrolled at all hours by fourteen police officers. A judge holds court every Wednesday night, and the dozens of people with traffic fines to pay to this microscopic suburb of St. Louis, Missouri, typically line up a full hour before the courthouse door opens. They shuffle their feet and check their phones in the summer evening heat. A disabled man named Ed Brandon is particularly anxious to learn his fate. He now owes $375 in fines after being cited by police twice in one week. "This is totally predatory," he tells me. "How am I supposed to pay this on a fixed income?"

The courthouse looks like a ranch home painted blue. When a blank-faced cop opens the door at 6:00 p.m., at least twenty people—all but one of them black—prepare to walk through the metal detector and take a seat on folding chairs in a gallery with the dimensions of a good-sized living room. Brandon approaches a glass window to try to pay down fifty dollars of his fine—all he can afford. Then he loses his temper.

"I'm telling you, I have no ability to pay this!" he yells to the woman behind the window. A court official leads him into a side room and calms him down, but he leaves without any idea of how he can dig himself out of the financial penalty for driving with a suspended license in a borrowed car that was not registered to him. Just another night in Calverton Park—a town that issued 4,494 arrest warrants the year before, which is more than four times the number of people who actually live there.

I next head over to the Normandy Traffic Court, which has been rented out tonight to serve the abundant judicial needs of the village of Cool Valley (pop. 1,175). In the parking lot, I meet attorney Jack Waldron of the firm Arch City Defenders, one of the only firms that takes on indigent clients caught up in the judicial maze of St. Louis County towns that habitually chisel motorists with aggressive police stops.

"This is not about public safety," he tells me. "The police find it very easy to find probable cause to pull people over—'I thought he was speeding, I thought the taillight was out'—and there's a good chance that person will have a warrant out for their arrest on another ticket. Then they wind up in jail. They are going to have to surrender hundreds of dollars and that just keeps them in poverty. These towns have to raise revenue in this disgusting way because they're about broke and they shouldn't exist. They can't squeeze any more out of property taxes."

Waldron goes off into a side chamber to confer with the prosecutor, who usually refuses to speak to a defendant unless they have an attorney—which is rare.

While I wait, I listen to multiple defendants, all of them African American, plead their case to Judge Kevin R. Kelley. The ritual does not change from person to person. They tell the judge they cannot afford to pay their ticket, and he tries to find out how much the town of Cool

Valley can secure from them immediately. "Are you working these days?" he asks one man. "How much can you pay? Can you afford $150?" The man stammers an answer, then goes off to pay what he can to the cashier. Then Waldron emerges from the side room, looking upset. The prosecutor had joked that many impoverished defendants had not shown up that night because they were "off at their summer homes by the lake." Such thoughtless jibes against the poor are par for the course. "I rarely leave here without being infuriated," he tells me.

Waldron's next stop of the night on behalf of his client is at the courthouse in the town of Olivette, and I tell him I'll follow him there. He tells me: "It's about a twelve-minute drive and we'll pass through about ten municipalities on the way."

As it turns out, his count of cities is a little high: we only pass through seven on the twelve-minute drive. I watch the signs go by for Normandy, Bellerive, Bel-Ridge, Chalant, Sycamore Hills, Overland, Olivette. Some of these municipalities are no bigger than a few residential blocks, and most have their own mayor, council, police force, and jail. Open up any map of St. Louis and you'll see a mess of these colorful pieces of confetti—ninety-three scraps of orange, red, blue, and yellow, each representing a tiny civic fiefdom, some of them no bigger than a handful of houses, all with their own sovereign powers to tax, fine, arrest, and incarcerate.

When I promised Waldron I would drive extremely carefully through this tangle, he didn't look up from his phone. "I don't think *you* need to worry," he said offhandedly. Meaning that I was white.

Americans are bred to understand the town or city as perhaps the most benign form of government: the supplier of tangible goods like parks, libraries, recreational leagues, sidewalks, and the like. It's far more likely for a common resident to be personally acquainted with the mayor (compared with a member of Congress or the governor) and to have a tiny bit of clout, and it's far easier to actually get something done.

The town occupies a privileged spot in American mythology—the very title of Thornton Wilder's *Our Town* is designed to sound a chord of lost togetherness. Even the old despairing expression "you can't fight city hall" signifies only minor frustrations: a code violation fine that must be paid or a building extension that failed to get a proper permit. For all of its irritating gossips and invisible hierarchies, the town is a national pastoral and a place of safety, the warmly lit cluster of fellowship set into the dark plain. It is a metaphor of life against death.

The town is, in fact, at the root of human civilization. The first stable groupings of non-nomadic humans in upper Mesopotamia, charted at around 9600 B.C.E., relied on a scale and an organizational form similar to that of a village: a heart of residential structures surrounded by cultivated grains and livestock pens, and overseen by an elite circle of strongmen who had organized defenses against predators and internal trouble. The leadership expected each citizen to contribute to the collective good and extracted tributes in the form of grain: the earliest taxes.

This big leap brought humanity out of its hunter-gatherer phase. Food storage and discipline acted as a hedge against drought, insects, and various other horrors. But the earliest towns also had a coercive element. The ethnographer James C. Scott in his book *Against the Grain: A Deep History of the Earliest States* argues that "city hall" was essentially a protection racket, relying less on the happy consent of the governed than on the strength of elites that would later be called "law" to prey on the wealth of individuals. The people set themselves apart from the barbarians or the neighboring towns through differences of religion or appearance. Public works were both an expression of ego and a method of bribing the population not to revolt.

The beneficent provider of jungle gyms for the park could also grow a Mafia-heart: this tension still exists within the marrow of an American town. Of all the governments in this country—from the federal apparatus down to the school board—the town is statistically the one most likely to commit a murder, in the form of a police shooting. Almost no other government entity can harass you so consistently and so easily. Urban violence, grit, crowds, pollution, scams, and noise have alarmed bucolic America for generations, and these imprints show up in the nation's stock of literary tropes. Theodore Dreiser's heroine in *Sister Carrie* takes a train to Chicago and almost immediately succumbs to moral turpitude. John Dos Passos spent his later career writing about cities, and not favorably. "The young man walks by himself," he wrote of a character in *The 42nd Parallel*,

> fast but not fast enough, far but not far enough (faces slide out of sight, talk trails into tattered scraps, footsteps tap fainter in alleys); he must catch the last subway, the streetcar, the bus, run up the gangplanks of all the steamboats, register at all the hotels, work in the cities, answer the want ads, learn the trades, take up the jobs, live in all the boardinghouses, sleep in all the beds. One bed is not enough, one job is not enough, one life is not enough. At night, head swimming with wants, he walks by himself alone.

T. S. Eliot used London as the primary locale of his poem *The Waste Land*, but he may have also had his native St. Louis and its Mississippi in mind when he wrote of urban lassitude. *The river sweats / Oil and tar / The barges drift / With the turning tide.*

Towns can become private rackets, in a way immediately recognizable to a large body of American literature. "The law enforcement in this town is terrific," wrote Raymond Chandler in *The Big Sleep*. "All through prohibition Eddie Mars' place was a night club and they had two uni-formed men in the lobby every night—to see that the guests didn't bring their own liquor instead of buying it from the house." Dashiell Hammett famously began his novel *Red Harvest* about a crime-saturated Montana mining city with these sentences: "I first heard Personville called Poison-ville by a red-haired mucker named Hickey Dewey in the Big Ship in Butte. He also called his shirt a shoit." More recently, Daniel Woodruff's *Winter's Bone* follows the trail of a girl in search of her missing father through the underside of a thoroughly double-dealing small town in the Ozarks. A virtuous individual going up against a worm-eaten Poisonville is a dynamic that runs deep in the American imagination; its hard lines and shadows stand for the darkness and psychological tension within our own consciousness.

Every dirty town in America, large and small, generally has a key feature in common besides systematic corruption. Most of these towns have malignant motives written into their beings from the start. Their nativity wasn't clean; their birth story is rotten with greed or prejudice. Which is how their journey toward seeing people as "grain" was so easy.

How the venomous little towns of St. Louis County got started is an or-igin story ingrained in the mentality of the mid-twentieth century and, in particular, in the consciousness of St. Louis itself, once a wealthy and powerful city home to major rail lines, shoe factories, grain elevators, breweries, rows of graceful town houses, and a train station as glorious as any medieval cathedral.

Future *Waste Land* author T. S. Eliot was the son of a man who grew wealthy manufacturing the red bricks that gave the city its distinctive federalist look, and the 1904 World's Fair had made what was then the fourth biggest city in the country internationally famous as a center of innovation, elegance, and fun, all astride the grand liquid freeway of the Mississippi River. But St. Louis remained firmly wedded to the march of the cotton economy and segregation. "There's definitely a Southern cast to what happens here," said local historian Harper Barnes. "Chicago always looked to the east for its inspiration and we looked down the Mississippi River. We can never forget the northern leg of the gateway arch rests close to where slaves were once put on the auction block."

When former sharecropping African Americans came up from the Deep South during World War I to work in the city's steel mills and packing plants, white residents threw up a forest of legal restrictions to keep them at bay, including writing restrictive covenants in their deeds that prohibited sale to "any member of the Negro or Mongolian race." The powerful St. Louis Real Estate Exchange encouraged its agents to steer black clients to certain neighborhoods and successfully campaigned for an ordinance to prevent anyone from buying a home in an area more than three-quarters occupied by another race. "Do you realize," they warned in a pamphlet, "that at any time you are liable to suffer an irreparable loss, due to the coming of negroes into the block in which you live?"

All-white neighborhoods erected decorative wrought-iron fences on private streets—a particularly St. Louis innovation—to give a physical reality to the invisible racial fortifications. The Federal Home Administration, meanwhile, made it nearly impossible for a black family to secure a guaranteed mortgage. The phrase "FHA Approved" in real estate ads was understood to be synonymous with "no black people allowed."

When a couple from Mississippi, John and Ethel Shelley, purchased a modest home at 4600 Labadie in 1945, a neighborhood group sued to enforce the "Negro race" clause in the deed. The U.S. Supreme Court ruled such language was unconstitutional in the resulting *Shelley v. Kraemer* case of 1948. The heart of St. Louis soon opened up to a growing tide of Southern black migrants looking for a better life, and the St. Louis Housing Authority made a bet on a futuristic solution to handle the influx. Architect Minoru Yamasaki designed the Pruitt-Igoe complex of thirty-three high rises as a "radiant city" of bright apartments and green spaces. Poor maintenance soon created a nightmare labyrinth of frozen pipes, malfunctioning elevators, vandalized galleries, broken incinerators, and an atmosphere where nobody wanted to raise children and police were reluctant to enter.

Whites had found a useful refuge on the margins: brand-new suburban governments where they could pass laws designed to keep out minorities. Missouri's "home rule" laws made it easy to incorporate even small patches of land and give them taxing authority. A ring of instant towns sprung up like crabgrass around the city core: places like Pine Lawn, Cool Valley, Pasadena Park, Glen Echo Park, Beverly Hills, Greendale, Bellerive Acres. Mayors and their councils held impromptu meetings in their living rooms, spent about five hours a week on city business, and found creative ways to be officially racist without sounding racist. Most of them quickly banned new duplexes—totems of density reminiscent of shift work and modest accommodation and now only meaning "black and poor." Lot sizes were kept no smaller than a half acre, which pushed away people below a certain income. Though they could not explicitly bar people of color, the suburbs could use a dodge such as mandating everyone to join a particular country club, which could then deny their applications for vague reasons.

The number of incorporated suburbs rocketed from thirty-five to ninety-five in the two-decade period between 1940 and 1960. Some were no more than glorified subdivisions with a part-time cop and an improvised "city hall" outside somebody's house. Among the strangest was Champ (pop. 12), seven homes and a church, which existed so that the mayor—a former track and field star—could apply for revenue bonds to build a domed stadium that never appeared.

The pop-up towns found a champion in Harland Bartholomew, dubbed the "dean of city planners" by *The New York Times*. He favored expressways, automobiles, parks, municipalities no bigger than twelve thousand residents, and zoning laws that favored big lawns and cookie-cutter homes. "The properties must be protected against obnoxious uses," he remarked. He had helped rezone predominately black areas of St. Louis as industrial, allowing for liquor stores, rooming houses, and polluting businesses barred from white neighborhoods. Among his other noteworthy accomplishments was the razing of early nineteenth-century homes along the St. Louis waterfront to make room for the Gateway Arch. Bartholomew was a midwestern version of New York's Robert Moses: aggressive scientific progressivism stained with racism. "Political fragmentation enabled local and parochial interests to tear the city apart and reassemble it as a crazy quilt of fiercely segregated industrial, commercial, residential and racial enclaves," concluded Colin Gordon.

By 1956, the view from the top of the Monsanto skyscraper downtown was so bad that a French visitor said it reminded him of a European city bombed to rubble during the war. St. Louis soon led the country in the highest central city vacancy rate of all major cities. Downtown became a place where, in the word of the hometown novelist Jonathan Franzen, "sparrows bickered and pigeons ate. Here City Hall, a hip-roofed copy of the Hotel de Ville in Paris, rose up in two-dimensional splendor from a flat, vacant block." He compared the downtown of what had been the country's fourth-biggest city to a meadow, or a backyard.

As African Americans eventually broke down the artificial barriers of segregation and settled in inner-ring suburbs like Jennings, Normandy, and Ferguson, majority-white city councils tended to hang on to power.

After the foreclosure meltdown of 2008, the property tax picture looked dire. The confetti municipalities of St. Louis County had to take radical fiscal action to keep themselves afloat.

And so they turned on their own residents, and anybody else who might have the misfortune to be poor and black and just passing through.

Candice Lloyd, the mother of five children, is nobody's idea of a criminal. She has a cheerful disposition, stands 5'2", and works as a medical assistant. Her main job is transporting elderly patients to their doctor's appointments, which means she has to drive through the maze of municipalities on a daily basis. Because she is African American in St. Louis County and drives a junky-looking car, this means—axiomatically—she gets a lot of tickets for no other reason, which once put her in jail for a week and almost cost her a job and her family.

Her troubles started when she was pulled over in Creve Coeur for a broken taillight on her green 2002 Mitsubishi Galant. The car was registered in her stepmother's name, which earned her a second ticket. But Lloyd lives on an income of just $1,948 a month to support a family of six. She couldn't afford to fix the taillight, and she had to do her job, whose core responsibility is driving. When Lloyd went over to Maplewood to transport another client on a cold day, she wore a hoodie because the heater had broken. Sure enough, a cop pulled her over, and he seemed surprised to see that Lloyd was a woman. He gave her a ticket for "improper lane usage" and told her the car couldn't be driven with a broken taillight. Lloyd walked to the bus stop to get home.

After Lloyd got her car out of the towing yard and went to the auto parts store to get a new taillight, she drove directly to a friend's house so he could help her install it. But she was pulled over in St. Johns on the way, and the officer told her that she should have had the light installed at the auto parts store, giving her still more tickets.

In order to keep her job, Lloyd took to renting cars from Enterprise. This didn't stop her from going to jail three separate times; every time she was pulled over, the police found all of her outstanding court warrants. She was in the city lockup in St. Ann's for an entire week before Christmas in 2015 before her friends and family could scrape together $300 to bond her out. She was terrified of losing her job, but her bosses were sympathetic and cut her a break. They, too, had been victims of the St. Louis County "round robin," which is the local term for getting pulled over for a trivial infraction then facing a gauntlet of outstanding warrants that must be cleared, often leaving the defendant several thousand dollars in debt and afraid to show up for court dates for fear of being arrested. "If I could afford to pay the fines, I would, but I couldn't. They were just too much," Lloyd told me.

Could it be that Lloyd is simply a bad driver who brought the tickets on herself? She laughed and pointed out that almost all of her offenses were for non-moving violations, and that she would never have kept her job for so long if she were incompetent behind the wheel. "I transport elderly people and they are not shy about speaking their minds," she said. Any patient complaints about her would have gotten her fired a long time ago. At one time, she had cases outstanding in eight separate towns. None of them were for moving violations; most were for paperwork matters common to the poor.

Lloyd now hates the anxiety of driving. "I get sick whenever I see a police car behind me," she said. "On St. Charles Rock Road, you go through four separate municipalities, and it's easy to get a couple of tickets a day." She must risk her freedom every time she goes to work.

St. Louis County has eighty-one separate municipal court systems (by comparison, the entire state of Arizona has eighty-eight). The rinky-dinkedness of them approaches the comical. One municipality shares its city hall and courthouse with a drugstore, and the drugstore gets top billing on the sign outside. Another has its court in a remodeled Pizza Hut restaurant. The city of Florissant—a particular bad offender— simply rents gymnasium space to hold court, and the judge sits up on a riser that seems more appropriate for a graduation ceremony. The rental fee for the gymnasium is passed on to the defendants in the form of a ten-dollar fee. At any given session, at least a hundred people show up.

"The courts don't have any interest in running as a real court and displaying due process," complained James Wyrsch, who takes on in-digent defense cases. "Judges ask them, 'What's $500 to you? You have to figure this out.' But they have no sense of the gravity of that expense to most of the defendants. We shouldn't be trying to wring out the last dollars from the poorest citizens. This is like debtor's prison."

The city of Ferguson was not a classic confetti town—it had been incor-porated in 1894 and had a coherent business district. But it exemplified the characteristics of a northern St. Louis County white-flight suburb, a "sundown town" in which African Americans were subject to harassment after dark. The city even barricaded a road leading into the predomi-nantly black town of Kinloch.

Back during Ronald Reagan's second term as president, Ferguson's population was three-quarters white. But within twenty years, that ra-tio changed dramatically as younger black residents, many of them fleeing the reviled housing projects, took their Section 8 vouchers to bland new apartment blocks with names like Northwinds and Can-field Green. By 2010, Ferguson was 67 percent black and operating with a virtually all-white town government and police force that took extraordinary measures against its own citizens.

One of the more striking aspects of the judicial system in Ferguson is how closely it began to resemble a sales corporation—with ticket revenue as the "product." Public officials began to sound like entrepreneurs. The finance director of Ferguson wrote to Police Chief Thomas Jackson: "Unless ticket writing ramps up significantly before the end of the year, it will be hard to significantly raise collections next year." The chief responded by saying he would tweak the patrol shifts to put more officers on the street, "which in turn," he said, "will increase traffic enforcement per shift." Three years later, the finance director wrote to the city manager in response to further attempts to beef up the budget. "I did ask the chief if he thought the PD could deliver 10% increase. He indicated they could try."

The pressure to ticket flowed downward. Lists of top performers began appearing inside the police station. Ticket writing was euphemistically described as "self-initiated activity," and it was explicitly held up as a criterion for promotion. Officers started to hold informal contests to see who could write the most tickets in a single stop. The municipal court system also took on the role of a profit center, mainly through issuing arrest warrants for the tiniest of infractions. Many residents came to believe they would be sent to jail simply for showing up to their appointed court date and thus accumulated a warrant that would show up in a later traffic stop. In Ferguson, where two-thirds of the citizenry is black, 96 percent of those arrested for the sole reason of an outstanding warrant are black.

"Ferguson's law enforcement practices are shaped by the city's focus on revenue rather than by public safety needs," concluded the U.S. Department of Justice. Even worse, Ferguson's police officers had begun to see people on the street "less as constituents to be protected than as potential offenders and sources of revenue."

The aggressive jailing and ticket-writing paid big dividends for Ferguson. "Municipal Court gross revenue for calendar year 2012 passed the

$2,000,000 mark for the first time in history, reaching the $2,066,050 (not including red light photo enforcement)," wrote Jackson to the city manager, John Shaw. He responded: "Awesome! Thanks!"

Citizens paid the price, and not just out of their pockets. In one egregious case, a thirty-two-year-old man named Fred Watson was sitting in his car after a basketball game in a public park. A police officer named Eddie Boyd III—who had been fired from a previous agency for misconduct—came over and demanded to see a driver's license. Watson's license happened to list his name as Frederick instead of Fred. The officer then asked for a social security number, which Watson said he couldn't give because he worked as a contractor at the National Geospatial-Intelligence Agency and had a security clearance. Boyd then drew his gun and ordered Watson out of the car at gunpoint. He suggested Watson was under suspicion for pedophilia, gave his car a thorough searching before having it towed, and jailed Watson on seven charges, including not wearing a seatbelt, failure to have a license, having windows tinted too dark, and failure to comply with a police officer. The U.S. Navy veteran lost his job and his government security clearance because of the incident. All charges were later dropped, but only after five years.

In another case, a fifty-two-year-old man named Henry Davis drove into a common St. Louis County fate—he was picked up on a warrant while sitting in a parked car. Except it was the wrong Henry Davis. The booking officer realized the trouble, but still put Davis into an occupied one-man cell and told him he could sleep on the cement floor until he could be bonded out. Davis objected, and three officers tried to force him inside. The officers punched and kicked him, leaving Davis bleeding from the scalp. When he left jail four days later, Davis did so tagged with four citations for "property damage." In an assertion worthy of *Monty Python*, Officer John Beaird said that Davis had bled on his uniform while he was being beaten.

Not every police officer enjoys being used as a collections agent for a greedy city. A man named Redditt Hudson told me he encountered a similar culture when he worked as a patrol officer for the city of St. Louis from 1994 to 1998. "It was always a push for numbers," he said. "And I would be one of those officers who would be quote-unquote counseled for low numbers."

He said he still regrets some of the unnecessary tickets that he gave to poor African American residents, knowing the turmoil they would cause. "The money they'd have to spend to get their vehicle fixed would be thousands of dollars and wipe them out. It would turn into a cascading series of events. We make poverty a self-fulfilling prophecy when we put them in situations they can't get out of."

Hudson now works for the Urban League and said he constantly hears from agonized suburban police officers from Ferguson and elsewhere who feel pressure from every side: low-boiling anger from the ticketed citizens, social shaming from their fellow officers, a threat of sanctions from the top brass if their citation numbers start to flag. "Those municipal courts function, in effect, as ATMs for those towns, and they cite their residents at outrageous rates," he said. "Every household has an average of three warrants. This is destructive to police-community relations on every level."

On the afternoon of August 9, 2014, an eighteen-year-old recent high school graduate named Michael Brown was caught on a security camera in the Ferguson Market stealing a package of Swisher cigarillos, and the call went over the police dispatch radios. Officer Darren Wilson of the Ferguson police approached Brown near the Section 8 blocks off Canfield Drive and asked him to move off the roadway to the sidewalk.

"Fuck what you have to say," Brown retorted.

In a set of events that would be relentlessly scrutinized, Brown reached into the Chevrolet Tahoe SUV to grab at Wilson, whose gun went off and the bullet hit Brown in the hand. Wilson ran down the street pursuing Brown, who turned around in a position that Wilson interpreted as an intention to attack. Wilson shot Brown four more times. A federal investigation later cleared Wilson of wrongdoing, but angry residents believed Brown had been murdered. Sporadic protests erupted for nearly four months. Police showed up in mini-tanks and dressed in riot gear; protestors broke windows, overturned cars, and torched stores.

For those who had experience with Ferguson's culture of nickel-and-diming, the explosion was not truly about the death of Michael Brown. It was in response to several hundreds of thousands of less newsworthy abuses perpetuated by the leadership of their own city over the course of two decades.

The spot on the American map that most resembles the spray of confetti outside St. Louis is the collection of eighty-seven municipalities in Los Angeles County, most of them in the wide basin to the south of downtown L.A.

They bleed into one another in an urban rug of freeways, warehouses, railroad tracks, strip malls, food plants, power poles, and trim residential blocks: South Gate, Bellflower, Paramount, Maywood, Gardena, Commerce. Few have coherent downtowns or strong senses of place, and it is hard to discern where one starts and another begins. They resemble Thomas Pynchon's fictional Southern California suburb of San Narciso in *The Crying of Lot 49*: "Less an identifiable city than a group of concepts—census tracts, special purpose bond-issue districts, shopping nuclei, all overlaid with access roads to its own freeway."

Why do they exist? It's another version of the old American short-hustle that left a permanent legacy on the map of Southern California. A belt of factories making auto parts, tires, and steel along the 710

Freeway—which competes with the New Jersey Turnpike for the most conventionally ugly stretch of road in the country—provided ample high-wage jobs after World War II, and homebuilders seeking to cash in on nearby orchard and farm land sought to incorporate private schemes into respectable legal entities. Under the cover of a new city hall, developers could raise taxes, lay down streets, rezone new neighborhoods, and get out as soon as possible. "To continue to earn profits, builders needed to rapidly organize new cities to subsidize the next wave of suburban construction and turn the county's pastures and fields into a new kind of factory floor," wrote Victor Valle in his book *City of Industry*.

The most onerous part of the start-up costs—a police department—could be sloughed off under the new Lakewood Plan, an innovation that allowed baby city councils to sign deals with the L.A. County Sheriff's Office to patrol their cities. Soon these "contract cities" were relying on the county for road repair, libraries, parks, garbage pickup, health clinics, and just about anything that an ordinary city hall was supposed to do— except keep taxing its citizens to pay itself.

Which is how the corruption started. When the jobs moved overseas and civic revenue declined, the small city of Bell needed a fix-it man and hired a corpulent bully named Robert Rizzo as a city manager. But instead of acting as a faceless bureaucrat, he functioned much like an old-time machine caudillo in the mold of Richard J. Daley or Boss Tweed. Rizzo diverted tax money into gargantuan salaries for a ring of complicit elected officials to the point where his total compensation was over $1.5 million a year, more than three times the salary of the president of the United States. Old-time party machines at least gave back a little something to the citizens in the form of charity or jobs in exchange for their votes. Not here. "There were no special favors or special attention paid to Bell's many poor, or the newly-arrived who desperately needed someone to help them navigate a strange new world," wrote political scientist Fred

Smoller, who argued the scam was able to flourish because nobody was attending city council meetings and the standard watchdogs of the press and community activists had long since retreated from the scene.

Rizzo was sentenced to twelve years in prison, but he wasn't the only one skinning the municipal kitty along the 710 Freeway. In the neighboring town of Cudahy, the longtime city manager—who also worked for the company that sold water to the city—was accused of rigging elections and being chauffeured to a Denny's restaurant to accept a bribe in a shoebox. One of the most notorious of L.A.'s industrial belt towns, Vernon, for years barred anyone from living in the "exclusively industrial" town who could vote to change the power structure in which officials collected big fees from factory owners and paid themselves huge bonuses. Valle documented a half century of official chicanery in the City of Industry, an awkward fourteen-mile tax shelter along the tracks of the Southern Pacific. A 2012 University of Illinois study measured the number of criminal convictions and declared the region the second most corrupt in the nation—second only to the historic snake pit of Chicago. The 710 corridor is like a modern hangover to the widespread graft that used to characterize Los Angeles's government in the middle of the twentieth century. "This isn't a city," said a former editor for the *Herald-Examiner* as he left on a train in 1935. "It's a goddamn conspiracy."

But towns with a predatory heart don't always fleece their own residents, and not all of them are close to major cities.

The village of Ludowici, in the deep piney lowlands of southeast Georgia, had a traffic light in the center of town with a habit of unexpectedly flashing from green to red—skipping yellow altogether—while cops lurked nearby. Legend had it that the light was connected via remote switch to a desk in the second-story office of a bus station, where a local stooge sat waiting to push the button and catch yet another driver.

The fast-changing "Ludowici light" was known all over the South and became the subject of more complaints to the American Automobile Association than any other traffic signal in the country. *Time* magazine called it "a magic lamp" in 1959 and noted that it brought in a quarter of the town's $15,000 annual income.

A town needs to have two things working in its favor for a scheme like this to work, and in the decades between the 1940s and the 1970s, Ludowici had both: an ideal location and a ring of conspirators who controlled the courthouse and the police. The town sat astride U.S. Route 301, which was once the main artery into Florida, traveled by a constant stream of tourists who weren't predisposed to stick around and fight a twenty-five-dollar ticket for doing a hair over the (unexpectedly posted) limit.

Ludowici's own Mr. Big was a county solicitor named Ralph Dawson, a stout little fellow with a porkpie hat, a soggy cigar, and a starched shirt gone to yellow. He kept stacks of zero coupon bonds under his mattress and wore a .38 pistol on his hip. Nobody won local office without his approval, and "the vote was whatever he said it was," according to longtime resident Brent Kleindeinst. Dawson took regular tributes from the tickets and the "clip joints" that flourished along U.S. Route 301.

These conniving gas stations and pecan stands lured in tourists for an unwinnable dice game called Razzle Dazzle, while one particular mechanic nicknamed "Cinch" would sometimes cut the unsuspecting customer's fan belt or drain their oil before charging a stupendous price for repair. Another gas station owner mounted a sign that said: Last Gas Before Entering the Swamp, even though the larger town of Jesup (and its many gas stations) was just fourteen miles distant. There was a truck stop on the route from Ludowici to Jesup where slinky waitresses offered, as one local put it, "cold coffee and other hot stuff." The highway's income-generating potential reached into the farm fields, as pigs and chickens were allowed to wander onto the asphalt in hopes that they would be struck by a passing car. When that happened, the guilty driver would be shaken down for on-the-spot payments for damages. In death, many a sickly runt was transformed into a blue-ribbon hog that was supposed to feed a family of six for the winter.

Courthouse thugs like Dawson derived their power from Georgia's antique "county unit" system, in which even the smallest county in the state was guaranteed a seat in the General Assembly, diluting and disempowering the growing urban concentrations of blacks. (This is why Georgia has 159 counties even today, a number that's second only to Texas.) Some of the counties never should have been created in the first place, like Long County, home of Ludowici, which was hastily carved in 1920 and named for the first surgeon in the world to use anesthesia. Nothing much ever grew there except oak trees, Spanish moss, and a few marginal fields of tobacco and corn. Water quickly seeped into any holes dug into the sandy soil. As the Long County seat, Ludowici had barely fifteen hundred people in its prime, though it still commanded outsized power for its ability to deliver votes to the Democratic machine in Atlanta.

The unlettered country cousins scoring a victory over the rich New Yorkers in their fancy cars also tapped into a body of "trickster" mythology common to both black and white southerners; the winking rogue who suffers from a position of powerlessness, but still manages to put one over on the hypocritical overseer. Jimmy Smith, a local political observer who knew Ralph Dawson, put it this way: "It's one of the poorest areas of the country, and here are all these Packards and Cadillacs coming through, and, well, a man's got to do what a man's got to do."

I went down to Ludowici to visit with Price Chapman Jr., the son of the man who built the town's now-razed bus station and is rumored to have been the person who switched the traffic light from green to red. Chapman denied the switch ever ran through his father's office (but acknowledged there had been slot machines in the basement). He took me around on a mini-tour of the town's historic roadside skullduggery, showing me the billboard that used to shield the motorcycle cops from view. He is a good-humored man and a pillar of the Jones Creek Baptist Church who didn't fleece any snowbirds himself. But he recalled the sense of righteous justification in the air.

"It was wrong what we did, but there's a big cultural thing in this city between North and South and they thought it was the right thing to do if they could put one over," he told me. "It was the victory of the southern mind over Yankee engineering . . . But that was just an excuse to pick people's pockets."

Just as the 710 Freeway has become a byword for L.A. corruption, there appears to be a tantalizing quality to U.S. Highway 301 that brings out the worst in southern towns. Approximately 142 miles down the road from Ludowici is the barely there town of Hampton, Florida, which annexed about a thousand feet of the road in the early 1990s, hired a squad of cops with radar guns, and walked away with a quarter million dollars in annual ticket revenue. And just a few miles to the north is the speck of Oliver, Georgia, which has an unusually aggressive police department. A politician from a neighboring county, ticketed once too often, erected a vengeful billboard at the border: Don't Get Caught in a Speed Trap.

None of the southern speed traps, however, could match the vicious little pimple of New Rome, Ohio, when it came to shamelessness. A town of just eight voting residents and three small blocks took advantage of an abrupt drop in the speed limit on its thousand-foot stretch of U.S. Route 40 to grab about half a million dollars for itself each year, with fines paid directly at the double-wide trailer that served as city hall. Most of the revenue wasn't even from speeding—that was merely the excuse of probable cause needed to pull a driver over and issue big fines for "safety violations" like muddy license plates, unlatched seat belts, cracked windshields, and the like. The state of Ohio received so many complaints it dissolved the town's charter in 2004.

One of the only remnants of the conurbation that *Car & Driver* magazine called "a chickenshit town, a little police state" is the New Rome Motel, which is still in business on the side of the highway. "The cops were nice to us, at least," the owner, Pat Patel, told me. "They would sit right under our sign to pick people off. Everyone in the government was in cahoots. You have to be to pull off a scam like that."

The state of Missouri took a few ameliorative measures after the Ferguson protests. The legislature passed a law limiting the amount of a city's budget that could be taken from fines, a measure targeting the out-of-control confetti towns of St. Louis County, which were collecting 46 percent of the monetary penalties in the entire state. (The state supreme court ruled portions of the law unconstitutional.) The 2019 election of the reformist Wesley Bell as chief county prosecutor also gave reason to think the town rackets might be broken up, or at least see their influence reduced.

Judges, meanwhile, have grown more circumspect about throwing defendants in jail for outstanding warrants. Some have embraced a legal disposition called "suspended imposition of sentence," in which violators are put on probation and subject to court monitoring, which can cost up to $3,000. This keeps the defendant from having a criminal record, but it still keeps the revenue stream intact.

Attorney Stephanie Lummus, who does legal services for Catholic Charities, said she hasn't noticed much of a difference since the Ferguson protests. When one of her clients recently pulled over when she saw the lights of a police car behind her, she was cited for failure to use her turn signal. The prevalence of what she calls "crimes of poverty"—the failure to have a registration at the correct address, for example—is still a part of the landscape.

"We have grandmas who get a flat tire and get dragged out of their car on warrants," she said. "You just can't gig your way out of the municipal court system. You are not going to be able to exit poverty."

Many of her clients are afraid even to go into court because of the practice—now somewhat curtailed—of the bailiffs handcuffing those who are found to have arrest warrants for traffic violations in other towns. That's public information: anyone with a person's date of birth or license plate number can make such a check through the Regional Justice Information Service database, or REJIS. This includes employers, who are reluctant to hire anyone who's been in trouble with the confetti towns.

When it comes to pumping out arrest warrants, no place outdoes the judicial maze that is St. Louis County, which issued 142,802 warrants in 2017, nearly all for minor traffic infractions. That's more than a quarter of the arrest warrants issued in the entire state of Missouri. Some of the police officers are also known to check the license plates of cars in the parking lot on traffic court nights—then meeting the drivers with handcuffs when they emerge after paying a ticket.

The night I sat in on Olivette Municipal Court, the prosecuting attorney was a well-tanned man in a crisp button-down shirt and blue tie named Sam Alton. Twenty years ago, he would have looked at home in a Sigma Chi fraternity house. The courtroom was plush; over the judge's bench was a motto in raised letters: Olivette . . . In the Center of It All.

Sam Alton worked during the day as a personal injury attorney and did traffic prosecution as part-time work. Defense attorney Jack Waldron asked to confer with him for a minute on behalf of his absent client, and they nodded to each other in agreement: a continuance and a future court date. The client still had five other warrants to clear. "This is just kicking the can down the road," Waldron muttered. Alton wasn't a bad guy, he told me, and he didn't moonlight as a judge. This common practice in St. Louis County leads to flagrant conflicts of interests when drivers are required to stand before the same officials—almost always white—who assume shifting roles in multiple courthouses. The well-connected law firm of Curtis, Heinz, Garrett, and O'Keefe supplies many of the judges, and nearly half the firm's revenue comes from traffic courts in the confetti towns.

"I feel by and large that the public in St. Louis County likes to have their communities," the firm's president, Carl Lumley, told *The St. Louis Post-Dispatch*. "Most of these communities have been around for a long time and have very distinct flavors to them." America's dirty towns, it seems, also depend on their own peculiar version of civic pride to keep the money coming.

Searchlight

The woman behind the bar hands me a piece of silver that she assayed herself—not perfect, as it bears a pimple of iron in the middle—but she got it for free, scavenged from a pile of mine waste and then cooked down into this blob of wealth.

"You put the rocks into the furnace and it goes into a kind of black sponge," C.J. says. "Every now and then you can see a flash when it shows platinum. There's rainbow colors, depending on what type of mineral you've got in there. It's awesome."

She's tending the bar tonight at Terrible's Roadhouse, one of two casinos in the town of Searchlight, which sits near the southernmost dagger-point of Nevada. The carpet bears a pattern of fleur-de-lis, faded and gummy with a thousand spilled drinks, and the stage in the corner—approximately the square footage of an average hot tub—is empty. No green velvet table games available here, only forty-nine slot machines winking in obedient rows. C.J. pours me another whiskey and keeps talking.

"Now you get these people around here who use cyanide. I don't fuck with that anymore. It killed my sister. My husband and I take walks all the time around here and look for gold and silver, picking up rocks as we go. You can tell by their weight if there might be something hiding in there."

Searchlight's motto is The Camp That Didn't Fail. Like almost every surviving town in Nevada, Searchlight was built around a mineral craze. A group of investors hacked into a Miocene-era bluff in 1897, and one of them, Fred Colton, snorted: "There's something here, boys, but it would take a searchlight to find it." They kept digging. A vein of gold materialized, and with it, more people. For years, the town had a tennis court but no churches. A midcentury hustler named Willie Martello built a gambling den and cathouse called the El Rey Club and flew in big spenders for weekend fun. Now the El Rey is a rectangle of ruined walls bleaching in the sun, and the town is at a population of 539, which includes the bartender C.J., who lives in a single-wide trailer with a load of broken computers stacked outside that she melts down for the metallic guts.

"I'm going to die here," she says. "This is the first land I've ever owned." She can supplement the $8.50 an hour plus tips she earns at the bar with the gold that lies around her. The land is blasted and sere in all directions; nothing grows but weeds and yucca. But the land can yield coin if you look at it correctly. "Right place, right time," C.J. told me. Money is nothing but labor stored in a little package.

I slept that night on a flat spot in the desert that I found in the dark and woke up to discover a green-and-red speckle of plastic shotgun shells around me, along with a mess of shattered clay pigeons and a pair of kitchen appliances that had been generously ventilated with gunfire—a makeshift shooting range on federal land, which is 84.9 percent of Nevada. For as much as the western constitutionalist desert rat likes to rail against the heavy fist of Uncle Sam, out here you can pretty much do as you like: camp, fish, hunt, shoot your guns, ride your quad. Freedom's banner flies high. The Battle Born State's unwritten ethic is that you can have anything you want at any hour, as long as you pay for it yourself and don't bother the other customers. I yawned, scratched, got a coffee at Terrible's Roadhouse, and drove north. My aim, eventually, was the Idaho border.

Statistical matters in which Nevada ranks number one in the country include: home foreclosures, court-ordered phone taps, bankruptcy, divorce, disposable income, active mining claims, child drowning, job growth, gambling revenue, IRS audits, gold, per capita suicides.

There is no better way to enter Las Vegas, I think, than to do it from having slept in the desert, with dirt in the hair and last night's whiskey still acrid in the mouth. I stopped at a suburban video poker chain called Dotty's and washed up in the bathroom. The neighborhood was Sun Belt bland, full of convenience stores, thirsty-looking palm trees, and doleful apartment blocks with polyurethane banners announcing rent deals and move-in specials; a phalanx of strip malls lined the broad streets—a lot like Phoenix, Arizona, just with slot machines in the gas stations.

I headed to the Strip, the gravitational center of Nevada and of the American pleasure principle. Above sunbaked streets, a view opened up of an Eiffel Tower, a New York skyline, a multicolored medieval castle, an Egyptian pyramid, a Grecian temple, a space needle, and a marching line of mirrored slabs all blaring their brand names at the top. A gold-windowed monolith proclaimed TRUMP.

Mandalay Bay, a resort that themed itself after South Asian jungles, anchors the southern end of the Strip. My room on the twenty-seventh floor—one of 3,039 in this megacomplex—had a view into the thickest cluster of themed casinos: the Egyptian pyramid, the Manhattan skyline, the Arthurian castle, the Eiffel Tower. I went downstairs and out to the artificial beach fronting the eleven-acre wave pool where I floated in the moving water, looking upward at the hard white sun and feeling the desert wash off.

Fantasy palaces like the Mandalay Bay were not the first kinds of casinos on the Las Vegas Strip, whose history of money and neon can be traced to a 1938 cleanup of Los Angeles by a reformist mayor cracking down on the backroom roulette, prostitution, and police corruption on the Sunset Strip. But squeeze a balloon one place and it'll bulge in another. A Californian named Thomas Hull took note of the L.A. vice raids and bought some near-worthless land ($150 an acre) off Nevada's U.S. Highway 93 and built the El Rancho resort, which featured all-night table games, dancing, horseback rides, a river of liquor, and the midnight all-you-can-eat chuck wagon beef cart—the birth of the casino bargain buffet. Others copied Hull's example, especially by playing up the cowboy aesthetic. Drummed out of the LAPD, former vice squad officer Guy McAfee—who himself owned a brothel on the sly and had married the madam—came to Las Vegas to found the mining-themed Golden Nugget.

But not until the Stardust opened on July 2, 1958, did the civic spirit really turn away from Wild West themes and toward European-style enchantment. The Stardust's mammoth road sign featured a capsule sputniking around a planet; the display used seventy-one hundred feet of neon tubing with enough electrical power to light four thousand homes. The show *Lido de Paris*, patterned after the lewd extravagance of a nineteenth-century French dance hall, featured fifty showgirls with tiny mirrors sewn into their costumes and crowned with headpieces that weighed up to thirty pounds. Few of them were trained dancers or singers; it didn't matter. Most went topless on stage. In the count room, out of sight from the public, goodfellas from midwestern crime families made sure that reported income from the tables was far less than the actual rake. The balance usually went out through the airport to Chicago or Kansas City stuffed into a mule's suitcase.

Vegas boosters encouraged gossip columnists to file their columns from the side of the hotel pools, dropping the names of the celebrities they spotted enjoying their own prepaid junkets. "People who come to Vegas expect spice and glamour," a manager told the *Chicago Tribune*. "They want the biggest, the most and the best in food and fun and entertainment. We have long since learned how to give it to them." When Jay Sarno used grimy money from the Teamster Pension Fund to open Caesars Palace in 1966, complete with fountains, cypress trees, marble statues, a triumphant driveway, and waitresses dressed in skimpy togas, he did so by selling the idea that every customer deserved to have grapes dangled into their mouth—they, too, deserved to be a winner. Sarno loathed straight lines and right angles, so he ordered all the bars to be made in oval shapes.

The more important illusion of effortless wealth helped turn card and dice games from seedy back-alley practices into respectable fun and made slot machines as innocuous as televisions. In the showrooms, Hollywood B-list cornballs like Wayne Newton and Shecky Greene played up nostalgic acts and sang ten-year-old songs. Elvis Presley, the poet laureate of this era, showed up only in brief bursts. He did terrible lowbrow material, and long past his best days—by 1970, he had to stuff himself into a white suit. But promoters turned his flagging image into a virtual Caravaggio and reaffirmed a central truth about Las Vegas: its unapologetic and barefaced *uncoolness*, its lack of regard for the tasteful, its defiant embrace of the over-the-top consumption of luxury and chintz, and its abiding interest in selling the inchoate hunger for a lost fortune, a promised country, an overseas dream city, a forgotten romance, a carelessly spent $1,000 that would come back with interest if the dealer would cooperate. Las Vegas reaches but never realizes. On weekend nights, the Strip is a parade of Ma and Pa America in shorts and rubber sandals, dazed, half-drunk, and looking for new amusements in other casinos that would only replicate what they found in the last one: foraging in the garden of desire.

Off the Strip, you find pawnshops. One of them is in a corner mall, neighboring a nail salon, a sports bar, and a video poker den. Five bank safes are behind the register. Mounted on the wall are thirteen guitars, and underneath them, a glass case of jewelry whose personal histories have been washed clean. The pawnbroker is a slow-talking man of middle age with a pistol conspicuously perched on his hip.

"I don't want to know the stories," he told me. "Suzy gets pissed off, comes in here to pawn her wedding ring. Maybe it gets picked up by someone who gives it to his own significant other. And then maybe that ends, and it's back here again. How the hell would I know? Am I supposed to give a $200 premium on a ring because it's been in the family three hundred years? I can't do that. They want money. So do we. And maybe there's a place where we can meet in the middle, to help them, as long as we can benefit from it."

Statistical matters in which Nevada ranks dead last in the country include: health spending, public school outcome, annual rainfall, flu vaccinations, affordable rental units, tornados, people who report "feeling safe."

The Stardust came down on March 13, 2007, after a company named Controlled Demolition, Inc., drilled more than a thousand holes in its concrete core and packed them with 428 pounds of explosives. "It has been notched, literally, like a tree," said the chief engineer, Mark

Loizeaux. After a four-minute fireworks show put on for the crowd that had amassed on the Strip, the blasts went off at 2:34 a.m. and the Stardust collapsed into 170,000 tons of debris to make way for a new resort that was never built.

Blowing up Strip hotels and turning the destruction into a street party was already a local custom before 2007. Howard Hughes's Landmark Hotel lasted twenty-four years and took thirteen seconds to come down. "All in all, it was a very proper, fitting demise of a grand old lady that deserved to go out in a splash of color," said Loizeaux of the Stardust. "I expected it to take a little longer," muttered a tourist from Alabama watching the Desert Inn crumble to the pavement in 2004. "This is not an execution," Steve Wynn insisted to the crowd just before the destruction of the Dunes on October 27, 1993. "It's a phoenix rising!" He then set off the flash cannons on the fake HMS *Britannia* in the lake in front of the new Treasure Island casino across the street to signal the final button-push on the Dunes. "Blow it up!" screamed the crowd of twenty thousand people. "Blow it up! Blow it up!"

I was in the lounge for the last night of the Riviera on April 26, 2015, watching a nostalgia artist named George Bugatti sing Rat Pack songs. The casino floor had the threadbare feel of a third-rate cruise ship with grubby golden bannisters; upgrades had been deferred for years. The ninety-three-year-old comedian Marty Allen was a few rows in front of me. "It's tough to see this place go," the drummer Gary Olds told John Glionna, the friend I was sitting with. "There's no longer any place on the Strip for this kind of music. We're losing our collective memory." The final pour at the bar was a Pabst Blue Ribbon to a guy who murmured, "Sad, very sad." Hotel guests were hustled out the next day, and the employees were offered access to the contents of the suite once occupied by Frank Sinatra. During a liquidation sale of the furniture, a woman named Karla R. Ostrowsky jumped to her death from the twentieth floor. Such conspicuous suicides are common in Las Vegas, and this one made the news only because it happened at a semi-public event—the end of the Riviera. The Las Vegas Convention and Visitors Association encouraged people to write down their worst personal secrets and submit them to be included in a vault to be tucked into the hotel just before its destruction. "As the Riviera's walls come down, the confessions will be concealed creating the ultimate 'what happens here, stays here' moment," they said.

Before the gallows fireworks for the Riviera on June 14, 2016, and the customary blast time of 2:35 a.m., the *Review-Journal* called up Michael Ian Borer, an associate professor of sociology at the University of Nevada, Las Vegas, who theorized "by destroying something, we create something else—certainly, that identity, that sense of belonging. Most importantly, by destroying a hotel, we're actually creating a sense of place. A person may not have a slew of memories of the Riviera, but they'll have this one now and that will create some connection to Las Vegas."

The connection obtained through vanishing is perhaps an appropriate epitaph for a place like a casino, where thousands of dollars change hands each minute in a storm of arithmetic without a word being spoken. The eye-in-the-sky cameras concealed within half domes on the ceiling log every visitor, cross-checking them against a facial recognition database of card cheats and troublemakers. But almost nothing is written down and never discussed in the open. What you want to do in the seclusion of your room is considered sacrosanct. A guest's privacy must always be protected. Discretion is of paramount value. Everyone is seen, yet never seen; remembered briefly, and erased.

The names of destroyed Nevada casinos include: Oasis, Silver Slipper, Gem, Key West, Northern Club, Apache, Royal Nevada, Dunes, Sahara, Riviera, Double-O, San Remo, Arizona Club, Desert Inn,

Aladdin, Meadows, Mint, Landmark, Castaways, Frontier, Stardust, Boardwalk.

A blinking light and a security station sixty-five miles north of Las Vegas denotes the border of Mercury, one of the only sealed towns in America, and the residential center of what is now called the Nevada National Security Site. It's not much to look at—cinderblock dormitories, Quonset huts, fire stations, a military-modern cafeteria that might as well have traveled in time from the 1950s, all looking disused and sunwashed. I'm on a bus full of nuclear waste-management experts who have been invited to tour this wedge of the Mojave Desert where the U.S. government exploded 928 atomic weapons in desert isolation before the end of the Cold War.

"That was back when we were still making the ground shake," says the guide, a genial and grandfatherly man named Joe Johnston. He's wearing Levi's 501s, a denim jacket, and a perpetual smile under a white goatee. He had worked at what was then called the Nevada Test Site only two years before the underground explosions stopped, and I got the feeling the transition had been greatly disappointing to him and his colleagues. Here was where cowboy bravado met the isotope. "It felt like we had unlimited money," he told us. "This was priority number one for the U.S. security profile. You can't go to war and cross your fingers and hope it's going to work. You need to know."

After we showed our badges to a blank-faced guard in body armor, our bus passed over a small gap toward the forbidden zone of Frenchman Flat. On the left were a series of warped-wood benches where the press and assorted VIPs used to sit to watch the atmospheric tests—a vermillion star blossoming in front of them with a brightness four thousand times the power of the sun. Those who didn't have welder's goggles were instructed to either turn away from the blast or put their hands over their eyes lest they be blinded. At the silent instant of detonation, the audience could clearly see the veins and bones in their hands as in an X-ray. Steam rose from the moisture that had been on their skin a few seconds later, and the shock waves were strong enough to knock people off the benches and onto the dirt. The echo of the explosion among the mountains would sometimes frighten spectators into thinking there was more than one bomb.

Mushroom cloud tops were visible from Las Vegas, and a few casino managers scheduled rooftop parties to watch the show. Windows shook and foundations cracked on those nights. A test code-named "Boxcar" caused the Hilton off the Strip to sway one foot back and forth. Some blasts created ugly dark clouds full of radioactivity that drifted eastward, burning the faces of cowhands and miners and seeding cancerous particles over towns in southern Utah. The NTS data professionals concealed the dangers through charts that showed "averages," insisting the risk was negligible.

The drive to test more and more, to play with Big Fire, must have been a force stronger than morality or reason. Testing shifted underground and out of sight in 1951. The crews tamped mega-kiloton bombs under the lake beds like plugs of pipe tobacco, and when they were lit off, they vaporized the bedrock and blew spectacular unseen chambers into being. When a weapon called Transom failed to detonate as planned in 1978, the scientists argued about how to safely extract the dud. The winning proposal was to carefully set another atomic weapon next to it and blow it into dust.

Johnston showed us the enormous crater left by the Sedan blast, meant to probe the capacity of nuclear bombs to carve out harbors and canals, and to dislodge underground reserves of petroleum. And then over to the remnants of Doomtown, the artificial neighborhood of wooden and stone houses built to be obliterated in the twenty-ninekiloton Apple II test. "We had school buses, propane tanks, refrigerators full of food, Sears and Roebuck clothes on mannequins, a whole town," Johnston told us. "Everything except lawns and sprinklers." Only two structures survived—the fireball had created an odd radial wedge of a non-destruction shadow that spared them. All else was pulverized.

We peered into the windows of one of the surviving buildings, a dilapidated tract home, before Johnston took us over to a second abandoned village of bent railway bridges, gas tanks, radio towers, a faux motel, abandoned bank safes that had been filled with phony bills, livestock pens that had been filled with pigs dressed in green army uniforms and doped up with sodium pentothal to see how the burns would affect their skin—porcine skin being similar in texture to human skin. Under the guise of research, this was high amusement.

Invited guests to the detonations often mentioned the strange colors they saw at the heart of the blasts: most often crimson, yellow, and violet, but sometimes green and black. Invited to watch the third test in the Buster–Jangle series on October 30, 1952, Gene Sherman of the *Los Angeles Herald-Examiner* saw "pinkish ribs not unlike orange slices" and a fireball that changed from "creamy white, reddish and orange" to "tinges of reddish-pink." Watching the same test, Chris Clausen of the *Los Angeles Times* reported the mass "shifted through the color spectrum from pure white to light red to dark red then to a malevolent purple. It looked like a large head of cauliflower. It was pure white and fleecy. Occasionally its white face was blotched with spots of unhealthy pink."

The man from the United Press, Max Miller, was watching from an airplane seven thousand feet in the air and saw a blossom of fire "blasted with rosy purple hue" with a scorching illumination. "When the bomb went off," he wrote in his dispatch, "it was just like somebody turning on a brilliant searchlight into our eyes at close range."

The code names of the nuclear test operations included: Teapot, Bedrock, Plumbbob, Crosstie, Musketeer, Touchstone, Latchkey, Flintlock, Bowline, Storax, Hardtack, Phalanx, Aqueduct, Sunbeam, Anvil, Charioteer, Quicksilver.

A few dozen miles north of the test site gate, I pause at a spot on U.S. Highway 95. On September 30, 1998, a twenty-one-year-old prostitute named Jamie Jean Ericsson was driving back to the Mustang Ranch, a legal brothel where she worked. At approximately 3:40 p.m., her car drifted into the opposite lane and struck a van full of people heading back to Arizona after a family reunion. Ericsson and three people in the van died in the grotesque tangle of metal, and the highway patrol suspected she had done it deliberately—impulsively killing herself in a grotesquely selfish manner.

In the wreckage, police found Ericsson's diary, which was apparently a litany of horror. A patrol spokesperson told the *Las Vegas Sun*, the entries "almost make you cry."

"Had we not found the very depressing journal, we probably would've just said inattention," he went on. "The way she went off the road—it wasn't real sudden, she drifted, but it wasn't a jerky movement. The van's driver tried to steer away to avoid the crash, but it didn't seem like she did."

Ericsson had been working for the Mustang Ranch in Lyon County, then for the nearby Old Bridge—one of approximately one thousand women in any given year who have worked as legal courtesans since 1971, when the Nevada legislature allowed prostitution on a county-by-county basis.

Though the illegal flesh trade in Reno and Las Vegas dwarfs the revenue from the aboveground establishments, the legitimate business rakes in about $75 million per year. The women work as independent contractors and kick back about half of their fee to the house (a twenty-minute act of coitus runs at a benchmark of $1,000). That's not counting the fees the workers must pay, not unlike that of a coal miner bound to the company store: each sandwich eaten in the café, every ride she's given for the weekly STD test and the payment for the test itself, rent on her room, cosmetics, and condoms. The sex workers are confined to the premises every night as virtual inmates; nobody can leave for more than a twelve-hour period without another mandatory STD screening (the baseline assumption being that she's gone out to have sex with someone). Federal investigations routinely turn up evidence that some of the women have been trafficked against their will.

The typical Nevada brothel is an over-decorated warren of rooms inside a stick building out in the desert that looks like a pioneer's home—though this model has exceptions: Mona's Ranch in Elko is barely two blocks from the town's stately Mediterranean-revival U.S. post office. The brothel facilities are often unconsciously done up in a Gay Nineties theme, which also happens to be the default syntax of a casino. When a customer walks in, a bell rings throughout the rooms and the women can gaze on the newcomer via a hidden camera—another Nevada tradition. If the woman doesn't find the customer repulsive, she comes out for the lineup, a ritual in which the women present themselves to the customer, who gets his pick. The selected one goes back into a room, a price is negotiated for what is universally known as the "party," the customer is led back to the entrance to pay at the desk, and the woman has access to a panic button that summons the house muscle should matters go awry.

Like so much else in Nevada, prostitution thrives on ephemerality. If a customer pays in cash, nobody knows his name. Credit card records are kept confidential. The women go by aliases or obvious masquerade names like Midnight Violet or Danger. Nobody at the Mustang Ranch remembers Jamie Jean Ericsson. "I've been here a while," the madam told me over the phone. "Never heard of her. Also, I don't know the real names of most of the girls here."

The coroner found no drugs in Jamie's system and ruled her death inconclusive. An official with the Nevada Highway Patrol told me that unless a dead person makes an explicit statement of intent, determinations of murder-suicide in collisions like this are extremely rare. The patrol sends its crash records to the state transportation department, which shreds and incinerates them after three years. Ericsson's diary is also gone, likely incinerated. Whatever stories she preserved in it have been lost. Her life—and the mystery of her death—is like the shapes of people in the hidden casino cameras, liminal souls drifting briefly into view, then out.

The names of Nevada's legal bordellos include: Dovetail, Desert Rose, Desert Club, Moonlight Bunnyranch, Alien Cathouse, Sagebrush, Love, Kit Kat, Stardust, Big 4, Sagebrush, Mustang.

The road from Jamie Jean Ericsson's unmarked crash site bends northward to Beatty, and the hot air on the pavement creates blurry light waves that fade away as you approach them, revealing new ones farther down the black ribbon of U.S. 95. The sky is colored pale azure going to indigo, and the mountains on either side are dull ochre fronted with a line of electric poles. Every now and then, a jagged non-natural hole in the slope presents itself, along with the slanted foundations of what had been a stamp mill: signs of another vanished town.

This is classic basin and range, the primary geological furniture of Nevada.

Dozens of mountain chains run parallel to each other in a north–south direction, resembling on a map what the nineteenth-century geologist Clarence Dutton called "a line of caterpillars marching toward Mexico." Restless tectonic plates stretch out and create faults in which some blocks ram together in collisions of rocks to form peaks and others subside into flat valleys. The relentless heat and violence of 450 million years ago created the volcanic seeps of liquidized minerals, like gold and silver, that hardened into veins waiting to be discovered by the generation of Anglo schemers in the 1850s who trickled into what was then a lightly held possession of the Mormon Church in faraway Salt Lake City. Busted refugees from the California Gold Rush came back over the Sierra Nevadas to try their luck anew, and a group of them, including the prospector Henry "Old Pancake" Comstock, zeroed in on a set of ragged claims on the side of a peak they called Sun Mountain. It turned out to be a lode of silver so big that the U.S. Mint eventually needed to open a branch nearby to strike its coins, though most of the profits went into San Francisco banks.

A persistent myth still taught in Nevada's schools was that the U.S. needed that silver wealth to finance the Civil War. But the war's outcome was already clear by 1864, and Abraham Lincoln needed two more Republican seats in the Senate to get his Reconstruction bills through Congress. Statehood for a patch of the Basin and Range Province with barely forty thousand residents was hustled through as a political fillip, but the hazy blend of myth and fact surrounding Nevada's side-door entry into the nation were memorialized in the state's motto, Battle Born. Torn off like a leg of Sunday chicken from Utah and later tipped with a southwestern triangle to provide steamboat access to the Colorado River, Nevada's state lines have a boxy form that nevertheless comes off looking sleek, like a shank that could be slipped into a jeans pocket or the top of a polished boot. Or, perhaps, a single open quote mark.

Nevada tells many other stories about itself that aren't true: the Strip was an idealistic dream of Bugsy Siegel (he muscled in on Billy Wilkerson's Flamingo and ran it into the ground); Las Vegas was safer and nicer when the mob ran it (Sheriff Ralph Lamb was the real peacekeeper of what was then a much smaller town); the mob brought prosperity (their counting-room skims stole the tax money that should have built local schools and roads); the place was built on western individualist grit (federal projects like the Hoover Dam and outside interests like the Central Pacific Railroad, Basic Magnesium, the Guggenheim copper family, and international hotel chains actually swung the weight); Virginia City got its name after a drunk named Old Virginny Finney stumbled on his way home and, spilling a bottle of whiskey on the ground, insisted that he had baptized the town and therefore had a right to name it for himself (no evidence for this).

One Nevada origin story that *is* true, however, is that the state was founded on the principles of low taxes, low services, and low government interference, and the *don't-tread-on-me* ethic reinforces itself every day in spirit and practice. Best of all, somebody else pays for it. "Nevada thrives on its make-believe business," writes local historian Deke Castleman. "The vast majority of state taxes are collected from people who don't live here. Sales, room, gambling, entertainment, rental car, airport—they're all 'export taxes.'"

In Beatty, a pleasant town next to the Amargosa River, I stopped for a lunch of chili and beer at a wooden storefront called Happy Burro and sat next to an older man with a porkpie hat and a Pittsburgh accent named Vaughn, who told me that his parents named him for a big band singer named Vaughn Monroe. He used to work in collision repair in Las Vegas and I asked him why he moved up here.

"One word, two syllables, seven letters," he said. "*Freedom*. I built a house up on the ridge. No permits, no inspectors. The county didn't give a shit. There's so many trailers around here, they were probably happy to see a stick house."

From an article by John Muir in the *San Francisco Evening Bulletin*, January 15, 1879:

*Nevada is one of the very youngest and wildest of the States; never-
theless, it is already strewn with ruins that seem as gray and silent
and time-worn as if civilization to which they had belonged had
perished centuries ago. Yet, strange to say, all these ruins are the
results of mining efforts made within the last few years. Wander
where you may through length and breadth of this mountain-barred
wilderness, you everywhere come upon these dead mining towns,
with their tall chimney stacks, standing forlorn amid broken walls
and furnaces, and machinery half-buried in sand, the very names of
many of them already forgotten amid the excitement of later discoveries, and now only known through tradition—tradition ten years
old . . . While traveling southward from Austin down Big Smoky
Valley, I noticed a remarkably tall and imposing column, rising like
a lone pine out of the sage-brush on the edge of a dry gulch. It seemed
strangely out of place in the desert, as if it had been transported
from the heart of some noisy manufacturing town and left here by
mistake. I learned afterward that it belonged to a set of furnaces
that were built by a New York company to smelt ore that was never
found. The tools of the workmen are still lying in place beside the
furnaces, as if dropped in some sudden Indian or earthquake panic
and never afterward handled. These imposing ruins, together with
the desolate town, lying a quarter-mile to the northward, present a
most vivid picture of wasted effort.*

The Amargosa River seemed to disappear once I left Beatty, which is
not an uncommon fate for water in the Great Basin that can unexpectedly slip underground and out of sight. Very few rivers flow out of what
amounts to a gigantic sink in the middle of the Mountain West, so it
really isn't going anywhere. Neither is a brief spatter of afternoon rain
that falls on my locust-smeared windshield. Windows of sun peep from

behind rain curtains, and I can see that breezes are stirring up vents of dust from a dry lake bed that look like wisps of steam, as if the ghost lake was boiling. The creosote plants of the Mojave have gradually turned to sage and bitterbrush and the occasional splash of Indian paintbrush as I approach the stumpy mesas of a formation that the map identifies as Slate Ridge.

A few more miles, past the telltale gashes in the slopes with a red wound of tailings tumbled down from them, and I'm coming into Gold-field, once the largest town in the state, and now down to about 270 people. It's one of the only county seats in the U.S. without a gas station, and consists of a stone business block, a magnificent eczema of battered wooden homes in a state of arrested decay, and—to the east—the Venusian landscape of what had once been the Florence Hill Mine: piles of sickly yellow tailings interspersed with shafts yawning open like bird mouths and protected only by flimsy squares of barbed wire, with silenced headframes brooding on hilltops and broken bottle shards—their pleasures long-emptied and possibly more than a hundred years old—glint up from the ground.

Few entities are more ruthlessly honest than gold camps. They are capitalism stripped away of all its pretentions and niceties, in the same way that a desert is honest and clean with all its verdure burned off to reveal the skeleton of land itself. The end of a gold camp resembles a corpse after an autopsy. The guts of the earth have been pulled out and piled to the side in a heap of bile and jaundice.

I had three whiskeys over ice in one of the town's two bars, The Hoist House, which Vaughn had told me about, and wound up in conversation with a road grader for Esmeralda County. He wanted to know where I was coming from, and I told him Las Vegas.

"They need to break off from the rest of the state," he said. And then he grew animated, though he had previously been soft-spoken: "It's all *me-me-me* down there. *Me-me-me.* Get all the fuckin' liberals out. They can go do what they like. Don't take my guns. And don't take my money."

I slept that night up a Forest Service road not far from the slopes of Montezuma Peak that afforded a view of the security lights of the Albemarle Corporation Lithium Operation, in which the clays embedded in a prehistoric lake bed are leached out for the chemical lithium carbonate, used for the production of ceramic glaze, and, in much smaller doses, to treat bipolar disorder. Just after sunset with the light fading, I took a walk up the rutty canyon road and about a half mile away, I found an abandoned stone kiln built against a cliff that had been used in the late nineteenth century to bake pine logs down into charcoal that could be used in the furnaces that assayed gold and silver. The kiln was in the shape of a turret, about twenty feet tall, and looked like a medieval frontier battlement.

As I drifted off to sleep, more comfortable than I would have been in any hotel, I thought of Nevada as a mammoth spill of basin and range with tiny smears of neon tucked into the folds. These little dabs of color represented the spots where minerals were exploited or the railroad had come through. But they do not necessarily represent wealth and safety, and the massive darkness that blankets Nevada does not necessarily represent danger.

The empty places are more intensely studied than we may realize. Down a 4WD-only road some twenty-five miles west of the town of Alamo, you can find a small mountain called Tikaboo Peak. I had camped at the base of it on a freezing night in late September 2016 and climbed it early the next morning. From the pine-covered summit, looking west, is the closest legal view of the secret government installation called Area 51.

Through the morning heat-shimmer emanating from the dry bed of Groom Lake, I could make out a line of white buildings twenty-five miles away. The U.S. Air Force uses the area to test classified aircraft, though its policy of silence about what happens there has fertilized hundreds of theories: reverse engineering of captured alien spacecraft, a movie stage for the faked moon landings, time travel research, planes that can turn invisible, and teleportation booths. With restricted federal land and mountain peaks sheltering it in every direction, it is hard to imagine a more isolated and private place for high-level tinkering.

The view from Tikaboo Peak gives away nothing except the row of hangars and other inscrutable structures, which seem to dance and blur in the light. Perhaps this is appropriate. Area 51 is an unfocused hole in the national consciousness.

I had been staring at it for more than fifteen minutes when an ordinary-looking Air Force F-16 soared overhead and banked hard above the summit, making a staggering roar. *I can see you*, this eye-in-the-sky seemed to be saying. *And I know what you're doing.*

Names for Area 51 include: Dreamland, The Ranch, Homey Airport, The Box, Groom Lake, Paradise Ranch, Watertown Strip, Home Base, The Container.

The Big Smoky Valley outside Tonopah is a panorama of heart-leaping views, with big alluvial fans covered in sagebrush sweeping up toward the escarpments, much harder and bigger and rougher than a child's view of a meadow. The multicolored folds of the Toiyabe Range lie under vaults of cumulonimbiform clouds, and the top ridgelines have abundant snow cover even in June.

As I drew closer to Seyler Peak, a mound of still-life volcanic fury, the northern view became slightly menacing; Mahogany Mountain behind it looks even more intimidating—a high wall of grayish-white without any one point on which to fix a gaze, like searching for something coherent within a mass of nothingness. The presentation of such a benign color as white can bring dread. Herman Melville called it "not so much a color as the visible absence of color; and at the same time the concrete of all colors; is it for these reasons that there is such a dumb blankness, full of meaning, in a wide landscape of snows—a colorless, all-color of atheism from which we shrink?"

Twenty miles more and I spot the flat-topped tables against the Toquima Range on the west side of the valley that look like half-finished Egyptian pyramids. This is the Round Mountain gold mine, which has been in operation since 1906; the ore body here ran deeper than any early geologist anticipated. The underground tunnels were spaded up like an ant colony when its owners converted it into a strip mine a half century ago. Gold keeps giving in Nevada: it yields more than $7 billion annually and adds fourteen thousand high-wage jobs to the payroll. I'd called ahead to ask for a tour, and after being issued a hard hat and a reflective vest at the administration trailer, I got into a pickup truck with John Miller whose job title was "Continuous Improvement Facilitator."

"This operation is pretty simple," he said, as we bumped up a dirt track at ten miles per hour. "We have geologists who tell us where they think the gold is and engineers who plan the sequence of mining. We set the blast, get the material loose, start piling up the tailings." He pointed to a giant man-made mesa covered with elaborate netting that recalled *Gulliver's Travels*. "Those are drop tubes, just like you have in a garden. A weak cyanide solution filters down through the rock. We figure that's a billion tons of rock up there."

The cyanide takes nearly three months to seep down through the rock, attaching itself molecularly to the .01 percent of gold hidden within all the useless waste minerals. Creeks at the base of the mesa called "gold ditches" ease the ammonia-smelling liquor over to a set of tanks where carbon attaches to the gold. Miller took me across a bed of tailings that looks remarkably like a prehistoric Nevada salt playa, and then past the grind mill where a motor originally designed to turn the screw of a cruise ship instead turns a drum full of steel balls that bang and crush the low-grade ore down to granules small enough to be added to the leaching pile.

Miller checked his cell phone. It was getting close to 2:00 p.m., the daily blasting time. He pointed his truck toward the side of a terraced pit where we could see a few tiny-looking people milling about a flat spot three-quarters of a mile down at the bottom of the earthen cone, conferring with each other. Miller's radio crackled. Though an afternoon storm was visibly kicking up over the Toquimas, the chances of lightning were deemed negligible. The sun made patterns on the hole as we waited. A crusher building had collapsed on the southwest side, a victim of "wall movement" on November 23 of the previous year, and its wreckage littered the slope.

At ten minutes past the hour, the workers in the pit below cleared the area, satisfied the charges of ammonium nitrate mixed with fuel oil were in place to move a quarter million tons of rock. Minutes later, a klaxon horn blared, sounding like an air raid siren from a 1950s movie.

"Fifteen seconds," said a voice from Miller's radio. Then a count-down and the words at zero: "Fire in the hole!"

Several dozen blasts went off in a closely timed series in a giant tic-tac-toe pattern of at least twenty squares, and a piece of ground that looked to be about two acres sunk several feet in a miasma of dust, in a way that reminded me of films of the underground H-bomb tests: a rapid subsidence. The muffled boom took nearly two seconds to arrive, even as the dust was already settling.

"That's the sound of business right there," said Miller.

He drove me back to the administration trailer, past a small metal statue of stacked gold bars that represented the volume of pure gold taken from the pit in the last three decades: about the size of a Ford Econoline van. What comes next for the displaced ore, I asked. "Got to break it up, got to get it worked over," he told me. "But it's dependable and steady. When you deal with any other product, you have to worry first about who's going to buy it. With gold, you never have to worry."

Deeper into the Toquima mountains, past the gold mine, is a triangular crack in the granite walls near a pine-covered summit. The ancestors of the Western Shoshone used it as a temporary shelter and a kind of cathedral at least fifteen hundred years ago and possibly as long as three thousand years ago. They painted shapes on the walls with ochre: wheels, bull's-eyes, human eyes, crosses, wavy lines, triangles—a baffling whirl of semiotics.

Archeological digs in the ground beneath the walls did not yield the expected trove of pots, weapons, or other prehistoric castoffs. This was not a place that people were permitted to stay, apparently, a restriction enforced by the priests. Was the art representational or abstract? A record of hunts? A calendar? No archeologist has been able to say for sure what these pictographs meant to their creators. Their key has been lost.

I camped about a half mile away from the cave after watching the explosion at Round Mountain. The spot was beneath the snow line at 7,687 feet, though the night was chilly and I shivered in my tent, not feeling the same sense of comfort as I had the night before. Nothing like flimsy walls against a yawning wilderness to make you feel like you could be smashed like a bug and never be missed.

In the early morning, I hiked back over to the cleft in the rock and looked again. What had seemed washed out and slightly dull in the previous evening's light now seemed to be resplendent with color: oranges and pinks, red circles, yellow lines, splashes of blue. Incredible hues.

What does art mean when the meaning is obscured?

Can we still perceive desire in the colors?

Samuel Langhorne Clemens followed his older brother Orion out to Nevada in 1862, hoping to escape a shameful past as a deserter from the Confederate Army and a potential life of drudgery as a small-town printer. He quickly tired of life in the capital of Carson City, and went up to one of the instant towns of brothels, bars, and gestures of respectability clustered around a silver discovery, a place its founders named Aurora. The twenty-one-year-old Clemens toiled in the shallow excavations, shivered inside a splintered cabin, and helped the mayor juice up his promotional speeches. "The only mistake George Washington ever made was that he wasn't born in Aurora," went one line. At night, he wrote letters to the Territorial Enterprise *in Virginia City in the persona of a broke miner named "Josh." The editor liked his style and offered him a job for twenty-five dollars a week. Clemens departed Aurora on foot. In Virginia City, another instant town encircled with mineshafts, he filled column after column of prose sketches and hoaxes, and invented the pen name of Mark Twain before absquatulating for San Francisco to escape a challenge to a duel. A fire in the offices of the* Territorial Enterprise *in 1875 turned most back copies into ash, and along with it, much of Mark Twain's formative writing, which is now lost. Aurora disappeared after the silver ran out, and its site can only be reached with a jeep. Bottle and tin fragments, one wall, and a cemetery are the only clues anything was ever there.*

Blackjack dealers keep impassive faces when they dispense cards. Perhaps this is because the job is so repetitive: when four players are sitting at the table, a good dealer can complete eighty-four hands in an hour. For occasional participants, the game is a novelty and a thrill, with perhaps a painfully large sum of money hanging in the balance. No less a gambling soul than Giacomo Casanova said that he loved the tables, where—in the interpretive words of the biographer Stefan Zweig—he found the "titillation of anxiety, with shuddering expectation . . . He never looks for a final relief of tension. What he wants is perpetual tension, the unceasing alternation of red and black, of spades and diamonds."

Games like this favor the risk-takers among us; enjoyment of peril is an evolutionary trait. Those who hazard big, win big.

But Nevada dealers typically seem bored almost to the point of melancholy. They have seen every possible combination of numbers and emotion the game can yield. Yet the game continues. The game can never stop—it is as constant as the revolution of the planets. The game mimics Darwinist nature because it is indifferent to whether we win or lose, whether we live or die. Nothing surprises a dealer.

I am now nearly to Idaho, and I have stopped in to play in at least twelve casinos. Each time I have walked out with more money. Blackjack is an easy-enough game in which to at least stay afloat for a good while as long as you observe basic strategy: stand even on garbage when the dealer shows a two through a six; don't split anything but aces and eights; hit on anything lower than a seven if the dealer has paint; double down on an ace even if it involves reaching into the reserves; walk away after doubling or losing a previously determined kitty.

On this trip, I seem to be untouchable.

Blackjack is the perfect casino game: more human than slots, less arcane than craps, less soul-deadening than video poker, not as visual as roulette, but a lot more sustainable over time. We demand endless variation in the numbers, but they must be wrapped within a cocoon we can understand. Because in our hearts, we truly don't want anything entirely revolutionary. We just want a rise in our fortunes within preexisting boundaries, an easy fattening of the account.

This is why casinos are, at bottom, all designed in the same basic manner with dependable rules and predictable layouts, and also why Nevada's trademark *uncoolness* has such enduring appeal. Under the engineered disorder and faux-spontaneity lies a soothing and familiar scheme. The hope of beating the system, stealing a march, getting away with something, taking the freebie, becoming the great exception if only once, perhaps an unconscious metaphor for humanity's paramount urge to cheat death.

Of course the game is rigged. But it doesn't need to be rigged against *us*.

Isn't this how we spend most of our lives? We chase a beam we barely understand. One of Nevada's many ironies is how the gaming halls, with their maroon bordello styling, are so closely packed in, almost always without windows, never with a good view of what lies outside, which is often a terrifying stretch of desert. Vice must be sequestered in a tight and warm place, safe from assault by thoughts of oblivion. Writer Mario Puzo once said that this is the place where America has outsourced all its unsavory impulses so they could be safely discharged in an arena far from home. "It is all a dream," he wrote. "It is a sanctuary away from the real world, real troubles, real emotion, and it is somehow fitting and proper that the city of Las Vegas is surrounded by a vast desert. A desert which acts as *cordon sanitaire*."

Casinos and their illusions are well suited to a place like Nevada. They hide the emptiness that looms in all directions.

The names of vanished Nevada mining towns include: Belmont, Rawhide, Wedekind, Pyramid City, Empire City, Mound House, Nordyke, Rhyolite, Elbow, Star City, Jumbo, Gold Park, Geneva, Diamond, Treasure Hill, Minerva, Montezuma, Gold Mountain, Oriental, Silver Peak, Acme, Candelaria, Metallic City, Whisky Spring, Lucky Boy.

With even more money in my pocket, I take the highway that parallels the Reese River into the Antelope Valley, one of the few splashes of cultivated green crops in the state. Dead locusts lie on the road in smashed patterns, and the alfalfa grows in circles off to the west: a sign of center-pivot irrigation tapping into an aquifer. To a cross-country jet passenger, they would look like giant green circles. The ghosts of played-out furrows display themselves outside the circumferences. And off to the north, presently, are the piles of the Lone Tree Mine, as stout and multicolored as a hoop dress at a pre-Lenten carnival.

In the town of Battle Mountain, I stop for a beer at the Owl Club next to the tracks. Eighteen years ago, Gene Weingarten of *The Washington Post* wrote a story in which he proclaimed this careworn city—with its initials BM painted in white on a nearby hill—"the armpit of America." The town responded with reluctant good humor and held a "Festival in the Pit" featuring the usual summer civic fare: bedframe races, a beauty pageant, funnel cake. They persuaded Old Spice deodorant to act as a sponsor. I asked a woman next to me playing an electronic keno game called Cleopatra when the festival was held. "Oh, we haven't done that for years. People who start stuff don't always keep it going." Said her friend a little more indignantly, "Hell no, this isn't an armpit, and even if it is, it's my hometown and I like it. So what?"

Bill paid, thanks given, and in a few more minutes, I'm eastbound on Interstate 80, which parallels the Humboldt River—and as a matter of nineteenth-century necessity—the route for emigrants on the California Trail and the builders of the Central Pacific Railroad. The northern tier of towns across Nevada is on this necklace and it remains a major freight corridor. A train full of Wyoming coal passes me in the other direction, heading for some utility in the San Francisco Bay Area.

The springtime had been uncommonly moist, and the perpendicular route over a series of ranges is a painter's study in greens and blues, with snowy peaks backing a wealth of juniper and sage. Eventually, the road splits off from the river, and we're now heading toward Wendover at the edge of the salt flats—the borderline keyhole into sinfulness for the Salt Lake City metro region. Standing at the edge of town is a sixty-three-foot sign in the shape of a smiling cowboy. He's named Wendover Will, a cousin of the lighted Vegas Vic cowboy mounted above street level in downtown Las Vegas who mechanically gestures with a thumb toward the vanished Pioneer Club with a cigarette glowing in his mouth and an air of seductive menace in his beady eyes.

On the horizon stands Pilot Peak, the strikingly solitary mountain that had been an important landmark for the Donner Party to get them through the salt flats in 1846. They were the victims of bad advice. A promoter named Lansford Hastings—a real Wendover Will of his day—who published a book called *The Emigrants Guide to Oregon and California* touting what he described as a surefire way to beat the system, a shortcut across the trickiest midsections of the intermountain West. The wagon collective headed by George Donner and James M. Reed took the bait and struggled mightily through the Wasatch range and blew out their oxen in the sticky salt plain, missing their window to get over the crest of the Sierra Nevada before winter snows boxed them in and they starved in wretched fashion. They had gambled on wispy information and paid the price. From August 27 to September 3 of 1864, they had slogged eighty miles across the alien wastes, aiming for the precipice of Pilot Peak, which promised springs of fresh water at the base.

I got into Wendover well before sundown and took a drive past the old airfield on the Utah side. Rows of decaying wood barracks fronted a giant hangar—one of the only structures here to be restored. It had once sheltered the Boeing B-29 Superfortress, called Enola Gay, that had dropped the first atomic bomb on Hiroshima. The pilots of the 509th

Composite Group had trained here in closely guarded secrecy for more than a year before their mission that made World War II a nuclear war. Wendover was home to an Area 51 of an earlier era; the surrounding desert had been the scene of hundreds of practice drops of mock Fat Mans and Little Boys.

Time to play again. Past the effigy of Wendover Will are five large casinos that call one hundred miles across some of the most desolate and dehydrated country in America toward the world headquarters of the Mormon Church. In his novel, *This Is the Place*, the author Peter Rock has his bored blackjack dealer protagonist think the following thought as he walks home from the Stateline Casino: "In Utah, you will learn morality and restraint and you will yearn for everything you deny yourself; here in Nevada, nothing is illegal, everything is permitted and encouraged and will make you feel hollow. Believe me, the states need each other to recognize themselves, to savor the knowledge that there is an unhappiness more desperate than their own."

The Stateline no longer exists by that name but its competitor, The Peppermill, is still going strong, with a sunburst of colored tubing at its entrance, and I walk in feeling confident. A spell at the blackjack table yields more winnings, and it seems like the right time to put my name on the poker list and wait for a seat at the long oval table where a heavyset dealer presides over a court of ten supplicants, all of whom have the same idea as me. At the next-door seat, a youthful tattooed drunk introduces himself as Nate and I shake his hand.

I'm not a particularly aggressive bettor at Texas Hold 'em, but I seem constitutionally unable to chase a set of moderate hole cards into the turn before giving up. Within five hands, and without once going the distance, I've lost half my winnings from the past week. Then comes a down pair of aces, and I'm staying reasonable and reserved all the way to the flop, when I have to go all in because I'm out of money and drunken Nate beside me—who has not won a hand either—is pushing in enough of his chips to outpace me. The river card is an eight, and when he shows, I know that I had read him right, but did not foresee his luck. The last eight had given him three of a kind, and the win.

He shakes my hand once more as I get up, having lost every dollar I'd made since I came into Nevada at Searchlight. I thought I saw a flash of empathy in his tipsy eyes. Or maybe he was sorry I didn't have more to put on the table for him.

When it legalized gambling and liberalized divorce in 1931, the Nevada Legislature also transformed the state into the easiest in the country in which to get married. No blood tests or waiting period; no proof of residency or any prior unions. A slew of instant chapels with pasteboard decorations popped up in downtown Las Vegas. On the Fourth of July in 1941, my grandfather impulsively drove my soon-to-be grandmother up from Arizona having already put a gold engagement ring on her finger. They arrived at 4:00 a.m. and married at the Hitching Post at 226 South Fifth Street. The troubled union lasted three years. On the site today is a branch of EZ Pawn.

The light is leaking away from the sky as I get into the car and head on a dirt road east of town, briefly into Utah and then threading back into Nevada. With the false confidence that comes from loud music, open air, a light car, a big moon in the sky, and a mild buzz from comped casino bourbons, I roared along up over a small pass and down by the side of a dry lake. In the morning I will discover that the bottom air shield from the car was torn off by the stalks of cheatgrass growing in the hump between the tire tracks.

When the road up a long crevasse called Miner's Canyon thins out to the point I can no longer drive it, and one of the rear tires is half-way-hanging off the edge of the fading road overlooking the creek, I do a seven-point turn and backtrack to the nearest level spot, set up the tent, and flop down to sleep with the summit of Pilot Peak crowding the purple sky. "Oh you magnificent bastard," I think. "You are mine."

And then I'm up at dawn, walking aside the same creek where I had almost dumped my car, which was also the same water source that charged the springs where the Donners and the Reeds refreshed their ox teams after slogging across the flats toward their date with starvation and cannibalism. I've got a small pack around my shoulders and vague directions on a cell phone screenshot. The jeep trail up Miner's Canyon takes me past the crumbling walls of a cabin that looks about a century old. Yet another Nevada bust-up.

A half mile more and the track disappears entirely. Just one logical way presents itself, which is to bushwhack up the southern walls of the creek, which becomes vertiginous in a hurry. Pickleweed and saltbush block the way. Because it's easier to climb than descend, I'm soon at least five hundred feet above the creekbed. I know the peak lies over to the north, so I force myself to cut over. At this point, the creek has disappeared under a vast stone blanket. I can barely hear it. Water tumbles down this mountain invisibly, like the cyanide solution on a gold leach heap.

The summit looks to be about one horizontal mile away from here, but demanding a tribute of at least three thousand more feet of vertical climbing. I will have to improvise a path across a long field of boulders and loose talus broken only by patches of bristlecone pine. My goal is a reef standing above a ridgeline that looks like a good route toward the conical point, and within two hours, I'm standing on top of it in patchy snow to see that what I had thought was the target is actually a false summit. The mountain has been nothing but a pile of loose rock thus far, and the deeper snows ahead in the couloir probably hide ten thousand ankle-busting traps. I now understand why I could find no good map of Pilot Peak: it is rarely visited for a reason. Seen but not really seen.

I'm ready for a shortcut. Below where I'm standing on the reef is a vertical crack that I can navigate without a rope, and I carefully descend about twenty feet before coming to a small platform at the edge of a cliff that I can't see over. The ridgeline appears to be about a fifty-foot drop from here. A few gingered steps away is a tantalizing possibility—another crack that I could use as a natural ladder, though I can't see down to the bottom of it. Without thinking very much, and wanting to keep injecting the drug of forward motion, I start down and realize this will end badly if the crack should terminate. It is far from clear whether I can get back up, and the pack hanging from my shoulders is now hogging precious inches, pushing me away from the wall and toward what is likely to be a catastrophic fall if I slip.

Now a choice. Do I commit? I could buy some maneuvering space by throwing my unwieldy pack with all the food and water down this rock stovepipe to retrieve it in a few minutes when I bounced down myself. This improvised route could result in a viable way down to the ridge and then a straight path into the snowfields still wreathing the summit. But it could be a fatal cul-de-sac, leaving me stuck in a tight fold of rock like a cork in a bottle and no way to get out. The only colors up here were the dull ivory of the Bonneville Salt Flats far in the distance and the gray of the cracked Cambrian strata at my back. I couldn't find a handhold; all that was keeping me aloft was balance. The drop to the nearest flat piece of ground looked to be about fifty feet.

"You possess everything right now," I thought, pressed up against the wall, my legs shaking with effort. "All limbs in working order, and just scrapes and ant bites thus far. Make a wrong assumption, make an incorrect move, and you will have nothing—worse than nothing—in the space of two seconds."

From an unpublished account written by Robert G. Brooks, a U.S. Army solider ordered to station himself in a trench thirty-five hundred yards away from ground zero of the Priscilla explosion of the Nevada Test Site on June 24, 1957:

> *Keep your head down, I thought. Two minutes, the voice announced. I was uttering a silent prayer. Please God carry me through this ordeal. One minute. Get ahold of yourself. This is no worse than combat. You're protected by this reinforced trench. What about the heat from the blast? Look what it did to Hiroshima and Nagasaki. The effects of the radiation, will it leave scars on me? Ten seconds, nine, eight, seven, six, five, four, three, two, one, ZERO—a blinding flash of bright white light penetrated my eyes even though they were closed. It was as if a bucket of flash bulbs had gone off in my face.*

I slid the backpack off, inch by inch, trying to barely move, and tossed it carefully up to a tiny flat spot above my head. Then I backtracked up the stovepipe. After twenty minutes of clawing, I was back up at the top of the reef and again looking at the summit that the Donner Party had viewed as a lamp as they struggled toward their promised California.

Now the colors seemed to have returned to the world; the peak beckoned with alpenglow.

Conventional climbing wisdom said I should descend to the other side of the reef and do a lateral traverse, in search of another angle of attack. But the next trap could be just as bad, or worse. And there was still that hole-pocked snowfield to consider. I spun risk/reward calculations without much useful data, as clouds marshaled up to the south: a potential foretaste of the lightning storms that kick up around desert peaks on summer afternoons.

I loathed the idea of giving up, but there seemed no reasonable alternative. My route down involved a shameful crabwalk across the boulder field and multiple plodding charges through clumps of thorny bushes and dead piñon. I had wanted that pinnacle; thirsted for it the way that keeps people taking risks when they know better, wanting to leave marks as they follow the retreating lamp in a country that seems to suck up all traces of their passing.

And now the car and the shameful road, and the front doors of the Love's Travel Stop in Wells, tinted in garish colors to blunt the impact of the sun. Inside past the lobby is a dark bar with the inevitable video consoles. A man in a baseball cap sits staring into one. "There's a system," he says, tapping the red key. "I play the same seven numbers every time. This guy I know in Elko had the idea for this and he won $1,400 on his very first day. I'm getting good at it. Put in forty dollars two hours ago and I'm at forty-one dollars right now. Plus four beers and they're $6.50 without the comp." I play a few hands of robot-dealt poker, and lose every dollar I play.

The Angus cows in the fields off the highway out of Wells are the first I've seen in this state, and the hills are more rolling and modest than the operatic peaks of the Ruby Mountains fading behind me. The light is of a soft quality falling on the prairie undulations that give an aspect of Sahara dunes; tawny yellow mounds wearing angular black sashes of shadows that move on and off. The afternoon thunderstorm I had worried about on Pilot Peak never materialized, at least not here. Off to the side are occasional signs from the Bureau of Land Management pointing the way down a dirt track leading to an unseen creek or lake. I'm not biting; I'm on my way out now.

There is not one single occupied house on the way, only the ruins of a streamside motel that looks like it last saw a customer in the 1980s, and I cross a bridge that shows the mirrored waters of Salmon Falls Creek in the gamboge light of sunset. And over a brief rise in the highway right before the Idaho border, after the trumpetry and alarums of a golf course and trailer park, it materializes as if a sunken city from an Arabian fable: one last smear of neon and colored plastic clinging to the topmost edge of Nevada, the unincorporated settlement of Jackpot (pop. 1,195), advertising HORSESHOE, FOUR JACKS, CLUB 93, CACTUS PETE'S, four casinos and one final chance to recapture what I had lost along the way.

King Philip's Shadow

A red cedar tree stands on the edge of a marsh near Sage Lot Pond. The tree is dying, and its browning edges show the effects of warm salt water flooding into its root system.

Approximately a thousand of these trees have been tagged and are being monitored by biologists attempting to understand the effects of climate change around Waquoit Bay on the southern shore of Cape Cod, Massachusetts. Rising sea levels have already caused enough erosion of the beach to reveal the stumps of an ancient cedar forest poking up from the sand.

In nearby marshes, the flooding is becoming frequent enough to eat away at the seaward line of salt marsh cordgrass (*Spartina alterniflora*) pushing into different parts of the marsh that acts as a natural barrier to storm surges. The rising waters spell the probable doom for salt marsh sparrows who lay their eggs during a precise twenty-eight-day period that is now disrupted by flooding. The sparrows are decreasing steadily by 9 percent a year, and without a secure place to lay their eggs, the species is now scheduled to go extinct by 2040.

I stood next to a spongy field of yellow-green cordgrass in a pond next to Waquoit Bay, along with a biologist named Megan Tyrell. "The grasses drive everything," she said. "They create the marsh. They are the food source. Everything flows downstream from them. We're seeing changes in just the short time we've been monitoring this. We are seeing more open areas, more pools. It's visible."

The level of Waquoit Bay is now rising 9.23 millimeters per year, and the bay waters are an average of six degrees warmer than they were fifteen years ago. New pools the size of football fields have opened up in the marshes. The nearby Santuit River no longer has trout. Southern pine beetles have migrated north and are taking root in pitch pine trees, sapping them from the inside. Apple trees are slower to bud during the earlier springs.

Climate change is lapping at the shores of New England, which experienced another transformative incursion in the seventeenth century that forever changed its landscape and helped define the terms of a new American nation.

A consequential act of diplomacy took place twenty-seven miles from Waquoit Bay on March 22, 1621, in a waterside settlement where a band of religious radicals from England had starved through their first winter.

They reached out to their neighbors, the Wampanoag, which means "people of the first light," and persuaded the tribe's leader, Massasoit, to come to Plymouth village for what amounted to a summit conference. He smoked a pipe of tobacco with governor William Bradford, and both sides agreed to come to the other's aid "if any did unjustly warre" against them. The governor gave assurance that King James I across the ocean "would esteeme of him his friend and Alie," and Massasoit was pleased to hear that the fair-skinned soldiers with their muskets would help him subdue their hostile neighbors to the west, the Narragansett. In exchange, Massasoit gave the new arrivals some seed corn and shared his knowledge of how to plant it. The peace held for forty-five years and gave the Plymouth citizens the critical time they needed to replenish their numbers by having big families, to take in more supplies and recruits from England, and to expand to new farmland.

The English denizens of Plymouth built their frame houses on the edge of a remarkably spacious forest that resembled a city park more than a tangled wilderness. Gooseberries, currants, and strawberries two inches wide grew on the ground, where sunlight poured down on them from a moderate tree canopy. Patches of oak and maple forest were interspersed with freshwater bogs and, in a few sandy spots on Cape Cod, even prickly pear cactus. Thin forests gave way to vast open spaces; it was said that a person could stand on the bald summit of what would become Boston's Beacon Hill and not see a single tree in any direction among the fields of bluestem grass.

The Wampanoag and Pequot had cleared the forest themselves through the traditional practice of burning the land periodically to create new fields and drive animals out to be hunted. Native Americans consumed enormous stacks of firewood during the winter months for heating their homes of bark and woven reeds, which could be packed up and moved within hours. To Puritan observers, the big evening fires were the equivalent of their "bed cloathes," and they did not understand the habit of moving entire villages of wooden huts with the seasons in order to take advantage of hunting and fishing grounds in the winter and the coastal planting regions in the spring and summer.

Not only had the fauna of New England been thinned out, the human population was also on the wane. Portuguese traders and French

fur trappers had been making visits for more than a hundred years before the Puritans arrived, and with them came exotic diseases like small-
pox, malaria, influenza, measles, and yellow fever—maladies that had
been cleansed from the indigenous people's biosystem more than twenty
thousand years ago during their trek across the Bering Strait and their
long years in the Arctic. Their lack of antibodies left them horrifically
vulnerable.

Entire villages disappeared; the indigenous population of New England dropped from seventy thousand to twelve thousand, and in some
places, the death rate approached 90 percent. Thomas Morton said the
number of skulls he encountered on Cape Cod was reminiscent of a "new
found Golgotha." Plymouth Township was itself built on the site of a
vanished Wampanoag village that had been called Accomack. By 1630,
the spacious forests of coastal Massachusetts had choked up with under-
brush and thorny plants. William Wood said some places had become
impassable "because it hath not been burnt." The more religious among
them were inclined to see the hand of divinity. "God had laid this country open for us," wrote John Smith, who had given the place the hopeful
name of New England on a previous visit. "Where I had seen 100 or 200
people, there is scarce ten to be found."

The colonists used rivers to push inward and claim new lands under
the doctrine of *vacuum domicilium* ("land belonging to no one") under the authority of King James I. They crept up the Connecticut River
Valley as surely as the march of cordgrass into the heart of a salt marsh,
pushing the tilling grounds of the indigenous people higher and higher
away from the shores. The colonists failed to recognize—or conveniently
failed to see—that lands tilled only seasonally were far from "vacant."

The Native American principle of land ownership was a more fluid
one than Europeans knew, generally stemming from the collective decisions of a clan group's leader—known as a sachem—and a council of no-

bles who assigned streams and fields to certain families on a basis of trust and kinship. Fences and written contracts were alien to them, and they were baffled with the idea that they should be bound to a set of written English laws from an overseas monarch.

A 1630s essay by an anonymous author entitled "The Ordering of Towns" provides an insight into the English mentality of land use in their new home. Settlements ought to be organized in six-mile squares, the basis of a modern township, with a chapel—or meetinghouse—at the center, surrounded by homes "orderly placed to enjoye the compfortable Communion." Past the ring of houses were small fields of wheat and barley, themselves surrounded with grazing lands for cattle, and out past them where nobody wanted to roam, the "Swampes and Rubbish waest grownds ... which harber wolves and ... noyesom beasts and serpents."

The new settlers particularly dreaded the "Swampes," such as the ones at the edge of Waquoit Bay, a geography in which Native Americans were especially adept at hiding during warfare and becoming practically invisible to English eyes. The word "swamp" became an ominous verb meaning to conceal oneself in the marsh—"and on the 2nd instance being ye Sabbath about sun an hour high made ye enemies place of residence, and assaulted them who presently swamped them selves in a great spruce swamp," wrote John Talcott of an enemy maneuver. The colonists tried to erase swamps as they could, digging out new channels and erecting earthen dams in an attempt to drain them for cultivation. Their desire to wrench new lands from what they considered "wilderness" turned into a collective obsession, and they soon turned the confusing tool of English law onto their new neighbors.

Whenever a Native person killed a wandering cow or pig, for example, they could be hauled into court and made to pay a hefty fine, usually a land concession. The English also offered inducements like metal knives, copper pots, muskets, and liquor as payment for land, often "sold" on the spot to an expansion-minded farmer with or without consent from the sachem. Even Massasoit himself participated in the frenzy, selling the title to a large tract near the new town of Duxbury under pressure in the name of keeping the peace with his English friends.

"All this land was unknown to the British," Roger Longtoe, the chief of the Elnu band of Abenaki in modern-day Vermont, told me. "It didn't belong to any of them. Really, did King James own anything? But you can say anything you want when you're trying to claim other people's lands. That's how Europe became Europe. What happened here is we suffered from the addiction of the goods. We wanted the knives and the guns and the axes, and all the other stuff they brought with them."

The land boom across Massachusetts was aggravated by the rise of a currency economy based on "wampum," a type of bead made from hand-drilled clamshells and strung together to make jewelry. Such finery could raise a person's status in Native society, a token just as powerful as the bigger farms the English wanted to be seen in an esteemed light by their fellows.

At the newly endowed Harvard College in Cambridge, the evangelist John Eliot set up a printing press to publish Bibles in the Anglicized languages of the Native Americans and set up a network to distribute them and preach the gospel. Native converts to Christianity were moved into special settlements known as "praying towns" like Mashpee, Ponkapoag, Natick, and Hassanamisco, where practices like fenced land and the keeping of livestock were encouraged, and customs that the English found distasteful like premarital sex and face-painting were driven underground. One of the praying towns near Worcester, Massachusetts, bore the name Chabanakongkomun, whose literal Nipmuc translation spoke loudly to the Native American concept of fluid land ownership: "You fish on your side, I fish on my side, nobody fishes in the middle and we have no trouble."

New England had become a creole society by that point, but mutual suspicions abounded. Natives chuckled at the ineptitude of the colonists and their insistence on building a single residence in one place. Colonists privately called their neighbors "talking squirrels" and, in their haste to be dominant over them, adopted a pseudo-biblical narrative of themselves as new Israelites locked in a cold war with "the devil's instruments." With their fixation on record-keeping, land boundaries, and written histories, they possessed what contemporary English chronicler Samuel Purchas called a "literall advantage"—the ability to commemorate words and deeds in writing, a version of immortality.

These inherent tensions only fueled the economic and biological forces threatening the peace forged over tobacco smoke in 1621. The decline in wild animal species, the loss of traditional sustenance lands, and the demographic weakness caused by strange European diseases all combined to put the Native way of existence in jeopardy within a decade of the first awful winter at Plymouth.

"Our fathers had plenty of deer and skins, our plains were full of deer, as also our woods, and of turkies, and coves full of fish and fowl," complained a leader named Miantonomo in 1642. "But these English having gotten our land, they with scythes cut down the grass, and with axes fell the tress; their cows and horses eat the grass, and their hogs spoil our clam banks, and we shall all be starved."

The ecological crisis mounted until an effusion of blood became inevitable.

Almost all wars have tawdry flashpoints, and the ignition of what became known as King Philip's War was the murder of a Native American informant named John Sassamon, who was found floating in a frozen pond on January 26, 1675. Somebody had twisted his neck violently enough to break it. This was politically explosive. Sassamon had just come from a meeting with the governor of Plymouth to warn him of an impending attack from Massasoit's son Philip, who had grown increasingly unhappy with the gobbling up of land.

His real name was Metacom, but the colonists called him "King Philip" because he had once been given the Christian name Philip in a gesture of solidarity during better times. The royal designation was a joke intended to make fun of his aloof bearing, which was markedly different from his more accommodating father. He had assumed the role of sachem for the Wampanoag when his older brother died, a possible victim of poisoning by the colonists, and he was outraged when the Plymouth colonists rounded up three of his associates and hanged them for Sassamon's murder after a kangaroo trial. Philip may have authorized a violent response, or his words may have inspired some of his most passionate followers to act on their own.

On June 20, 1675, a team of Wampanoag attacked the village of Swansea and killed nine people. The governors of the Massachusetts Bay and Plymouth Colonies ordered their small patrols into action, even as the Wampanoag raided and burned more towns. The gifted military leader Benjamin Church tried to prevent Philip and his advisors from escaping their redoubt near the present-day town of Bristol, Rhode Island, but Philip slipped through their grasp and headed north to rally the Nipmuc tribe to his cause. The fighting spread to Springfield, Northampton, and Deerfield in Western Massachusetts and into Abenaki territory in present-day Maine. Stacks of John Eliot's Native Bibles were tossed into the fire. What started as a localized dispute quickly became a pan-Indian war, and panicked English colonists threw everything they had into building a thousand-man army, even amid the quarreling between Massachusetts Bay, Plymouth, and Connecticut.

Their combined units marched into southwestern Rhode Island to intimidate the powerful Narragansetts into remaining neutral, even though colonial administrators thought them an "accessory in the present bloody outrages of the Barbarous Natives." At midday on December 18, in one of the most shameful military encounters of colonial America, the united forces crossed the frozen waters of a swamp and poured into the single opening of a fortified encampment of Narragansett. At least a thousand Natives were gunned down and hacked to death inside the wooden palisade, even as they tried to surrender. Women and children were burned alive inside their huts. This atrocity only drew the surviving Narragansett into a conflict they had hoped to avoid.

Philip had gone so far as to try an alliance with the hated Mohawk to the west, but the governor of New York, Edmund Andros, had beat them to the mark. Though he was a proud Anglican, Andros overcame his hostility to the Puritan zealots to his east and enlisted the Mohawk to join the campaign against rebellious King Philip.

The Wampanoag and their allies continued their surprise attacks against isolated English towns like Sudbury, Lancaster, Groton, and Worcester, even under pressure from the Mohawks. They had no forge to repair their muskets or make new bullets, and they had little time to hunt during the winter. Benjamin Church managed to secure a peace with the Sakonnet tribe, and sensing that his western campaign was over, Philip led a retreat to the Rhode Island swamps to regroup. A Native defector led a party of soldiers—including Church—to Philip's hiding place on August 12, 1676, and Philip tried to swamp himself. A Native marksman named Alderman killed Philip with a well-placed shot and was given his severed hand as a reward—Alderman later charged people a fee to see it floating in a pail of rum. Philip's head was displayed in Plymouth on top of a pole. The United Colonies of New England—a forerunner of the eventual United States—heralded the assassination as the official end of the war, even though sporadic fighting continued in the North for several months as refugees streamed out of the ravaged countryside.

"We took in a lot of people," said Longtoe, speaking for his seventeenth-century ancestors. "The war didn't really end. It moved north into Vermont and New Hampshire, and took in all these refugees who didn't want to be under England's thumb. There is so much of an innocence there—that people could be so bad to you."

The war had ruined a planting season and claimed twenty thousand Native lives. More than half of New England's ninety towns had been hit by Philip's raiders. Entire regions were left deserted. The religious hostilities of the Puritans had been threatening to create an early attempt at a revolution from the crown, but the carnage on the frontier drove them back into an alliance of skin color and mutual affection with the House of Stuart that extended royal rule in the colonies for more than a century.

Preachers viewed the carnage as a warning against sin. "O New England, shall it be said of thee the Lord hath poured out the fury of his Anger," lamented Increase Mather. When measured by the ratio of casualties to total population, it was the costliest war in American history, and it set the benchmark for the gore and greed that would characterize Indian Wars into the late nineteenth century.

The Kiowa chief Kicking Bird wrote a letter to the Bureau of Indian Affairs in 1871 seeking an end to the wars on the southern plains. "The white man is strong," he wrote, "but he cannot destroy us all in one year, it will take him two or three, maybe four years and then the world will turn to water or burn up."

King Philip's War dealt a harsh ecological blow to the Wampanoag, but it did not destroy them. The "praying Indians" in the towns estab-

lished by Eliot were mainly free of harassment, even though the English arrested their relatives believed to have participated in the war and
sold them into slavery in the West Indies. Other Wampanoag melted
into the Abenaki or Narragansett clans willing to take them in. In two
Massachusetts settlements—Mashpee and Gay Head on Nantucket—
the survivors of the Wampanoag tribe adopted English customs of dress,
religion, and agriculture, and managed to keep elements of their culture alive. In 1834, Josiah J. Fiske predicted that Waquoit Bay would be
enough to sustain the surviving band for perpetuity.

"It is hardly possible to find a place more favorable for gaining sustenance," he wrote in a letter to the governor. "It is situated on a sound, cut
into necks of land with inlets from the sea, being well watered with beautiful
ponds and fresh water streams running from the central parts of the planta-
tion. On sea shores are sea-fowls, shell fish and lobsters in abundance. The
salt water bays abound in fish of a larger kind, and the fresh water streams
and ponds in trout and herring and small fish of every variety."

This is no longer true, thanks to climate change. The fauna and flora
of Waquoit Bay have changed at a speed almost as rapid as the entire
countryside of New England morphed within a generation of the coming
of the Puritans. The salt marshes now filling with cordgrass used to be
so full of waterfowl that William Wood bragged of killing fifty of them
with a single musket shot. As recently as the 1960s, tribal citizens made
regular harvests of shellfish and derived many of their meals from the
oysters and quahog clams that could be plucked from the shallows.

"If you knew what you were doing, you would never go hungry,"
said Casey Thornbrugh, a member of the Wampanoag tribe who works
as a liaison for the Northeast Climate Adaptation Science Center in Am-
herst, Massachusetts. "But now when you go out onto the marsh, you see
stumps where red cedar used to grow. People who have lived here their
whole lives have seen changes."

The Wampanoag Natural Resources Department maintains a network of conductivity, temperature, and depth sensors throughout Waquoit Bay. The staff also monitor the cedar trees at the edge of the water and look warily at the certain changes coming to Cape Cod. Some Wampanoag people wonder if their coastal settlement will one day have to be abandoned as sea levels rise, which stirs a memory of the migration patterns that used to define existence before the *Mayflower* arrived.

"Our ancestors were able to make smart decisions to keep the generations going to this day," said Thornbrugh. "So I look at it through the lens of resilience. You remain where you are despite chaos around you. Sometimes all you can do is move—but you try every alternative before that."

King Philip's War did as much to define the current shape of America as the Revolutionary War a century later, but it lacks a landscape of memory. There is no Freedom Trail, no Concord Bridge, no Valley Forge of King Philip's War, so unlike the major tourist sites in the northeast associated with the 1775–1783 independence movement. Locations associated with the nation's first full-blown war are nearly all erased and unmarked, perhaps because of the shame associated with them.

One of the creepiest monuments in this country—a rough granite shaft on the edge of Rhode Island's Great Swamp—stands a few miles in a clearing down a closed dirt road, almost never visited, celebrating the slaughter and death by arson of a neutral people who weren't even at war. Approximately sixteen Amtrak trains pass by less than a mile away every day on the Northeast Regional tracks, but the enclosing woods make this monument invisible to anyone who might be gazing out the window. The spot where King Philip himself was brought down is commemorated by an obscure tombstone-shaped marker in another patch of Rhode Island wetlands, almost impossible to find without precise directions.

Stories of King Philip's War are almost unknown among surviving groups of Abenaki, especially after a misbegotten eugenics program in the 1920s in which hundreds of Native women in Vermont were sterilized. Their families took pains to erase their own identities to escape a similar fate. "It stymied the population from talking about anything Indian related," said Arthur Hanchett, an Abenaki farmer from Strafford, Vermont. The oral traditions handed down from the seventeenth century disappeared during this forced forgetting.

Yet King Philip still casts a shadow. The conflict to which he lent his name was America's first environmental convulsion; an arena in which conflicting ideas over proper land use ended in miserable combat and a victory for bounded dominionism. The landing on Cape Cod in 1620 was one prong of a biological invasion from Europe that began slowly on a narrow beachhead and built itself into an unstoppable force. Rising ocean water flows through porous limestone underneath Miami Beach and routinely floods large portions of town on rainless days. Extreme heat waves in the Midwest have stressed the ability of wheat fields to produce harvest. Hurricanes are increasing in their power and frequency, and even milder storms will dump huge "rain bombs" on coastal cities ill-prepared to cope with the inundation. The American West now sees nearly sixty-seven thousand wildfires per year in forests dried and weakened by migrating beetles; ashes from those fires drift north and create huge dark pools of water on melting glaciers in Alaska, where scorching summer days are now a permanent reality.

Farmers tend to notice it the most; Hanchett said the cloudy summers of his youth have given way to relentlessly clear skies and more infrequent rains. The nation may be on the way toward a more nomadic way of life, as populations on the coast are forced to move out of the way of rising waters and new methods of agriculture develop to move crops away from desiccated soil. Puritan fixedness may give way in the end to Native American seasonal mobility. Our hunger for more lands and more goods is as insatiable as it was in the 1620s, and it also points us toward an ecological reckoning.

This isn't happening all at once. It is happening in fragments and in checkerboard squares, in upticks of degrees, in species shrinking, in forests thinning out, in water rising. We are losing land in imperceptible measures, just as the Wampanoag lost it to the settlers.

In America, there is a temptation to think of New England as the "oldest" part of our nation because it was the first point of contact between the indigenous and the English ways of existence. It was also the kiln of our basic principles of liberty and subjugation. But the Spanish were busy colonizing what is now Florida, New Mexico, and California a long time before the *Mayflower* arrived. The North American craton—its rock core—is 600 million years old; it was home to millions of Native people for tens of thousands of years, and it all remains physically interconnected today. If one part burns, it all burns.

Our desire for property and material goods has again outpaced the ability of the land to absorb the impact, just as it had in 1676. We can mitigate the damage, we can ease the burden, we can move away from the burning parts, but we can't make war among ourselves any longer, because today we're all standing on the shore watching the approach of sails from a faraway place.

Home Ground

Evergreen Cemetery is a strip of bumpy land the size of eight large city blocks, surrounded with rusted barbed wire on all sides and dotted with palm trees. The oldest operating necropolis in Los Angeles lies here in genteel decay, with some of its nineteenth-century tombstones leaning akimbo like fence pickets in a wind.

Like many urban cemeteries of its era, it is arranged into pockets of ethnicity and hierarchies of wealth. There are eighteen paved avenues of separation, precincts with names like "North Park," and dedicated barrios for Armenians, Japanese Irish, African Americans, and Chinese, many of whom had to pay extra for the democratic privileges of death. The WASP quarter features the resting place of forgotten mayors and bankers; hundreds of carnival workers lie in a precinct called Showman's Rest. The poorest dwelling of all is in the southeast corner where the city peeled off a triangle of land for unclaimed bodies. When the ground grew too full, the authorities built a crematorium with a smokestack to chuff the bodies into ash for internments on a nearby slope called, in the inevitable biblical phrasing, the Potter's Field.

The city transferred the Potter's Field to the county the year before the worldwide outbreak of Spanish influenza in 1918. Los Angeles was comparatively lucky; its farsighted health commissioner Luther M. Powers convinced the city council to order citizens into their homes for most of the autumn. Most people wore masks in public. Movie producers protested: How was the local economy supposed to function? But the collective solitude helped keep fatalities low compared to places like San Francisco and Philadelphia where World War I victory parades were held with disastrous results. Still, half of 1 percent of the population of Los Angeles died: at least 2,713 people gone from what amounted to a young boomtown. Burials at Evergreen turned into rushed and panicked affairs. An unknown number, mainly indigent, went namelessly into the Potter's Field.

Approximately seveneen hundred people per year still die in L.A. without anyone knowing their names. They lived alone, mainly on the streets of virtual refugee camps like the Skid Row east of downtown, and they mostly died without company. The unmourned lonely are gathered in a communion of ash and buried together under a stone tablet bearing only the year as an identifier.

Their solitude lies not at the tail of society but at its vanguard. When isolation descended across the country in the COVID-19 pandemic, approximately 28 percent of American households had only one member. Personal geographies shrank even further. The insides of apartments, townhouses, detached houses, motel units, or tents became for a time the boundaries of the cosmos. Other means of delineating the self grew weaker and withered. The nation had been sent to its room.

Do we like what we see there? Katherine Ann Porter wrote of the homebound condition during the 1918 flu epidemic in her novella *Pale*

Horse, Pale Rider; her newspaper reporter heroine Miriam catches the virus and is banished, delirious, to the room where she had been having a love affair with a soldier. Her existence closes in and turns to the shabby surroundings, hating "the dull world to which she was condemned, where the light seemed filmed over with cobwebs, all the bright surfaces corroded, the sharp planes melted and formless, noiseless houses with the shades drawn, empty streets, the dead cold light of tomorrow."

That chasing after lost yesterdays, the recovery of the true self that drifted away in the river currents: such a quest is central to an astonishing number of American pursuits. The Mexican poet Octavio Paz spent two years in California reflecting on the ironies and contradictions of his native country and wrote a biting 1957 book called *The Labyrinth of Solitude* in which he reflected on the universal and permanent state of the individual: solitary, suspicious, and trapped in endless rumination and nostalgia. This condition of humanity was even sharper in Mexico, he theorized, because of the traumatic sixteenth-century origin of the modern country: the conquistador dagger put against the throats of the indigenous. The mingled bloodlines and the lasting heritage of physical and cultural rape created a profoundly divided nation of individual souls who each concealed a private chamber of secrets behind a colorful front parlor.

"He builds a wall of indifference and remoteness between reality and himself," wrote Paz, "a wall that is no less impenetrable for being invisible. The Mexican is always remote, from the world and from other people."

Paz argued that outside these rooms, the "true Mexican" can only take off the mask and come out during times of community celebration, weddings, *quinceañeras*, festivals, and, especially, funerals. Paz admired what he considered a relative openness to the American mentality, composed of layered elements: seventeenth-century Calvinism, the Enlightenment attitude of the eighteenth-century Constitution, and nineteenth-century Victorian morality.

But where was this "true American" in the spring of 2020 when planes mostly disappeared from the sky, cars generally stayed off the roads, and other people were seen, if at all, through screens, behind masks, or standing a somber six feet apart? The pandemic only exacerbated an American solitude that was already there, already growing stronger, not just in an era when social media and computerized entertainment were pulling the national garment thinner but as trust in old principles and institutions was faltering under fevered hallucinations creeping even deeper into the country's amygdala. Civil servants had become the deep state, once-valued immigrants had been cast as an invasion, straight-laced information sources were fake news, experts were frauds, doctors were greedy liars, the killing virus itself was some kind of hoax.

Every pillar of the American soul that Octavio Paz had identified seemed to be crumbling. The Calvinism had been shorn of every restraining quality leaving only economic sociopathy; the goodwill that lubricated the Constitution had dehydrated into abrasive sand; the Victorian morality had become liberated beyond all recognition into tawdry gold-plated spectacle. Before the virus parted the waters and created physical separations, many Americans had already taken themselves into a spiritual and informational cocoon, disgusted with their neighbors and tired of the quest for common ground. Polls show roughly half the members of our opposing political parties have a level of extreme personal distrust for one another; fewer than one American in ten says they have multiple friends of different political beliefs, to say nothing of other races. The social distancing had begun a long time before COVID-19. As Porter wrote of her characters, "Every step they took toward each other seemed perilous, drawing them apart instead of together."

Pandemics conceal faces, but they also tear away social illusions and expose what lies underneath. Perhaps what it tells us most of all is that the American origin story contains its own labyrinth of solitude that Octavio Paz did not fully appreciate. The country experienced two trans-atlantic foundings at roughly the same time: the Massachusetts Bay Colony in 1620 and the Colony of Virginia in 1607. Divergent ideas sprung from these landings. The northern branch gave us a concern for charity, an interest in democratic government, a disdain for royalty, a hazy idea of equality, a zest for education and self-betterment. The southern branch gave us an inheritance of proud individualism, a code of personal honor, a commodities economy, suspicion of central authority, an idyll of country squires, the first shipment of enslaved people from Africa.

What might be termed the long contest between Plymouth values and Jamestown values reconciled themselves in an imperfect Constitution and then erupted into a civil war eighty years later. The conflict never really went away, even though these distinct strands of thinking are permanently braided together, uneasily mingled like the ashes at Evergreen Cemetery.

After the virus of 1918 burned itself out, a curious silence descended in the midst of the renewed social energy of the Roaring Twenties. Almost nobody wanted to talk about, write about, or think about the pandemic again. Virtually no literature, with the exception of *Pale Horse, Pale Rider*, emerged from the trauma. National forgetting commenced. Very few monuments were erected. At Evergreen Cemetery, only the outsized number of headstones bearing "1918" provides a physical clue to what happened. Historians have supposed the amnesia was due to the terror and inexplicability of the flu; that such grief so close to home was better left papered over.

Perhaps there was another reason. The collective retreat into our rooms may have also been terrible enough in itself, revealing the fraying bonds of what draws us together, making us aware of our baseline loneliness, the neighbors we don't know or understand, the fragility of our social contract, and how much we depend on those nearby on our home ground whom we never really accepted. When the experience was over, it was over for a century. American masks went on again in 2020. But the masks also came off.

At the End
There Will Be
Strangers

My grandmother lived for sixty-one years in a hand-built ranch house on Mockingbird Lane in Paradise Valley, Arizona. I had known it all my life: playing there as a child, staying there for long periods of time between jobs, coming over for dinner on Monday nights.

Grandmother died at the age of ninety-six from a swarm of maladies that prey on the elderly—congestive heart failure, diabetes, complications from a broken hip—and after we buried her ashes, we went about selling the house in our usual dilatory way. This took four years. Eventually, a buyer stepped forward: a wealthy Canadian family who would tear down the house and erect a mansion more congruent with what the neighborhood had become.

Though grandmother had died almost penniless, the land beneath her house was now far too valuable to be anything other than a platform for another rambling faux-Florentine palace common to the eastern margins of metropolitan Phoenix, where the city's big money had come to settle. Her grandfather had acquired the land under the Homestead Act before Arizona was even admitted as a state in 1912 and had tried to farm the brittle soil without luck.

I had enjoyed the fact that our adobe and tarpaper house was now among the lowest-assessed properties within the richest zip code in Arizona, looking like a chunk of defiant Appalachian poverty had been bivouacked in the midst of private tennis courts, infinity pools, and emerald lawns. Now our house faced its invariable destiny: it was to be erased.

I had called up the buying family to see if I might be told the date of the demolition. They complied, though without enthusiasm. And here was a dilemma: What good would it do to watch this destruction? What did I hope to gain? The end of life is nearly always bad for objects and people alike; the romance of the deathbed is a famous lie of literature.

Guilt drove me toward a decision. My grandmother, with whom I had been close, broke her hip getting out of the car when she was coming to watch me at a public event. That fracture was the beginning of her decline, as it is for most nonagenarians who break a hip—the bones there deteriorate to thin glass. At last confined to her bed, in the same room where her second husband had put a gun to his head one night in 1962, she lived only about eight more months, sleeping longer and longer, fed and changed by my Aunt Diane.

Most of us will end like this, broken and helpless. I had waited with her for three days through a period of non-responsiveness, then decided to slip out for a few hours to go on a hike with a friend. Her breath quickened, shortened, and stopped while I was away, an absence that has haunted me since. Perhaps it was also the morbidity of knowing that if I missed the destruction of the house, there could never be a repeat, just as I had not been there for my grandmother. I would never have a second chance. It is hard not to anthropomorphize a well-loved house—especially a little one—and I didn't want its death to be unattended.

So on the night of April 25, 2017, I taught a graduate course until 9:00 p.m., then got into my car for the six-hour drive across the Mojave Desert and into Arizona. On the way, I stopped at a sad little convenience store off the highway for a six-pack. I would have gotten Coors, my grandmother's favorite beer, but they stocked only Bud Light. I stole into town shortly after 3:00 a.m. and turned off Mockingbird Lane into the driveway to see that every piece of vegetation had been scraped away from the lot. The pepper tree I had climbed as a boy. The *Larrea tridentata* plants known as greasewood that live for centuries and release fragrant wafts of creosote after rainstorms. The orange tree with the white-painted trunk in the backyard. All gone, as though they had never existed.

Three powerful sprinklers were set out like howitzers in strategic places around the property, sending out curtains of water to keep the dust down. The sight was post-apocalyptic, looking like nothing so much as a federal reclamation of a uranium mine. The spiky palm trees of the much-wealthier neighbors next door peered down onto a lunar surface. In the middle of it all was the house, or what was left of it.

The front door had been torn off. I went into the entryway, and there was the slightly sloped corridor and the venue of one of my earliest memories: riding a Playskool toy car. On the wall there had been a cherished object: a certificate signed by the governor of Arizona congratulating my grandmother on thirty-five years of civil service. To the left was the rock-walled indoor planter, once full of lantana flowers, anchoring an empty living room stripped of carpet. This was the only part still mostly intact. It was in this room that my father picked up my mother on their very first date. He had stumbled on the four-inch step that separated the living room from the hallway, a gesture that had weirdly charmed my mother. I was then eight years away from conception, though neither of them could have foreseen it that night.

My grandmother had always said she was leaving the house "feet first," by which she meant she'd never go to a nursing home, which she dreaded. The night she died, two young men had shown up from the mortuary in a white van without windows. They wore white shirts, dark pants, cheap ties. They bagged up my grandmother's body in a zippered bag. "I have an odd request," I told them, and they agreed to carry her out the door leading with the feet, which put me in mind of the Wallace Stevens poem about a lonely woman's funeral wake, "The Emperor of Ice Cream." *If her horny feet protrude, they come / To show how cold she is, and dumb / Let the lamp affix its beam/The only emperor is the emperor of ice-cream.*

The two young men from the mortuary had looked no older than college age; one was Filipino, the other white. They were grim and clumsily efficient. I could smell cigarettes on one of them as I held the door open so they could accomplish grandmother's small victory of place and longevity.

When the body had been loaded into the white van, the doors closed, they shook my hand as if in conclusion of a transaction. At every end, there will be strangers like this. They will handle the details. They will clean up the mess. Not only will they not know your story, they will barely know your name. They disappeared in the van and I never saw them again.

Now, I peered into the wreckage of the bedroom. The roof had been knocked in by one of the backhoes, and the internal beams lay exposed for the first time since they had been nailed in place and covered with plaster when Harry Truman was president. They spread open diagonally like the spines of an insane fan. The bathroom wall had been completely collapsed; the submerged pink bathtub had been pulled out like a tooth, bits of wallboard and wood and insulation lay everywhere. Vertical blinds fluttered in the space where a sliding patio door used to be. I felt as though this room was blaming me for its mortal wound; I felt it was not wrong.

The family room was even worse; the roof totally ripped away, the scene dominated by a mound of mud that had once been adobe bricks made by my step-grandfather, a surreal pattering of rain coming from the open sky every thirty seconds or so. It took a few passings of this for me to realize it was not coming from the sky but from the outside construction sprinklers. The room that had been the scene of tens of thousands of dinner conversations and a long series of annual Christmas mornings looked like it had been bombed in an air raid. The chimney, the kitchen counter, the pantry with the door that had felt like corduroy: all of it appeared in 4:00 a.m. shades of dark gray, a state of neither being nor not being. I had always loved the view out the back window of the McDowell Mountains; now I couldn't even see them because a pile of debris blocked them from view.

Another dousing of water from the sprinkler drove me from the ruins of the living room, back out the front door to the antiseptic plain of what used to be seventy years' worth of desert vegetation, which lay bulldozed and squared off in a tidy heap at the corner of the lot. I went over to the bald place where the vanished carport used to be and to the half-broken south wall of the bedroom where my uncle Fred had spent nearly all his life. He had been a brilliant ne'er-do-well; a college dropout and a charming loner who never found a job up to his talents and whiled away his time tinkering with obsolete electronics and watching great glurts of network television. Growing up on the edge of the sixties' upheavals turned him into an admirer of Hunter S. Thompson and Kurt Vonnegut, though I never saw him read anything other than the newspaper. He had been a strict atheist with an aversion for talking about death or larger meanings, and he succumbed to a sudden onset of acute leukemia one year after marrying for the first time at the age of sixty-two and bringing my new aunt Diane here. This space had been his cell for almost all of his life. The closet had been stuffed with ancient motherboards; the workbench had drawers with a hundred varieties of alligator clips and screws.

He didn't perish in here like grandmother—that happened in the intensive care unit at nearby Scottsdale Osborn Medical Center—but the broke-open state of his room reminded me of the death ritual of the Navajo. Their traditional homes made of mud and branches are called hogans, and nobody is supposed to die inside one because their spirit, or *chindi*, will be trapped in the structure. The sick are taken outside to perish in the open air. If somebody accidentally perishes inside, the family has to punch a hole in the north wall to let the *chindi* escape and then never live in the house again. I collected a mud brick as a souvenir and put it in the trunk of the car. Then I sat in the driver's seat and drank a lukewarm beer, toasting my vanished relatives.

In the last hour before dawn, I went twice more inside the vacant living room, not wanting to leave the house just yet, not wanting it to be the final time. I touched the cold stones on the planter, peered into the wreckage of my grandmother's bedroom, unable to really see the spindly fan of what used to be the roof. Within a few hours, even that would be gone. Dumpsters lay outside to receive the scattered materials of what had been the house. The particles would exist, but the essence would be forever destroyed. What made it whole—the thing I remembered— could never be replaced.

From a long-ago college course on Renaissance poetry, I could remember a line from John Donne: "And to your scattered bodies go." He had been talking about the Last Judgment and the old Christian folk belief that the resurrection of the dead would be a pell-mell dash of spirits around the globe, looking for the dust and bone fragments that had once been the suit of flesh worn when they were alive.

Two months before this night, I had been on a hiking trip to the
Grand Canyon with a friend I had known since I was nine years old. I
could see the wrinkles fanning his eyes, the years on his face, the same
way he probably saw the age creeping on mine. We had a spare two
hours before he dropped me off at the Phoenix airport and—thinking it
might be the last time I would see it—I asked him to drive me past the
Mockingbird house, which had looked then slightly less vulnerable and
pathetic, though it had been marked for destruction. The electrical wir-
ing had been stripped from it already; it was being dressed like a corpse.
In a sardonic mood, I mentioned this comparison to him, and he told
me about how, during his work as a U.S. diplomatic officer in Morocco,
he had been responsible for supervising the repatriation of the bodies of
Americans who died overseas. Eventually he got used to it. "They are the
shells," he told me. "You can't think of them as people. The life has gone."

Arizona isn't big on monuments. Since the 1950s, the economy has
relied on perpetual homebuilding and *newness*. There is not a lot of room
for the unbeautiful residue of a different time. My grandmother was the
daughter of a minor courthouse official who made extra money deliver-
ing laundry. She worked as a civil servant all of her life—for the Civilian
Conservation Corps during the Depression, then for the county and the
state highway department. She suffered two flawed husbands, her father's
early death, a life of thankless work, watching eastern Phoenix shift from
the end of its agricultural frontier into a sprawling blanket of semi-urban
prosperity and absentee ownership. I never heard her complain about
anything. Once I asked her if she ever resented all the outside wealth that
had sprung up around her tiny square of earth, and she answered with an
emphatic no. "Because I was here first," she said.

As the sky began to lighten, I went back to my car and drank one
more beer, staring at the rectangular form of my grandmother's house.
Eventually I fell into a thin soup of unconsciousness and came back to

awareness with the sun beating down into the car's interior and a guy who had come onto the property. I got out, blearily, and said hello. His name was Laswavian, a temp laborer who had gotten to the job site early, and we made conversation. He had worked as a motel manager for the last decade, gotten divorced, and arrived here on the bus for this temp gig that paid eleven dollars per hour. Then the guy who would be doing the destruction drove up. His name was Matt, and he shook my hand and looked away. The neighbors had complained the other day when the workers started to strip the vegetation from the yard in the early morning, Matt told me, and they agreed not to destroy the house until 11:00 a.m. The wreckage would be loaded into the large dumpsters and taken to two separate landfills.

Despite the circumstances, I wanted to be friendly and told him: "Take it down gently." He only said: "Uh-huh."

A car slowed down as it passed by, the driver gawking, and I wondered if it might be one of the neighbors. Perhaps one who had not liked the sight of my grandmother's modest house in the midst of such a posh enclave. *So that unsightly thing is finally coming down,* they might have thought. *Good.* My eyes burned with lack of sleep.

At 10:30 a.m., Matt began removing the yellow caution tape from around the house. A black BMW came into the driveway, and out stepped a burly man of about sixty years old. He was wearing Birkenstock sandals with no socks, and I took him to be the scion of the Canadian family. He regarded me suspiciously and I went to introduce myself. We had spoken on the phone, I reminded him. I was the representative of the family who had owned the property and he had given me permission to be here. "Great, great," he said. They would be building their own house soon, and though he didn't describe it, I imagined the same rambling Arizona mansions that had gone up all around the valley, with wine cellars, spiral staircases, and turrets fashioned after the castles of eighteenth-century Italian strongmen.

"We want to get closer to the amenities you guys have enjoyed all these years," he said.

Amenities, I thought. A luxury real estate term. Grandmother had worked as a civil servant for thirty-five years, keeping her two children fed and clothed while hovering just above the poverty line. Her first husband had deserted her; her second husband had shot himself in the bedroom. Who did he think we were? I suddenly felt bright vermillion hate for this person on the land that was no longer ours. But it was now his property, this ground of my childhood, and I was only an invited guest who could be asked to leave at a moment's notice.

As it happened, this purchasing family had made their money through a chain of nursing homes designed for Alzheimer's patients. The concept was called "Memory Care." As the resident loses their ability to recall basic details of how to brush their teeth, go to the bathroom, or recognize their relatives, the staff is supposed to be on hand with brain-fitness exercises and social activities to make their recollection last as long as possible.

This Mockingbird house was a chamber of recollections, and like the brain itself, it would not endure forever. Because my mother grew up here and went to the nearby university where she met my father, I came about. And one day I will be gone, along with the last people who recalled the pleasant damp odor of the foyer; the poky straw in the adobe bricks; the refrigerator on the patio with the pull-handle; the smell of oranges, dogs, cigarettes, and enchiladas. Photographs in albums show the family project that erecting this house had been: the mixed concrete, the trowels and plaster, my uncle Fred as an eight-year-old playing on the rafters of the little structure where he would spend his reclusive life; all of which would have such an outsized role in my personal history: a dependable geography. Now it was headed for the landfill; obliteration written in its essence.

The new owner walked over to Matt, who was getting ready to fire up the John Deere 554K Wheel Loader.

"Now it's starting to look like a building pad, huh?" he said, turning to me with a grin that was, I think, intended to be friendly. "Now you can see what it looks like without all the growth."

A building pad. He had not asked me anything about this house that was about to be wiped away, or anything about those who had lived here. His face was childlike, delighted even. I decided I didn't want to talk to him anymore, not a single word more, and I walked off to another part of the emptiness that had been the front yard. And then Matt moved in with the Wheel Loader. The clawbucket reached toward the living room window like a grasping hand. The window broke with an audible crash, and the sun-stained ivory blinds fluttered, alarmed, in the new wind, as though they were panicking.

I had been cautioned ahead of time that houses come down fast. In the next sixty seconds, the rock planter was completely broken up, its brown stones tossed to the side on a heap of dead rabbitbrush. Insulation that had not been exposed in six decades spilled out into the sun. The roofbeams made loud clapping sounds as they fell into the cavity of the living room, and the kitchen window that faced the street—out of which my grandmother had looked as she cooked sixty-one years of meals— collapsed in a barely audible tinkle amid the grumble and whine of the Wheel Loader. Matt used it as a battering ram against everything that stood.

The last intact part to go was the chimney, which was the first part of the house to be built by Fred von Blume, a newly returned veteran of World War II who had married my grandmother. He carried with him the traumatic stress of combat that would eventually take his life, but this had been a happy and hopeful time for him. Western landscapes had been his passion since he was an orphan growing up in a charity home outside Chicago, and he excitedly had called this two-acre lot "The Lazy B Ranch" and insisted that all of the family members answer the phone that way. His home-taught masonry wasn't perfect, and there were little bits of horse and cow dung embedded in some of the bricks he patted into shape, but the chimney had been the visual centerpiece of the house, with a wood mantel inlaid with diamond-shaped apertures backed with copper leaf and a starburst clock fastened to the face. When it collapsed after several hits, it went in a spray and downpour of light brown powder, the bricks atomizing into the soil they had once been.

The entire operation took six minutes. What had been our house lay heaped in an unruly pile that looked shockingly diminutive. I glanced at the Memory Care scion standing next to his black BMW and felt the anger the dead might feel toward the living, the fury of a grieving parent toward a drunk driver who had killed their child, the heartsick powerlessness that a serf might feel when a royal had exercised *droit du seigneur* on his wife. I felt sorry that I had shaken his hand.

None of my anger was logical. Better manners on his part would not have changed the reality even a tiny bit. Possession was the entire law. The strangers at the end are powerless to help or hurt; they are as indifferent and constant as the state of matter itself. He paid me no attention as I walked toward my car.

Memory is as fragile as a dirt brick, staying solid for years then demolished in a few seconds. I wondered how long the Canadians' new mansion would last and what might happen on the day it fell for whatever might replace it, the mute and uncomprehending ground beneath it turned once again into a building pad. By then, I would likely be gone, too, and there would be nobody who could piece together the layers underneath or who would even remember that a scruffy modernist ranch house had been there in the latter half of the twentieth century, and it had been the gravitational center of lives that nobody would bother applauding but are still worth something. On my way out of Paradise Valley, I could not help but picture a clawhammer bucket ramming against the side of every elephantine manor house I drove past, even the freshly built ones, and all of them collapsing in an enveloping cloud of brown dust.

And this is America, too—a country of destruction and reinvention where the scythe sits on the table next to the blueprint. We think we own the land, but the land survives while we and our sand structures do not. The raw physicality of the ground pulls at us like an undertow, reminding us of where we stand and who we are. More than a flag, a tribe, an ethnicity, a legal agreement, a cluster of art, or a production of culture, America is a civilization of whereness. Our shared geography between the oceans is the lowest common denominator within this clashing territory of strangers. The land that we gain and lose in endless cycle is the substance of our national communion; this road of constant change is our blotchy and beautiful inheritance.

Acknowledgments

I am indebted to hundreds of people for the content of these essays. This is an extremely partial list of those who were generous with their conversations and insights: Scott Dickinsheets, Geoff Schumacher, Dayvid Figler, Charles Bock, Joshua Wolf Shenk, Abby Ellin, Michael Cooper, Dan Buecke, Sudip Bose, Claire Dederer, Nate Liquor, Alissa Quart, Dan Shearer, John D'Anna, Kevin Gass, Steve Shockey, Bob Etter, Barbara Kreiger, Melissa O'Rourke, Sonya Naumann, David Garner, Mary Woolsey, Kit Rachlis, Sewell Chan, Denis Boyles, Don Pease, Alex Corey, Christine DeLucia, Sean McCoy, Ellie Duke, Jake Downey, Sugi Ganeshanathan, Greg Cullison, Tom Lutz, Boris Dralyuk, Kevin Poch, Kristi Coulter, Rachel Barnhart, David McGlynn, Brian Smith, Meghan Daum, Phillip Hagerman, Brad Tyer, Amy Silverman, Paula Neuhaus, Bathsheba Demuth, Larry Peterson, Lawrence Viele, Mike Sager, Colin Calloway, Roger Longtoe, Amanda Gokee, Brian Lawver, Scott Timberg, Karl Jacoby, Deke Castleman.

The primary inspiration for this collection was the work of the journalist John Gunther, whose book *Inside U.S.A.* (Harper & Brothers, 1947) still ranks as a staggering achievement and the best tome about this nation ever written. American identity has never been summarized in a single volume, but this one came close. I also should cite his *A Fragment of Autobiography: The Fun of Writing the Inside Books* (Harper & Row, 1962) as a look into the reporting method of one of the true savants of the U.S. press corps.

Preexisting bodies of knowledge are both starter fluid and firewood for nonfiction, and I am grateful to have had access to the books and articles listed here not already credited in the text. Additional notes are also appended.

"Late City Final" was informed by a speech called "Journalism Under Siege: What Is Its Future?" given by Kit Rachlis to the Los Angeles Institute for the Humanities on April 12, 2019. The studies *The Expanding News Desert* (University of North Carolina, 2018) and *Losing the News* (PEN America, 2019) were depressing and educational. I also benefitted from the books *Breaking News: The Remaking of Journalism and Why It Matters Now*, by Alan Rusbridger (FSG, 2018); *Merchants of Truth: The Business of News and the Fight for Facts*, by Jill Abramson (Simon and Shuster, 2019); *Late City Edition*, by Joseph G. Herzberg (Henry Holt, 1947); *Don't Stop the Presses*, by Patt Morrison (Angel City Press, 2018); *On Press: The Liberal Values That Shaped the News*, by Matthew Pressman (Harvard University Press, 2018); and the collection *The Press*, by the incomparable A. J. Liebling (Ballantine, 1961).

"Your Land" drew from *Landscapes of the Sacred: Geography and Narrative in American Spirituality*, by Belden C. Lane (Johns Hopkins University Press, 1988), and *The Necessity for Ruins and Other Topics*, by J. B. Jackson (University of Massachusetts Press, 1980).

"The Whole Hoop of the World" relied most heavily on *The Mountain World: A Literary Journey*, by Greg McNamee (Sierra Club Books, 2000). I also consulted *Pilgrims to the Wild*, by John P. O'Grady (University of Utah Press, 2002), and *How the States Got Their Shapes*, by Mark Stein (Harper, 2009).

The essay "King Philip's Shadow" benefitted from many histories of colonial America, most notably *Changes in the Land: Indians, Colonists, and the Ecology of New England*, by William Cronin (Hill & Wang, 1983); *Our Beloved Kin: A New History of King Philip's War*, by Lisa Brooks (Yale University Press, 2018); *In the Name of War King Philip's War and the Origins of American Identity*, by Jill Lepore (Vintage, 1998); *Regeneration Through Violence*, by Richard Slotkin (University of Oklahoma Press, 1973); *King Philip's War: Civil War in New England*, by James David Drake (University of Massachusetts Press, 2000); *King Philip's War: The History and Legacy of America's Forgotten Conflict*, by Eric B. Schultz (Countryman Press, 2000); *King Philip's War: Native Resistance, and the End of Indian Sovereignty*, by Daniel R. Mandell (Johns Hopkins University Press, 2010); and *Memory Lands: King Philip's War and the Place of Violence in the Northeast*, by Christine DeLucia (Yale University Press, 2018). I also credit the author of this last work, in addition to Colin Calloway, for the use of the term "shadow" to describe the lasting influence of America's seventeenth-century environmental clash.

A section of "Welcome to Dirtytown" was adapted from an article I wrote for the *Oxford American* magazine of Summer 2014 called "The Ludowici Trap." I also consulted *From Kleptocracy to Democracy: How Citizens Can*

Take Back Local Government, by Fred Smoller (Cognella, 2018); *Dear Los Angeles: The City in Diaries and Letters, 1542 to 2018*, edited by David Kipen (Modern Library, 2018); *My Blue Heaven: Life and Politics in the Working-Class Suburbs of Los Angeles, 1920-1965*, by Becky Nicolaides (University of Chicago Press, 2002); and *City of Industry: Genealogies of Power in Southern California*, by Victor Valle (Rutgers University Press, 2011).

For "Searchlight," I wish to thank Joe Johnston of the Nevada National Security Site who provided me with a copy of the account of the atomic bomb explosion written by Robert G. Brooks. The history *Searchlight: The Camp That Didn't Fail* by Harry Reid (University of Nevada Press, 2007) was indispensable. I felt smarter from reading *Sun, Sin and Suburbia: An Essential History of Modern Las Vegas*, by Geoff Schumacher (Stephens, 2010), in tandem with *Bright Light City: Las Vegas in Modern Culture*, by Larry Gragg (University of Kansas Press, 2013). The stories about Jamie Jean Ericsson ran in *The Las Vegas Sun* on October 3 and 7, 1998; they were written by Karen Zekan. I also consulted *Roadside Geology of Nevada*, by Frank DeCourten and Norma Biggar (Mountain Press, 2017). The lists of state firsts and lasts were drawn from multiple government documents.

"The Valley" drew on the academic studies *Smutty Little Movies: The Creation and Regulation of Adult Video*, by Peter Alilunas (University of California Press, 2016), and *Hard Core: Power, Pleasure and the Frenzy of the Visible*, by Linda Williams (University of California Press, 1999).

"Drive" appeared in *Red Earth Review* in July 2018.

"At the End There Will Be Strangers" appeared in *Tin House* on April 24, 2018.

The California portions of "The National Road" have been adapted from a story I wrote in the *Los Angeles Times* titled "Dollar General throws a lifeline to hard-pressed communities. Not all welcome it," published October 5, 2018. I also drew information from *Five and Ten: The Fabulous Life of F. W. Woolworth*, by John Winkler (Robert M. McBride and Co., 1940), and *The Great A&P and the Struggle for Small Business in America*, by Marc Levinson (Hill & Wang, 2012).

"Spillville" is a revised and expanded version of the magazine story "No Harmony in the Heartland" in *The American Scholar* of Winter 2019. The quotes from Dvořák's letters are taken from *Dvorak in America: In Search of the New World*, by Joseph Horowitz (Cricket Books, 2003). This essay is dedicated to the memory of David Godfrey, with whom I first visited Spillville in the spring of 1991.

Grateful thanks to Dan Smetanka at Counterpoint Books, who believed in this project from the start, production expert Jordan Koluch, and agent Brettne Bloom at The Book Group. Erin Dunkerly displayed astounding patience, care, and thoughtfulness all the way through; she is my hero.

© Erin Dunkerly

TOM ZOELLNER is is the author and coauthor of seven previous books of nonfiction. He teaches at Chapman University and Dartmouth College and serves as the politics editor of *The Los Angeles Review of Books*. His writing has appeared in *The Atlantic, Foreign Policy, The American Scholar, Men's Health, The New York Times, The Wall Street Journal, Harper's Magazine*, and many other places. Find out more at tomzoellner.com.